MIDDLE EASTERN MONOGRAPHS: 8

THE EGYPTIAN
AGRARIAN REFORM
1952–1962

MIDDLE EASTERN MONOGRAPHS

The following have been published in this series:

THE EGYPTIAN
AGRARIAN REFORM
1952–1962

BY

GABRIEL S. SAAB

Issued under the auspices of the
Royal Institute of International Affairs

OXFORD UNIVERSITY PRESS
LONDON   NEW YORK   TORONTO
1967

Oxford University Press, Ely House, London W. 1

GLASGOW NEW YORK TORONTO MELBOURNE WELLINGTON
CAPE TOWN SALISBURY IBADAN NAIROBI LUSAKA ADDIS ABABA
BOMBAY CALCUTTA MADRAS KARACHI LAHORE DACCA
KUALA LUMPUR HONG KONG TOKYO

PRINTED IN GREAT BRITAIN
AT THE UNIVERSITY PRESS, OXFORD
BY VIVIAN RIDLER
PRINTER TO THE UNIVERSITY

TO
JAQUELINE ARIDA SAAB

PREFACE

AGRARIAN reform as a device to bring about greater social equality and to promote dynamic agricultural policies commonly refers to a variety of measures such as land redistribution, changes in the status of tenancy and of agricultural labour, land consolidation, co-operative organization of agriculture, and the development of agricultural credit, land reclamation, &c. It was instituted in Egypt in September 1952, hardly six weeks after the revolution started. During the following nine years the revolutionary government firmly established its grip throughout the country and carried out a large part of the agrarian changes advocated in September 1952. The original legislation promulgated in 1952 was completed by several laws and by a series of measures in the economic and social spheres which aimed at filling gaps, extending its scope, and facilitating its practical implementation.

The prime objective of this book is to review the Egyptian Agrarian Reform during 1952–62. This Agrarian Reform is important not only for the changes it has brought about in Egyptian rural life, but also because it has decisively influenced land tenure policies in the Arab countries of the Middle East and North Africa. It will doubtless remain a landmark in their socioeconomic history. Moreover, many fruitful lessons can be derived from a study of the various measures which were devised in Egypt to implement the first Agrarian Reform Law of 1952 and the laws which were issued during the following nine years. Some of these measures may prove to be of significant practical importance, not only to developing nations but also to those fully developed nations where agricultural problems remain an obstacle to a balanced growth of their economies.

Numerous studies by foreign experts have already been devoted to reviewing the new pattern of agrarian structure, but so far no attempt has been made to analyse the operation of the Egyptian Agrarian Reform at close range. The author has, therefore, ventured to study it during a nine-year period to attempt to appraise the extent to which the various laws and measures had been effectively implemented and to determine the immediate effects. For this transitional evaluation[1] all the available published

---

[1] 'Although the evaluation of effects of Agrarian Reform should be considered a continuous process from the early stage of initial implementation, different stages of evaluation have to be distinguished corresponding to different stages of implementation proper, i.e. issues closely related to the immediate objectives of legislation will be dealt with in the transitional evaluation; issues relating to more remote effects are subject to "subsequent evaluation". The two stages of

and unpublished documentation was collected and analysed, and comprehensive field surveys were carried out in rural areas throughout 1959 and early 1960 to obtain additional information and to witness the day-to-day operation of the land-distribution programme. Though the field surveys and interviews were not carried out on a statistical basis, they were used as a basis for the establishment of estimates by the author. The areas visited mainly consisted of estates and lands expropriated since the enactment of the 1952 Agrarian Reform Law, and entrusted to the super-vision and control of various Agrarian Reform regional ad-ministrative centres (*mantiqat*) specially created to this effect. In 1959 there were forty-three of these centres of approximately 10,000 feddans each. Their jurisdiction extended over approxi-mately 450,000 feddans scattered throughout the country but mostly (85 per cent) in Central and Lower Egypt. Seventeen *mantiqat*[1] situated in Central and Lower Egypt were visited in order to obtain a representative picture of the prevailing con-ditions in expropriated areas. In view of the similarity of the agronomical, sociological, and economic factors governing agri-cultural activity in the various regions of Central and Lower Egypt, the results of the field surveys in these seventeen *mantiqat* were extrapolated to the other *mantiqat* of Central and Lower Egypt not visited; information obtained from reliable sources about recent developments in these other *mantiqat* indicated that the choice of this method did not result in material error. The *mantiqat* established in Southern Egypt, in the provinces of Asiyut, Girga, Qena, and Aswan, where conditions were com-pletely different, were not visited because time did not permit of this.

Other areas in Central and Lower Egypt not subject to the land-

evaluation are distinct from each other, because of difference in emphasis and in criteria, but where the dividing line should be drawn rests exclusively with the evaluating agency as this decision has to be made on the merits of the individual case and with reference to the progress achieved in implementation of each specific measure.' For further reference see *Methods for Evaluation of Effects of Agrarian Reform; Report of the Working Group of the Government of India and FAO* (New Delhi, Aug. 1958).

[1] These were:

Mantiqa	Province	Mantiqa	Province
Idfina	Buhaira	Simbilawain	Daqahliya
Alexandria	,,	Sabarbay	Gharbiya
Abis	,,	Shibin al-Kawm	Minufiya
al-Khazan	,,	al-Marg	Qalyubiya
Itay al-Barud	,,	Sharq al-Fayyum	Fayyum
Dasuq	Kafr al-Shaikh	Giza	Giza
Za'faran	,,	Bani Suwaif	Bani Suwaif
Damira	Daqahliya	Minya	Minya
Bahut (Nabaruh)	,,	Liberation (Tahrir)	Tahrir

distribution programme were also visited to study the implementation of the Agrarian Reform Law tenancy and sharecropping regulations, and to examine the important experiment in crop consolidation undertaken in the village of Nawag, Gharbiya province, which was to be the basis for future plans of consolidation in 50 per cent of the area under cultivation in 1959. The so-called Liberation (Tahrir) province was also visited to survey one of the most important attempts to reclaim desert land since 1959.

It is clear that this evaluation of the various aspects of the Egyptian Agrarian Reform programme during 1952–62 is not a statistical survey and that it cannot be considered final; the author merely hopes that it will serve as a basis for future large-scale research work. Moreover, problems connected with a 'subsequent evaluation', i.e. relating to the more remote social and economic effects of the various Agrarian Reform measures in the regions where they have been implemented, have only been superficially studied, and the same is true of the effects on national income. However, if a thorough and complete 'transitional evaluation' were to be carried out by a team of impartial scientists, it would be possible to construct the framework for conducting a 'subsequent evaluation' and for undertaking studies seeking to determine the national income effects of the Agrarian Reform laws and measures.

As the cornerstone of agricultural development since September 1952, these laws and measures aimed at solving Egypt's most pressing agrarian problems by tackling them along four main lines of approach:

1. Landownership and farm operation were limited and regulations laid down for the expropriation and redistribution of lands in excess of the legal limit.
2. The conditions of tenure of farmers and sharecroppers were drastically changed and the formation of agricultural labour unions was legalized.
3. Co-operative efforts to prevent fragmentation of landownership and farm operation were encouraged, and a new system of agricultural co-operative credit was introduced.
4. Land reclamation by private individuals or by companies was submitted to state supervision and control, and the way was paved for large-scale state intervention in this field.

To facilitate the understanding of this multi-purpose programme of agrarian reform, this book, which starts with an introduction describing the characteristics of Egyptian agriculture in 1952, has been divided in three Parts. Part 1 covers the limitation of landownership and farm operation with special emphasis on land

x   *The Egyptian Agrarian Reform 1952–1962*

redistribution in areas expropriated by the state. Part 2 is concerned with the various other agrarian reform measures introduced throughout Egypt, i.e. in all the areas not affected by land redistribution; these measures included changes in tenancy and sharecropping and in the status of agricultural labour, co-operative efforts to prevent fragmentation, improvements in agricultural credit, and the development of land reclamation under state supervision. Part 3 contains a review of agricultural and agrarian policies during 1952–61, and describes the second Agrarian Reform Law enacted in July 1961, giving a brief account of its subsequent implementation.

The author expresses his deep gratitude to all who helped and advised him while he was undertaking this study, as well as those who helped in writing and editing, or commenting on this book. He is particularly indebted to all the officials of the UAR Ministry of Agrarian Reform, to the Egyptian farmers interviewed, to the Research Committee of Chatham House, to Professors Charles Issawi and Yusif Sayegh, and to Mr Albert Hourani. Last but not least gratitude is hereby extended to Miss Hermia Oliver, who was responsible for editing the final draft, and to Mr Alex Noujaim who typed the manuscript.

G. S.

December 1965

CONTENTS

Contents

PART 3

AGRARIAN POLICIES AND THE SECOND
AGRARIAN REFORM

TABLES

ABBREVIATIONS

ACS	Associated Co-operative Society
Ann. stat.	*Annuaire statistique*
Ann. stat. FI	*Annuaire statistique Federation des Industries*
EARIS	Egyptian–American Rural Improvement Society
Ég. contemp.	*Égypte contemporaine*
GCS	General Co-operative Society
Issawi, *EMC*	C. Issawi, *Egypt at Mid-Century: an Economic Survey* (1954)
ME Econ. Papers	American University of Beirut, *Middle East Economic Papers*
Min. AR	Ministry of Agrarian Reform
NBE, *Econ. B.*	National Bank of Egypt, *Economic Bulletin*
Saab, *Motorisation*	G. Saab, *Motorisation de l'agriculture et développement agricole au Proche Orient* (1960)

UNITS OF MEASUREMENT

1 feddan = 4,200 sq. metres = 0·42 hectares = 1·038 acres
1 kassaba is a unit of length equivalent to 3·35 metres
1 rotl = 449 grm.
1 oke = 1,248 grm.
1 kantar = 100 rotls = 45 kg.
1 kantar of unginned cotton = 315 rotls = 141·520 kg.
1 kantar of ginned cotton = 100 rotls = 44·9 kg.
1 ardeb of cotton seed = 2·70 cantars
1 dariba of rice (husk) = 945 kg.
1 ardeb of rice (husk) = 292·5 kg.
1 ardeb of beans = 155 kg.
1 ardeb of wheat = 150 kg.
1 ardeb of maize = 140 kg.
1 ardeb of barley = 120 kg.
Egyptian pound (£E) = 100 piastres = 1,000 millièmes = US $2·87156
= £1. 0s. 6d.

I

INTRODUCTION

It is soil equivalent to that of European market gardens, but while in Europe such soil has been wholly created by the industry of man and covers only a minute area, in Egypt it covers 2·5 million hectares.

P. FROMONT, *L'Agriculture égyptienne et ses problèmes* (1954)

CHARACTERISTICS OF EGYPTIAN AGRICULTURE[1]

IN 1952 Egypt was a predominantly agricultural country with nearly three-quarters of its population (70 per cent) living in rural areas; most of its exports (90 per cent) and a large share of its national income (30 per cent) were drawn from agriculture, which employed 63·2 per cent of its active population[2] and absorbed 66 per cent of the national capital. Despite efforts to industrialize the country, industry played only a minor role in the national economy, its main function being the processing of the principal agricultural products—cotton, rice, wheat, sugar-cane, milk, vegetables, and fruit. The scarcity of tapped mineral resources and the absence of a cheap source of energy had until then condemned Egypt to concentrate on its agriculture, which was completely dependent on cotton cultivation and therefore exposed to the violent fluctuations of the world cotton market.[3]

But since the turn of the century, and especially during the last fifteen years, the agricultural economy had miserably failed to keep pace with the ever-increasing demographic pressures. Egypt was thus faced in 1952 with a population problem that was growing yearly more explosive, the latest census taken in 1947 having revealed an acceleration of the rate of demographic growth which even the most pessimistic experts did not expect.[4] The population, which was estimated at 2,490,000 early in the nineteenth century, reached 9,715,000 in 1897, 15,933,000 in 1937, and slightly more

[1] For a full review of Egypt's socio-economic problems see Issawi, *EMC* (1954), and *Egypt in Revolution* (1963).

[2] *Ann. stat. FI 1954–5* (Cairo, 1956), p. 225.

[3] '70 per cent of the population was directly affected by the fluctuations of the prices of cotton and 30 per cent indirectly' (Gamal al-Din Sa'id, *Iqtisadiat misr* (1951), p. 32).

[4] See *Ann. stat. 1951–4* (1956), p. 10. The rate of population growth during the period 1873–1947 was as follows (per thousand): 1873–82, 29·23; 1882–97, 28·52; 1897–1907, 16·19; 1907–17, 12·96; 1917–27, 11·50; 1927–37, 12·06; 1937–47, 19·86.

than 19,100,000 in 1947. This extraordinary population increase shows no signs of slowing down. Indeed, by 1952 the population was estimated to be over the 21 million mark, while the annual rate of growth was said to have soared to nearly 2·5 per cent and even higher in rural areas, especially in the Northern Delta. Official extrapolations of approximately 45 million inhabitants in 1982 were even claimed to be too low in view of the expected improvement in sanitary conditions and fall in the death-rate. As a result of this demographic tidal wave, the average area cropped per inhabitant had fallen from 0·83 feddans in 1896 to 0·53 in 1937 and 0·47 in 1947, while the net agricultural income,[5] if calculated on the assumption of an egalitarian distribution among the rural population, amounted in 1952 to £E22 per head. This figure is revealing and clearly demonstrates the magnitude of Egyptian development problems, and in particular of agricultural development. These problems, which sprang from numerous causes, some institutional, some social, and some economic, were all linked to the various characteristics of Egyptian agriculture, which may be summed up as follows.

1. *Uniformity of Factors of Agricultural Production*

The Egyptian climate is temperate and extremely favourable for intensive agricultural production, especially in the Northern Delta where the average temperature in summer is around 27·4° C., and where annual rainfall averages 150 mm. This stable climate, allied to a highly organized system for the utilization of hydraulic resources, makes possible in the fertile soils of Egypt the continuous production of abundant crops, including forage crops and fruit and vegetables, throughout the year. Agricultural production is thus governed by three dominating factors: a stable and relatively uniform climate, uniform conditions of drainage and irrigation, and the uniform chemical composition of the heavy clay soils. The development of perennial irrigation in the last half-century further increased the uniformity of conditions, and by 1952 the rhythm of the cropping pattern was very much the same throughout the country, most of the arable lands being farmed in a system of either biennial or triennial crop rotation,[6] with slight variations in the rice-producing regions of the Delta. The development of perennial irrigation had also made necessary the use of specialized irrigation and drainage techniques; but lack of attention to this problem both on the part of the state and on the part of farm operators had adversely affected agricultural productivity.

[5] i.e. after deduction of the value of all inputs.
[6] See J. Anhoury, 'Les grandes lignes de l'économie agricole de l'Égypte', *Ég. contemp.*, no. 199 (1941) and nos 238–9 (1947).

The wasteful use of irrigation water by farm operators, which had become a notable feature of Egyptian agriculture[7] despite the shortage of water, was not only the source of grave drainage difficulties but also an obstacle to the development of large-scale land reclamation. It was a consequence of the absence of any plan to limit the use of free gravity flow irrigation water and to promote the utilization of the important underground water resources of the Central Delta.

2. *Scarcity of Arable Land and Low Productivity*

Although the area of alluvial soils of nilotic origin covered 7,300,000 feddans spread out on both sides of the Nile valley from Aswan to the sea, and though 2,300,000 feddans of sandy desert soils could profitably be reclaimed,[8] only 6,025,000 were under cultivation in 1952, i.e. less than two-thirds of the potentially productive area. Moreover, despite the legendary high fertility of Egyptian soils, average crop yields were disappointingly low[9] and well below the averages obtained on some well-managed Egyptian farms; they had also remained stagnant for a considerable length of time.

Land reclamation had proceeded on a fairly satisfactory scale in the opening decades of the century thanks to the establishment by the state of large irrigation, drainage, and road schemes and to the initiative of big land development companies; by 1935 the cultivated area had increased by over 10 per cent and the cropped area by over 25 per cent. Due to the massive use of chemical fertilizers, crop yields had increased by approximately 25 per cent during the period 1921–39 alone.[10] The resulting rise of 30 per cent in agricultural output was, however, hardly sufficient to alleviate the mounting pressure of population on land and was in any case not to last. During the period 1939–52 land reclamation slowed down to a snail's pace because of government interference, procrastination, and delay in the implementation of state sponsored irrigation, drainage, and road networks and because of the political instability in the Middle East after the war. At the

[7] See A. F. Money-Kyrle, *Agricultural Research and Development in Egypt* (1957), p. 60; also his 'Irrigation in the Middle East', *Spam* (London), iii/3 (1960).

[8] See Saab, *Motorisation* (1960), pp. 2–7.

[9] For a comparison of yields in Egypt and other countries see FAO, *Yearbook 1950*.

[10] See Anhoury, *Ég. contemp.*, nos 199 and 238–9; also A. el Tanamli, 'L'évolution de l'économie rurale égyptienne', ibid. no. 302 (1960), p. 48. The increase in crop yields at the national level had concealed a net decline of productivity in Egypt's most fertile lands in the last two decades, attributable solely to poor drainage conditions. This decline was estimated to be equivalent to the loss of 10 per cent of the cultivated area (see L. Balls, *The Yield of a Crop*).

same time crop yields fell by 4 per cent,[11] mainly because of the shortage of fertilizers during the war. While this was compensated by a 15 per cent increase in the area cropped and by an 11 per cent increase in agricultural production,[12] in the meanwhile the population had again increased, this time by 37 per cent. Thus in 1952, on the eve of the Agrarian Reform, the pressure on land was at the maximum. The density of population had risen to 650 inhabitants per square km. and was well on the way to becoming one of the highest in the world, so that Egyptian rural problems were becoming more and more similar to those of the most densely populated regions of China and South East Asia.

Nevertheless, however grave the plight of rural Egypt may have seemed in 1952, it was still not desperate. Additional water resources could be tapped, a more rational use of existing ones was possible, and substantial areas were available for rapid reclamation. The margin for improving land productivity through good drainage, increased use of organic and chemical fertilizers, and the widespread use of selected seeds and pesticides[13] was also considerable.[14]

3. *Predominance of Cotton and Cereal Crops*

The predominance of one cash crop, cotton, occupying 21·45 per cent of the cropped area, and of cereal crops such as wheat, maize, rice, and barley, occupying 43·4 per cent of the cropped area, was another of the important characteristics of Egyptian agriculture in 1952.[15] The loose biennial or triennial crop rotations commonly practised combined cotton with cereals and leguminous crops, with little thought for a balance between requirements of soil fertility, maximum gross and net returns, and a full utilization of manpower and livestock resources per unit of area (or per unit of irrigation water). Moreover, they did not yield comparatively high gross or net returns and were not really labour-intensive as

[11] The general index of crop yields declined from 100 in 1938 to 96·4 in 1952 (see *Ann. stat. 1951–4* (1956), p. 178).

[12] The general index of agricultural production increased from 100 during the period 1935–9 to 111 in 1952 (ibid. p. 179). Part of this increase was due to an increase of 40 per cent in livestock production (see A. R. Sedki, *Livestock Industry in Egypt* (Cairo, 1951), p. 32).

[13] The use of unselected seeds was annually responsible for a loss valued in 1942 at over £E4·2 m., i.e. nearly 2 per cent of gross agricultural income. The annual loss caused by pests and parasites was estimated in 1952 at an average of £E25 m. annually, i.e. well over 5 per cent of gross agricultural income.

[14] It has been said that 'the level of land productivity is already so high in Egypt that there is not great scope for increasing agricultural production on the present land area'. For further reference see D. Warriner, *Land Reform and Development in the Middle East* (1957), p. 21 and also Issawi, 'Egypt Since 1900: a Study in Lopsided Development', *J. Econ. Hist.*, xxi/1 (1961), p. 15. The views expressed by both these authors were in the author's opinion unduly pessimistic.

[15] See Saab, *Motorisation*, p. 233.

they only absorbed annually a maximum of 55 man days and 60 child or woman days per feddan. This was principally due to the extent of the acreage devoted to cereal crops which often hardly covered the costs of production and used relatively little labour. A biennial crop rotation which would have combined cotton, vegetable and leguminous crops, and livestock production, without any cereal crops, could have yielded very much higher gross and net returns and could have raised the annual rate of absorption of manpower per cultivated feddan to 80 man days and 120 child or woman days; it would also have been less exhausting for the soil. Fruit, flower, and medicinal crops offered other and more profitable[16] alternatives and were more labour-intensive[17] and well adapted to Egyptian agricultural conditions, but in 1952 fruit and vegetables represented a meagre 3·75 per cent of the cropped area.[18] Archaic methods of disposal of livestock products, vegetables, and fruit, the absence of co-operative marketing channels, poor transport facilities, the dearth of agricultural industries, and insufficient agricultural research were major obstacles impeding the development of an intensive Dutch-type agriculture.

4. *Abundant Manpower and Animal Draught Power*

The abundant manpower and animal draught power which could be used for farm work were other salient features in 1952. Some 170 man days and some 130 woman days of labour were available annually per feddan, i.e. 3·2 times the normal needs of cultivation for man days and 2·1 times for woman days. In addition, the majority of the 3 million odd children of 5–14 years living in rural areas were available for agricultural work during the peak seasons. As a result, there was a high rate of unemployment in the countryside, agricultural wages were depressed and at a subsistence level, and the conditions of work to which casual labourers were submitted were beyond description.

The superfluous animal draught power stemmed mainly from the big increase in bovine stock,[19] a large part of which consisted of dual-purpose cattle used for draught operations and for the production of milk and meat. It also resulted from a definite trend towards mechanizing irrigation and the preparation of seed-beds, which had raised the number of fixed irrigation pumps to over

---

[16] See Sa'id, *Iqtisadiat*, p. 347 and Saab, *Motorisation*, pp. 120 and 196.

[17] A crop of roses, for example, absorbed annually up to 750 man and child days of labour per feddan.

[18] Saab, *Motorisation*, pp. 233–4.

[19] See Sedki, *Livestock Industry in Egypt*. A similar situation has developed in Asiatic countries: see R. Bergmann, 'Problèmes de développement agricole au Bengale de l'Ouest', *B. de la Soc. française d'économie rurale*, Sept. 1959, pp. 37–44.

15,000 and of tractors to over 10,000 in 1952,[20] making draught animals redundant. But despite the large number of cattle, and notwithstanding the importance of the acreage reserved for green fodder (23·7 per cent of the cropped area), the production of milk and meat was quantitatively and qualitatively insufficient. Even with a very low standard of living, Egypt was already importing livestock products at a cost of £E3 million per annum. In fact the possibilities of improving Egyptian livestock had been extensively explored since the late 1930s. It had been proved experimentally and on private farms, that by crossing local breeds with pedigree cattle (imported Friesian or Jersey stock or selected buffaloes), milk yields could be increased by 100–250 per cent in 10–15 years, and beef yields by 60–100 per cent in 5–7 years; both these objectives could be attained without loss of profitability given adequate veterinary and nutritional care and relief from the burden of draught operations.[21]

5. *Lack of Managerial Skill and Low Productivity of Labour*

Though Egyptian farm operators had an innate understanding of agriculture, on the whole they lacked managerial skill and were unable to cope with all the problems that had arisen with the introduction of perennial irrigation. Only a small minority obtained yields that could be considered satisfactory given the fertility of the soil. This was especially true of small operators of less than 20 feddans, who constituted the largest part of the farming community (95·9 per cent of farm operators) and who occupied at least 48 per cent of the cultivable area.[22] The high percentage of illiteracy (77 per cent of the population over 5 years old) and the quasi absence of vocational training in agriculture[23] considerably hampered agricultural progress. They were, moreover, important additional factors contributing to the low productivity of agricultural labour, which was estimated before the Second World War at one-twenty-seventh of that of a labourer in New Zealand and one-seventh of that of a labourer in Holland. Calcu-

[20] For further reference see Saab, *Motorisation*. The value of the capital invested in fixed and mobile irrigation pumps and in tractors and implements was reckoned at approx. £E25 m. in 1952.

[21] For further reference see ibid. pp. 334–88.

[22] See below, p. 14. This opinon differs from that expressed by Issawi (*EMC*, pp. 188–95). Saab, *Motorisation*, pp. 188–95, includes the results of two surveys of mechanized and non-mechanized farms carried out in 1956 by members of the Egyptian Min. of Agriculture with the co-operation of an FAO expert, Mr C. Taylor. These established (among other things) that the highest net and gross returns per feddan in the area surveyed were obtained by farms of over 20 feddans, whether mechanized or not.

[23] In 1952 there were only 19 schools of agriculture throughout the country; 7 of these were preparatory and the remaining 12 were secondary schools; total attendance was slightly over 4,900 pupils.

lated in monetary terms, the gross productivity per tiller (and members of his family excluding children under 10) was hardly £E65 per annum during the period 1947–52. The bad health of the vast majority of rural inhabitants, afflicted by endemic diseases such as bilharzia[24] (90 per cent of the population), ankylostomia (15 per cent), and other parasites (50 per cent) and the addiction of a very high percentage of the agricultural population to the consumption of narcotics of various kinds were additional factors which should not be underestimated.[25]

6. *Limited Working Capital and Shortage of Credit*

The working capital (inclusive of cattle and farm implements and capital invested in the land and buildings) invested in farms of less than 20 feddans was extremely small and did not exceed £E12–15 per cultivated feddan, i.e. 3–4 per cent of the total capital invested.[26] Even on the larger farms, though investment in farm machinery and cattle was substantial, invested capital rarely exceeded £E30–40 per feddan, i.e. approximately 10 per cent of total capital invested. The disproportion between the working capital invested and the total capital outlay which thus characterized Egyptian agriculture was to a large extent attributable to a shortage of agricultural credit (especially medium and long-term credit) which affected nearly all farm operators but more particularly the very numerous small tenants and share-croppers.

During the first two decades of the twentieth century, ample long-term credit had been made available for agriculture, but most of it had been appropriated by the large landowning class who either diverted the funds borrowed to consumption purposes or utilized them for the purchase or enlargement of agricultural estates;[27] investment for agricultural development was exceptional. After 1929 funds for long-term credit considerably diminished.[28] The state attempted to compensate for this by creating an agricultural mortgage bank, the Crédit Hypothécaire Agricole, whose scale of operations in the field of long-term credit remained limited, and by setting up an Agricultural Credit Bank for the provision of short-term credit to small and medium-sized operators and co-operatives. This institution, which was more successful,

[24] The annual cost to the Egyptian economy of this illness has been estimated at £E80 m.
[25] The consumption of narcotics such as marijuana and hashish and of tea boiled until it became jet black was common throughout rural areas before 1952.
[26] This estimate is based on an estimate of the price of agricultural lands prior to 1952.
[27] See G. Baer, *A History of Landownership in Modern Egypt 1800–1950* (1962), pp. 99–112.
[28] See Saab, *Motorisation*, p. 299 and Tanamli, *Ég. contemp.*, no. 302 (1960), p. 53.

was founded in 1931 with a capital of £E1 million, 50 per cent of
which was subscribed by the government and the rest by the
principal banks.[29] Co-operative societies in particular were to
enjoy the privileges of lower interest rates and special discounts on
loans in kind (selected seeds, fertilizers, &c.) granted to them by
the bank for distribution to their members. A 2 per cent refund
on interest rates and a 5 per cent discount was planned accordingly.
Interest owed by individual clients of the bank was not to exceed
5 per cent per annum, an extremely favourable rate if compared
with that of commercial banks or village money-lenders.

By 1952 the volume of its loans had risen to £E15·6 million
(approx. one-thirtieth of the value of gross agricultural production),[30] but though the bank had partly fulfilled the need for
short-term credit, it had not lived up to the great expectations that
had accompanied its foundation. State influence remained paramount in its management, despite the importance of the share of
its capital owned by the private sector, and its lending policies
were mainly directed to satisfying the demands of the large landowners or the village *umdas* who had contrived to monopolize its
services. The loans in cash and in kind they obtained from it were
frequently passed on to small farmers, but not without charging
them exorbitant interest rates. Even the 2,000 odd agricultural
co-operative societies, which had sprung up all over the countryside between 1940 and 1950 under the auspices of the Ministry
of Social Affairs and which dealt extensively with the bank (20
per cent of its annual transactions in 1952)[31] were in fact tightly
controlled by the families of big landowners or their followers.
Moreover, the bank was precluded by statute from dealing with
tenants or sharecroppers without the written approval of their
landlords or the provision of some other collateral. Small tenants
and sharecroppers who had no access to commercial banks thus
fell prey to village money-lenders, merchants, and cotton and
grain brokers who extorted interest often exceeding 100 per cent
per annum.

7. *Lopsidedness of the Agrarian Structure*

The slow but steady disintegration of holdings in Egypt prior
to 1952 had made the whole agrarian system top-heavy. In the

---

[29] See Issawi, *EMC*, p. 221.

[30] In a fully developed economy such as the French, funds (short-, medium-,
and long-term) available at the Crédit Agricole were equivalent in 1955 to one-
quarter of the value of gross agricultural production (i.e. commercial production
plus production consumed on the farms).

[31] 300 agricultural co-operative societies existed in 1932, the volume of their
transactions with the Agricultural Credit Bank amounting to 5 per cent of its
turnover.

half century between 1896 and 1945 the number of landowners had increased fourfold, while the area owned had increased by less than 20 per cent. Most of this increase was in the category of small landowners, whose numbers had increased four times in that period, while the number of those possessing over 10 feddans remained much the same. Some 900,000 feddans of newly cultivated land had been added to the area owned and were appropriated by the very small landowners, who also gained possession of some 76,000 feddans surrendered by other categories of landowners. Owners of holdings of 5–10 feddans slightly increased in number, while owners of larger holdings lost some 100,000 feddans, though the number and size of the medium and large holdings varied little during this period. The increase of small landowners (5 feddans and less) was the result of population growth and of the application of the inheritance rules prescribed by Quranic law, which provide for the equal division of property between male heirs. In fact the steady increase in the number of small landowners combined with a reduction of the size of their holdings was not a specifically Egyptian phenomenon but was also characteristic of other underdeveloped countries (China, India, North Africa), where the same disparity between rural population and cultivated lands prevailed.

In 1952 2,760,661 landowners owned 5,964,000 feddans, with an average of 2·2 feddans per landowner. The very big landowners (over 200 feddans), representing less than 0·1 per cent of the total, possessed 20 per cent of the cultivated area, while they together with medium-sized landowners (over 5 feddans), who represented slightly less than 6 per cent of all landowners and who numbered less than 162,000 persons, possessed 65 per cent of the cultivated area. On the other hand the small landowners (under 5 feddans), representing the vast majority of landowners (94·1 per cent), possessed only 35 per cent of the cultivated area although they were 2,600,000 strong.

Two distinct institutional factors[32] contributed to aggravate the lopsidedness of the agrarian structure; the first of these derived from the Muslim practice of endowing private individuals or pious foundations with grants of money or real estate (buildings or land) known as *waqfs*, which were then held in perpetual trusteeship for their beneficiaries. By 1950 the area thus owned had increased to over 550,000 feddans, i.e. nearly 10 per cent of the cultivated area. It was held in trusteeship by individuals when private *waqfs* (*waqf ahli*) were involved (some 400,000 feddans) and by the state

---

[32] For further reference on the role of these institutional factors see *al-Magallat al-Zira'iyat*, 1959, p. 66; also Saab, *Motorisation*, p. 13; E. Lahita, *National Income* (1951), and *Ann. stat. 1956–8* (1959).

Ministry of Waqfs when pious foundations (*waqf khairi*) were concerned (approx. 150,000 feddans). Moreover, the greater part of this area was in large holdings which totalled nearly 22·5 per cent of all holdings of over 50 feddans. *Waqf* lands were in general grossly mismanaged and their trustees, whether private persons or officials delegated by the Ministry of Waqfs, took little interest in improving anything but their own profit. In the ministry's large estates the lands were leased to big operators who then divided up their holdings and sub-let them to small tenants and sharecroppers. Extortion, bad management, and low productivity of land and labour were the result, always to the detriment of the poorer section of the rural community. The second aggravating factor was the large area of cultivated and waste lands owned by the state itself, which totalled some 1,196,000 feddans in 1952, most of which was to be sold and reclaimed. But government sales of land for reclamation, though substantial, rarely benefited small farmers, who lacked the necessary financial backing and were unable to obtain credit or to pull the appropriate political strings; indeed, though 182,683 feddans were sold during 1935–50, only 3,100 feddans were sold to small farmers.

Despite the extent of large landownership, small-scale farm operation prevailed throughout most of Egypt, and the average area operated per farm unit was only 6·1 feddans in 1950. As has been stated, official figures indicate that 95·9 per cent of Egyptian farmers operated units of under 20 feddans in 48 per cent of the cultivated area in 1950, but the actual area operated by molecular-sized farms was probably very much larger since many large holders rented part of their lands to small cultivators on a seasonal basis. The problems arising from the predominance of small-scale farming were made more acute by the excessive fragmentation of the units operated; these were often broken up into several plots, scattered in different areas of the same village or even among different villages; losses in production due to frag-mentation have been estimated at 30 per cent of gross production.

Owner operation was relatively rare, for many landlords, whether large or small, found that it was more profitable to run their estates by letting them out to small tenants and sharecroppers. Leasing of large estates to intermediaries who divided them up into smallholdings allocated to sharecroppers or to tenants was frequent and one of the most obnoxious forms of absentee land-ownership. Legislation regulating tenancy and sharecropping was non-existent; the offer of land was limited, while population pressure kept demand constant. Landlords were thus in a monopo-list position with respect to agricultural rents and wages and exploited this situation to the maximum. They adjusted rentals to the fluctuations of the prices of agricultural products, while keeping wages at a subsistence level.[33]

TABLE I

Average Indices of Rents in the Various Provinces and of Prices of Principal Agricultural Products

(1938 = 100)

Years	Av. Index of rents	Av. Index of prices
1949	270·4	288·10
1950	288·4	366·4
1951	353·0	350·5
1952	397·4	327·1
1953	271·2	354·8
1954	278·2	317·7
1955	278·2	344·3

Sources: Rents calculated on basis of figures from *Monthly B. Rural Econ., Statist. & Legislation* (Cairo); prices from *Ann. stat. 1951–4* (1956), p. 330.

Even this table does not fully reveal this phenomenon, for in some of the highly populated provinces of Upper Egypt rents reached astronomical heights during the Korean cotton boom, the rate of increase being much higher than that of prices; in the province of Girga, for example, the index of rents in 1951–2 was over 547.

The number of tenants is reported to have increased between 1939 and 1949 as a result of the growing population and it has been claimed that 60 per cent of the land was tenanted in 1949 as against 17 per cent in 1939.[34] Rents between 1948–52 fluctuated between £E20 and 60 per feddan, and were equivalent to 75 per cent of net income. While constituting the major item of

[33] In the large estates owned by four members of the Tusun family at Damira (11,987 feddans), Daqahliya province, the increase in cotton sale prices between 1945 and 1952 was approx. 108 per cent while the resulting increase in rents was 86 per cent (see Min. AR publications on Damira, p. 224 below). At the al-Khazan estates (10,000 feddans also owned by the Tusun family in Buhaira province) the system applied by the ex-landlords for the calculation of rents was such that any variation in cotton prices automatically brought about a variation of rents for the whole of a holding. A basic rent per feddan was assessed on the assumption that the cotton price was £E3 per kantar of Karnak. Every increase of £E1 above this basic price automatically raised the rent per feddan of the whole holding by 10 per cent; a rent of £E9 established on the basis of a sale price of £E3 was raised to £E9·9 if the price increased by £E1. For a sale price of £E30 per kantar the corresponding rent increase was 270 per cent. In al-Khazan an elaborate approach had also been devised to facilitate the collection of rents. Tenants were not only responsible for their own rents according to the sliding scale, but also for those due by their colleagues whose holdings lay in the same block of lands as their own. This system was called *al-tadamun*, i.e. 'solidarity'.
[34] M. R. Ghunaimi, *al-Matba' al-Salafia* (Cairo, 1956). Issawi (*EMC*, p. 125) quotes a figure of 75 per cent.

annual expenditure (some 60 per cent of total annual expenses)[35] they absorbed up to 50–60 per cent of gross income from the land, leaving hardly anything for the tenant or the sharecropper. For example, the average net income per feddan of owner-operated land was £E16·19 during 1946–8 but the average cash rent was £E22–23,[36] a clear proof that it was more advantageous to lease lands than to owner-operate them. A typical example of this situation was to be found in Daqahliya province, where the clover and maize crops were rented annually at £E40 whereas gross returns very rarely exceeded £E50 (including the value of livestock production), the margin being hardly sufficient to cover operating costs.

Sharecropping arrangements were no more favourable to tenants. They have been described not as a contract between landowner and tenant to divide the profits of the farm but as

a method of reducing the costs of management and labour supervision and of cutting labour costs by reducing wages. . . . Different divisions of the gross product were used for different crops. A common arrangement was for the landowner to take all, or all but a small fraction, of the cotton crop, half or more of the wheat crop, leaving the maize and berseem for the cultivator and his buffalo. Blank agreements, with no division of the crop specified in advance, were sometimes made. Working capital was usually provided by the landowner, in the form of seeds and fertilizers for the cotton crop; the fixed capital, including the irrigation channels, is maintained by him. . . . The status of the small tenant-cultivator on a holding of 2 or 3 acres was that of a labourer rather than that of a tenant. Formerly he had no security of tenure, and no incentive and no means to invest, since the landowner undertook this function, and his income barely covered his needs. His position was better than that of the casual labourer only in so far as he was more regularly employed.[37]

The high level of rents resulted in tremendous inflation of land values. This was not offset by a rise in productivity, which on the contrary deteriorated between 1939 and 1952. Speculation was responsible for a diversion of available savings to land purchase, a most unproductive form of investment; £E500 million are reported to have been frozen by the purchase of farms at abnormal prices between 1913 and 1952.[38] Capital outlay on agricultural improvements was ridiculously small during the same period, except for the wider use of fertilizers[39] and a trend towards mechanization of draught operations already mentioned.[40] There was in addition a quantitative (but not qualitative) increase of livestock.

[35] See Saʻid, *Iqtisadiat*, pp. 170 and 352.   [36] Ghunaimi, p. 8.
[37] Warriner, *Land Reform*, p. 27; see also Issawi, *EMC*, p. 127.
[38] Ghunaimi, p. 7.   [39] Tanamli, *Ég. contemp.*, no. 302 (1960), p. 51.
[40] Saab, *Motorisation*.

The high price made it difficult for the small tenant cultivator to purchase land, commonly valued in 1951 at an average of £E400 per feddan.[41] Land not yet reclaimed, and therefore very cheap, could only be bought by smallholders with the greatest difficulty. As a result of the grossly inequitable distribution of ownership, a large share of agricultural income was absorbed by absentee landlords. This share has been estimated at nearly 21 per cent of the gross income in 1951–2, which totalled £E421 million. Of a total of 2,716,000 landowners, only 796,000 operated their lands—29 per cent of all landowners. It is fair to note, however, that absenteeism was particularly common among the class of small landowners of less than 1 feddan, many of whom were city-dwellers, unable to operate their minute holdings.[42]

The share of net agricultural income available for distribution after deduction of inputs (£E115 million excluding wages) and rentals paid to absentee landlords (£E85 million) is estimated at no more than £E220 million in 1951–2.[43] Of this the 1,003,000 odd farm operators (slightly more than 5 million people including families) obtained approximately £E165 million. The lion's share went to the big farm operators of 20 feddans and over who, though they represented only 4·1 per cent of the total, occupied 52 per cent of the cultivated area. The 8 million landless rural inhabitants were left with a bare £E55 million, i.e. £E7 per person.[44] The social consequences of the extremely uneven distribution of income need not be detailed. Tales of misery, human degradation, and disease are a pale description of the grim reality of Egyptian rural life. It is in fact extraordinary that revolution should not have occurred earlier than in 1952, by which time the legendary passivity and good nature of the Egyptian peasantry were wearing thin and signs of unrest were appearing.[45]

[41] Warriner, *Land Reform*, p. 30.

[42] In 1950 214,300 farmers operated holdings of less than 1 feddan, whereas 1,981,000 landowners owned holdings of less than 1 feddan.

[43] See NBE, *Econ. B.*, vols vi–xi.

[44] A more sophisticated breakdown of the distribution of agricultural income has been attempted by a research team of the Institut pour l'Étude de Dév. Économique et Sociale (IDES), Paris. But this breakdown suffers from the following weaknesses:

    (a) The figures quoted for the distribution of holdings are those of 1950 while reference is made to them as if they were for 1957.

    (b) Rural population in this study has been estimated at 19 m. in 1959, whereas in fact it was only 16 m. as late as 1960.

    (c) The figures quoted for agricultural income relate to 1958/9.

(See 'Pression démographique et stratification sociale dans les campagnes égyptiennes', *Tiers-Monde*, July–Sept. 1960).

[45] Peasants of the village of Bashmur, near Dakarnas, Daqahliya, occupied the 700-feddan Averoff estate twice in the space of three years. Agitation did not subside after the sale of the holding by its foreign owners, and only brutal intervention by security forces reduced the would-be squatters to submission. Similar incidents are reported by Baer, p. 221.

TABLE 2

Distribution of Holdings According to Size

| | 1950 | | | | 1956 | | | |
| | Area | | Holders | | Area | | Holders | |
Size of holding (feddans)	000 fedd.	%	000	%	000 fedd.	%	000	%
Under 1	112	1·8	214·3	21·4	142	2·3	405·3	32·3
1 to under 5	1,311	21·4	572·5	57·1	1,427	22·9	619·8	49·4
5 to under 20	1,524	24·8	174·9	17·4	1,681	27·1	187·7	15·0
20 to under 50	792	12·9	26·5	2·6	707	12·8	28·7	2·3
50 to under 200	1,142	18·6	12·4	1·2	1,040	16·7	11·0	0·9
200 and over	1,263	20·5	2·4	0·3	1,125	18·2	1·9	0·1
Total	6,144	100·0	1,003·0	100·0	6,212	100·0	1,254·4	100·0

TABLE 3

Distribution of Holdings According to type of Tenure

| | 1950 | | | | 1956 | | | |
| | Area | | Holders | | Area | | Holders | |
	000 fedd.	%	000	%	000 fedd.	%	000	%
Ownership	3,720	61	657	66	3,690	59	730	58
Tenancy (ownership)	1,223	20	207	20	1,351	22	346	28
	494	8			546	9		
Mixed (tenancy)			139	14			178	14
	706	11			626	10		
Total	6,143	100	1,003	100	6,213	100	1,254	100

Note: This table reveals that a very high percentage of holdings were owner-operated, which seems to contradict previous statements about the percentage of the area tenanted. This apparent contradiction can probably be explained by the fact that big farm operators, who generally reserved for themselves the cotton crop (and sometimes the wheat crop), often leased large areas of clover, maize, or rice, divided into small plots, to tenants or agricultural labourers on a seasonal basis. These seasonal tenancy arrangements were not taken into account at the time of the farm census. Moreover, even in the case of sharecropping arrangements, holdings were frequently classed as owner-operated.

Source: NBE, *Econ. B.* x/1 (1957).

PART 1

AGRARIAN REFORM IN
AREAS EXPROPRIATED
BY THE STATE

II

LIMITATION OF LANDOWNERSHIP
AND FARM OPERATION

One yardstick for the appraisal of a tenure system is its capacity to promote economic progress. Land tenure systems and agrarian reform measures may therefore be judged according to their contribution to the process of economic development.

FAO, *Interrelationship between Agrarian Reform and Agricultural Development* (1953).

BEFORE 1952 tremendous political and economic power had been wielded by large landowning groups, who were often accused of wilfully preventing the introduction of social reform in rural areas.[1] The Agrarian Reform Law of September 1952 aimed, therefore, at breaking the power of these groups by imposing a maximum ceiling on landownership, which would also correct the lopsidedness of the agrarian structure. Landownership was limited by the new law to a maximum of 200 feddans per person: over and above this limit, the law granted landowners the right to transfer to their dependants a maximum of 100 feddans, on condition that the area transferred did not exceed 50 feddans per person; the law further stipulated that, to benefit from this exemption, landowners whose property was not requisitioned had to carry out the transfer within five years of the promulgation of the law.

After 1952 many landowners desiring to enlarge their holdings evaded the provisions of the law by buying land above the legal limit in the name of their dependants. Consequently in 1958 an amendment to the 1952 act was passed, which stipulated that thereafter the maximum area which could be owned by a person or his dependants was to be 300 feddans. This limit was only applicable if land was being transferred as a result of a purchase. It did not interfere with the transfer of property as a result of inheritance, testamentary dispositions, &c. In these cases each member of a family retained the right to enjoy ownership within the 200-feddan limit set by the law.

---

[1] For example, rumours that certain big feudal landlords had gone to extreme lengths to delay the establishment of schools in areas close to their holdings are not wholly unfounded. It is interesting to note, however, that the same landlords, were not loath to sponsor the establishment of hospitals, when need be, at their own expense.

In September 1959 another far more sweeping amendment was enacted; it limited the area operated by a person (including his wife and his minor children) to that which he was legally entitled to own in full ownership, so that anyone holding lands partly in ownership and partly in tenancy was entitled to do so only if the area he operated (whether in ownership or tenancy or both) did not exceed 300 feddans. Any addition to the area operated, if accruing after 1958 (as the result of a tenancy contract or inheritance, &c.) was to be expropriated. This amendment was bound to have far-reaching effects on the size of farms, for it must be remembered that as late as 1956 0·1 per cent of farm operators still held 18·2 per cent of the cultivated area, or an average of 602 feddans per single farm operator. A further step was taken in September 1959, when a new law was enacted which limited total landownership to 200 feddans per person.

The abolition by law of *waqfs ahli* in September 1952 completed the agrarian reform legislation aimed at correcting the agrarian structure. The *waqf ahli* lands now reverted to their current beneficiaries, some of whom thus immediately became subject to the 200-feddan legal ceiling on ownership. But it was not until 1957 that a new law (no. 152) was issued subjecting the *waqf khairi* lands to the general provisions of the Agrarian Reform Law. Some 150,000 feddans which despite the revolution had remained in the trusteeship of the Ministry of Waqfs were thus released for distribution to landless peasants.

EXEMPTIONS FROM CEILINGS ON LANDOWNERSHIP

The Agrarian Reform Law when it was promulgated in 1952 was received with a howl of dismay in landowning circles, even though Article 2 had specified a number of exemptions to the ceiling on landownership.[2] In fact two of these exemptions were of prime importance. First, an exemption was granted to industrial companies in existence before the promulgation of the law or who had obtained the necessary permission from the Agrarian Reform authorities entrusted with the study of each individual case and the laying down of appropriate conditions. In practice, this exemption does not seem so far to have been claimed by more than a handful of companies, and until 1959 it involved only minute areas. Another exemption was granted to companies and individuals owning waste land; this will be discussed in Chapter XI.

It is of interest to note that no exemptions were provided for well-managed 'pilot' farms, i.e. farms where crop yields or the rate of capital investment or of absorption of labour per unit of

[2] See law no. 178 of 1952, Art. 2, paras. a–g.

land were well above average, or to farms where the peasants were provided with a minimum of social services. Yet few such farms existed in Egypt before the reform.[3] According to conservative estimates the total area which would have been involved by such an exemption could not have exceeded some 20,000 feddans, i.e. one-thirtieth of the area subjected to the law, and no more than 100 farms are likely to have benefited from it, since it would mainly have affected owners of 200–700 feddans who owner-operated their farms and showed a certain pride in their professional achievements. The absence of this exemption is a regrettable feature of the legislation, especially after the imposition of a ceiling on the size of farm operation in 1959. The possible effects of such an exemption should not be underrated; it would have encouraged efficient and productive farmers and could have provided an example of sound and progressive farm management to all the neighbouring small farms. In Italy, by contrast, this form of exemption was clearly specified by the Agrarian Reform legislation[4] in order to preserve some of the most efficient farms of the peninsula and with the openly stated desire of securing adequate leadership in farm management, especially since this leadership could only be supplied by state-run model farms with the greatest difficulty. In Egypt the scarcity of large, well-managed, relatively highly capitalized owner-operated farms, such as orchards, for example, and the low standards of productivity of state-operated farms, were arguments in favour of total or partial exemption of orchards from the legislative ceilings. Control of exemptions granted on a small scale would have presented no additional problems than those resulting normally from expropriation, distribution, compensation, and the setting up of state-run model farms.[5]

EXPROPRIATION

The lands in excess of the legal limit were to be requisitioned by the government over a period of five years. There were exceptions, such as the disposal by sale of the lands of medium-sized landowners (which were not included in the first requisitioning operation) in so far as this complied with conditions specified by Article 4 of the 1952 law. These landowners were given the opportunity to dispose of their extra land by sale to small farmers

---

[3] See Warriner, *Land Reform*, p. 30.
[4] A procedure adopted by the Mexican Agrarian Reform.
[5] On the difficulties encountered with the expropriated orchards, see below, p. 32. See also, for a different opinion as to the opportunity of exemption provisions in the Agrarian Reform legislation, M. Darling, 'Land Reform in Italy and Egypt', *Year Book of Agricultural Co-operation, 1956* (1956).

within the five-year period, at the end of which expropriation and requisitioning was to be completed. In the interim period, between the promulgation of the 1952 law and the registration of the sales (or requisition of the land), landowners were to pay on land subject to expropriation a supplementary tax equivalent to five times the basic land tax.[6] The disposal by sale to small farmers was, however, subject to the following conditions:

1. They had to be working in agriculture.
2. They had to be tenants or farmers cultivating the land disposed of, or inhabiting the village in which the land lay.
3. Their total ownership was not to exceed 10 feddans.
4. Lots so disposed of were to be not more than 5 feddans each.
5. Lots sold were to be not less than 2 feddans unless all the land sold was under this limit, or unless the land sold was in the immediate vicinity of villages or rural settlements.
6. In cases of sale to graduates of agricultural institutes, and on condition that the object of the sale consisted of orchards, the ownership limit of the buyer was raised to 20 feddans, but the area sold was not to be less than 10 and not more than 20 feddans.
7. Only adults with records of good conduct could buy such land.

Spurred on by the threat of requisition and to evade the payment of the additional taxes, landowners frantically attempted to rid themselves of their extra land. Large tracts of land were immediately sold, and values fell by 50 per cent or more. In the sparsely populated regions of the Delta[7] panic-stricken landowners were compelled to extend ample long-term credit (up to fifteen years) to prospective buyers to encourage them to purchase land. There were also cases of fraud, not only on the part of sellers but also on the part of buyers anxious to evade the stringent conditions of Article 4. By the autumn of 1953 it was clear that drastic action by the state was imminent, not so much to prevent fraud as to stop the excessive fragmentation of some of the most fertile estates in Egypt. The landowners had been driven to tear them to pieces in an effort to cut their losses and collect the value in cash rather than in government bonds. When action came on the 31 October 1953, with the prohibition of any further sale, much of the harm had already been done, and 145,000 feddans of highly fertile land had been split up and sold to small farmers.[8]

[6] Art. 25 of the 1952 law.
[7] Such as Buhaira province, where 25 per cent of the cultivated area was subject to expropriation.
[8] In an attempt to evade the tenancy clauses of the law, some landowners with tenants occupying their lands transferred them to the areas put up for sale;

A brief survey of these holdings in 1959–60 revealed an excessive fragmentation which had not been compensated by the introduction of a consolidated crop rotation similar to that made compulsory in the Agrarian Reform areas, as will be shown.[9] Yields were often not as high as they had been before, and in a number of cases the new owners, having made big cash-down payments, seemed to be short of working capital. They had been left to fend for themselves, no special co-operative organizations (for supplies, farm operation, or marketing) having been set up for them. After purchasing their holdings they had in general found themselves in the same position as that of all other small landowning or tenant operators; true some big landowners, having disposed of their estates on a credit basis and having retained in the neighbourhood the residual holding permitted by law, continued to provide seeds, fertilizers, and advice to the new occupants, in the hope of retrieving the purchase price more rapidly, but this was exceptional.

A detailed study[10] of the social and economic conditions of the owners and operators of the lands (145,000 feddans) purchased in conformity with the provisions of Article 4 of the 1952 law would provide a wealth of invaluable information and demonstrate that it is important when implementing land-distribution measures to establish and develop simultaneously adequate co-operative organizations.

REQUISITION

A few weeks after the promulgation of the 1952 law, orders were issued to requisition 187,000 feddans belonging to 112 very large landowners. The owners of these estates were, however, left with their residual holdings, as permitted by law, i.e. 200–300 feddans according to the number of their children. A year later, in November 1953, it was decided to confiscate without compensation all property belonging to members of the ex-royal family. In accordance with this 180,000 feddans of land were to be confiscated, some of which had already been included in the first batch of lands requisitioned in November 1952. The area thus taken over in November 1953 totalled 60,000 feddans, but part of these lands

they then disposed of these tenanted areas to other farmers, so contriving to rid of their occupants the lands they retained within the 200-feddan limit. As a result of this manœuvre a number of small farmers who in 1954 had purchased land according to Art. 4 of the law were still unable to lay hands on their property, which was being operated in 1960 by large and small tenants protected by the tenancy clause (see *al-Ta'awun*, 16 Feb. 1960).

---

[9] See below, pp. 32–34.

[10] In April 1960 the Ford Foundation allocated to the University of Alexandria a sum of US$200,000 for the creation of a department of study and research in agrarian reform. It may thus be hoped that impartial studies on this subject will be forthcoming in the future.

had already been disposed of in compliance with Article 4 of the 1952 law, while another part had been sold without restriction by ex-members of the royal family disposing of their lands within the limits of their 200-feddan residual holding. In the autumn of the following year new requisition orders directed against other large landowners were issued; by November 1956 the last 60,000 feddans were taken over from private individuals owning more land than permitted by law.[11] The whole of the area requisitioned (including lands expropriated from private individuals and lands confiscated from members of the ex-royal family) was reported to have totalled 462,663 feddans in July 1959; of these some 4,280 feddans were lands planted with orchards. In addition to this, and in compliance with law no. 152 of 1957, lands were requisitioned from the *waqfs khairi*; a first batch of 64,853 feddans was taken over in the spring of 1959 and another 80,000 feddans in 1960 and 1961.

TABLE 4

Area Expropriated by 1960

(*feddans*)

Province	Lands expropriated in compliance with the 1952 law	Mortmain lands expropriated	Total
Aswan	13,065	—	13,065
Qena	35,499	3,487	38,986
Suhag	4,419	—	4,419
Asyut	9,864	—	9,864
Minya	41,812	6,541	48,353
Bani Suwaif	7,970	5,110	13,080
Fayyum	29,792	—	29,792
Giza	7,441	—	7,441
Qaliubiya	5,729	2,189	7,918
Sharqiya	52,984	20,859	73,843
Minufiya	7,273	—	7,273
Daqahliya	77,504	8,812	86,316
Kafr al-Shaikh	24,568	22,642	47,210
Gharbiya	16,528	10,403	26,931
Buhaira	113,936	21,933	135,869
Alexandria	6,120	2,335	8,455
Western Desert	23,504	—	23,504
Total	478,008	104,311	582,319

Source: *Agrarian Reform in Nine Years* (1961).

The year 1959 was also to witness two important steps to widen the scope of Agrarian Reform. The first of these was the implementation in May of a decision to transfer to the Ministry of Agrarian Reform an area of 135,000 feddans of state-owned lands dispersed throughout Egypt and divided into 54,000 different lots.

[11] See *Agrarian Reform in Seven Years* (1959), p. 57.

These state lands, formerly under the management and super-vision of the department of State Domains (a subsidiary of the Ministry of Finance), were to be assigned in full ownership by the ministry to smallholders and landless agricultural peasants, in conformity with the usual agrarian reform regulations.

The second step, taken during the autumn of 1959, was the implementation of the amendment to the 1952 law relating to the imposition of a ceiling on farm operation equivalent to that on landownership; the lands held in excess of the limits set by law were to be surrendered to the Ministry of Agrarian Reform even if they were held in accordance with a tenancy contract, and this within a maximum period of three months or after the harvest of crops planted before the promulgation of the new amendment. In cases of delay, the Agrarian Reform authorities were empowered to requisition the excess lands. When taking delivery of such lands, or on the completion of the requisition procedure, the authorities were to operate them until they were redistributed to small-holders or landless peasants on a tenancy basis. The latter, on receiving their new holdings, were to become the tenants of the legal owners of the lands previously occupied by the big farm operators, if these themselves had been tenants; in this case the relationship between the tenants installed by the Agrarian Reform authorities and the legal owners of the land was thereafter to proceed without further intervention.

Difficulties Encountered

Many difficulties were encountered during requisitioning.[12] Some of these were the result of discrepancies in the title-deeds of the expropriated owners. Often these owners held land in joint ownership with others not subject to expropriation. Several of the requisitioned estates were dotted with splintered holdings—partly as the result of sales to small farmers in compliance with Article 4,[13] partly as the result of the sale of part or all the residual area left to landowners, and partly as the result of random disposal by panicky landowners.[14] In most cases too the landowners had picked for the 200-feddan holdings to which they were entitled the most fertile parts of their property; they took all mobile farm machinery and kept a large number of the farm buildings. Some landowners objected to expropriation measures on the grounds that their lands lying within the boundaries of urban centres were

[12] See ibid. pp. 61–62.

[13] See above, pp. 19–20. These sales occured in the twelve-month period to which Art. 4 of the Law applied.

[14] Many landowners who were members of the ex-royal family sold part of their residual holdings before the promulgation of the legislation confiscating the property of all the Muhammad 'Ali family.

not agricultural lands subject to the Agrarian Reform Law. Other objections were made on the grounds that the lands were waste lands under reclamation and therefore not immediately subject to the ceilings on ownership. Disputes arising between land-owners and the Agrarian Reform authorities were referred for investigation to a Judicial Committee consisting of a Counsellor (chairman), the notary, and delegates of the State Council, the Survey Department, and the Agrarian Reform authorities. The judgments issued by this committee were said on the whole to have been fair, though some cases of pressure exerted on disputing landowners were reported to the author.

COMPENSATION

Lands in excess of the legal limit were to be expropriated against payment of compensation equivalent to 10 times the rental value. This was assessed at 7 times the basic land tax; compensation per unit of land was therefore 70 times the basic land tax.[15] As the average land tax on the relevant areas was about £E2·3, the average expropriation price worked out at £E161 per feddan. This valuation corresponded in the majority of cases to 40 per cent of the actual market value of the expropriated lands in 1952.[16] It must be stressed, however, that land values since 1948 had increased by nearly 50 per cent as a result of the tremendous rise in cotton prices during the 1951 Korean war boom. The sharp fall in cotton prices after 1952 would anyway have depressed land values, with or without Agrarian Reform. It is therefore fair to say that the valuation of the expropriated lands corresponded to approximately 50 per cent of market value. But in quite a few cases where the landlords had in the past connived with the land tax evaluation committee to obtain an abnormally low assessment of the basic land tax, the expropriation price approached the confiscatory level. In these cases landlords suffered a capital loss of as much as 80 per cent. The value of trees, farm buildings, and fixed and mobile farm machinery was supposed to be added to the compensation paid for the bare lands. Compensation was to take the form of non-transferable bonds payable in thirty instalments and carrying an interest of 3 per cent per annum. But in 1958 a new law decreed that these bonds would be redeemable in forty annual instalments bearing an interest of 1·5 per cent. Lands expropriated from the *waqfs khairi* were exempted from this

[15] A similar system has been followed in Cuba by the Castro régime (see *The Economist*, 18 July 1959, p. 137).

[16] In Italy compensation was theoretically to have been made at 70–75 per cent of market value, but in the Maremma region was said to have actually equalled 28 per cent of market value (see Darling, *YB Agric. Co-op.*, *1956*, p. 3).

drastic treatment after 1957; compensation was to be paid in ten annual instalments bearing 3 per cent interest.

Total compensation due on the whole area expropriated (462,663 feddans) in July 1959 was approximately £E73·2 million. To this must be added the value (£E1·57 million) of 13,000 feddans of lands taken over from English and French owners in 1956, against payment in ten annual instalments. Compensation for trees, farm buildings, and fixed and mobile machinery expropriated was esti- mated at £E3·85 million. By 1959 official statements[17] claimed that compensation to the value of £E42·4 million (in the form of bonds) had been remitted to the former owners of 214,000 feddans. Compensation due for the 180,000 feddans confiscated in Novem- ber 1953 from members of the ex-royal family was said to have been remitted by the Agrarian Reform Fund to the state treasury, which was free to dispose of it as it pleased. The payment of further compensation was said to be pending, but nothing was yet disclosed about actual payment for the *waqfs khairi* which, valued according to normal Agrarian Reform procedure, were worth well over £E20 million. Statements in the press[18] expressed the view that compensation was to be paid according to the Agrarian Reform regulations, the bonds being redeemable in thirty years and bearing 3 per cent interest per annum. The redemption price was to be reinvested by the state Economic Organization when the expropriated property was a *waqf* in the trusteeship of the state Ministry of Waqfs. In these cases the Economic Organization was obliged to pay to the ministry a minimal annual income equivalent to 3·5 per cent of the value of the redeemed bonds.

In all cases the payment of compensation proceeded very slowly. It was not until late 1955 that the first bonds were remitted to some of the expropriated landowners; as late as 1959 numerous claimants were complaining that they had not yet received satisfac- tion. In fact all expropriation procedure, whether related to Agrarian Reform or not, was four to five years late in 1959, principally because of the intricacies of government administra- tion.

Though the compensation clauses of the Agrarian Reform legislation did not at first appear too drastic, by 1958 they had taken a definitely confiscatory form. Whereas the owners (includ- ing the ex-royal family) of the 462,660 feddans before 1952 received at least some £E10–15 million in annual income,[19] they received only £E1·1 million net after 1952 and the lengthening of the redemption period together with the reduction of the interest rate

[17] *Agrarian Reform in Seven Years.*
[18] *al-Ahram,* 2 Mar. 1960.
[19] The annual income of the landowners fluctuating with cotton prices.

decreed in 1958[20] (including the ex-royal family share taken over by the state treasury). This was a very drastic cut indeed, and the more so since the bonds were not negotiable. The bonds could, however, be used to pay death duties or the extra land tax on estates to be expropriated but which were not immediately requisitioned, or even to pay for uncultivated land purchased from the government for reclamation. The first two options were taken up by the expropriated landlords, some of whom paid the extra taxes with the value of bonds to be remitted to them while the heirs of others paid death duties with their share of bonds. But the third alternative does not seem to have tempted any of them not only because of the uncertainties about land reclamation policies until 1956[21] but also because of the massive state intervention in this field since.

[20] Previously this sum had been estimated at £E2·1 (see W. Thweatt, 'The Egyptian Agrarian Reform', *ME Economic Papers, 1956*).
[21] See below, Ch. XII.

III

THE DISTRIBUTION OF THE EXPROPRIATED ESTATES

The general feature of land ownership in the UAR is that the average size of ownership is very small, amounting to little over 2 feddans due to fragmentation through inheritance. The Agrarian Reform will not correct the disparity between land and population.

M. K. HINDI, *Reorganization of Land Use* (1962)

AREA DISTRIBUTED DURING 1952–61

FROM July 1953 some 60,000 feddans of land expropriated from private individuals were distributed annually to smallholders in holdings of 2–5 feddans. By July 1959 the total area allocated in full ownership to 118,938 farmers had risen to 333,782 feddans. The remainder of the area requisitioned, i.e. 128,881 feddans, was mostly tenanted by farmers who had received provisional occupation rights from the Agrarian Reform authorities.[1]

According to Agrarian Reform publications, the average area of holdings distributed in full ownership was approximately 2·8 feddans in July 1959; the total number of people to benefit from the redistribution programme (i.e. allocation in full ownership) amounted to about 700,000. If to this figure is added those who benefited from the purchase of smallholdings disposed of by landowners in compliance with Article 4 of the 1952 law, the total comes to nearly 1 million persons.[2] The loss suffered by the dispossessed large landowners, of whom (including their families) there were less than 10,000,[3] was thus supposed to be more than compensated by the advantages reaped by a million human beings.

In July 1959, seven years after the promulgation of the Agrarian Reform Law, the distribution of land was said to be as follows:[4]

Feddans

Area subject to 1952 Agrarian Reform law   .   .   .   650,000

---

[1] *Agrarian Reform in Seven Years*, p. 88. See below, pp. 31 and 35.

[2] This figure would be approx. 1·2 m. persons, if the families of the persons having obtained provisional occupancy rights (i.e. tenants) in Agrarian Reform lands are added.

[3] This figure would be much larger if it included the families of the intermediaries subletting the lands of the big landowners, as well as the families of the medium and large-sized farm operators renting these lands.

[4] *Agrarian Reform in Seven Years*.

Area sold by landowners to small farmers, according to
provisions of Art. 4 of the 1952 law. (The Ministry of
Agrarian Reform did not exercise any control or supervision over this area.) 145,000
Area requisitioned by the Agrarian Reform authorities from
private individuals. (This area was supervised by the
Agrarian Reform authorities as soon as it was requisitioned.) 462,663
Area requisitioned from private individuals and distributed
to small farmers in compliance with the general provisions of the 1952 law. (This area remained under the
supervision of the Ministry after distribution.) . . 333,782
Area expropriated from pious foundations (*waqfs khairi*) and
about to be requisitioned. (This area was to be supervised by the Ministry as soon as it was requisitioned) . 150,000
Area taken over by the Ministry from the State Domains
and about to be sold to small farmers 135,000
Area reclaimed by various organizations under the supervision of the Ministry and about to be sold to small
farmers. 60,000

These figures reveal that nearly 955,000 feddans of cultivated
lands had been or were in the process of being transferred to small
farmers, i.e. over 15·5 per cent of the cultivated area. The claim
made in Agrarian Reform publications[5] that small farmers (i.e.
94·7 per cent of owners) owning under 5 feddans would own
nearly 50 per cent (as against 35 per cent in 1952) of the cultivated
area at the close of the redistribution operations was therefore
about to be justified. The improvements in the agrarian structure
were, however, accompanied by a tentacular growth of the
Agrarian Reform administrative apparatus, which since 1957 had
become a full fledged Ministry. Indeed, by 1959 this Ministry
controlled and supervised some 807,000 feddans, i.e. over 13 per
cent of the cultivated area (145,000 feddans having been transferred to smallholders, in accordance with the 1952 law, without
any state interference). During the following two years approximately 120,000 feddans, most of it composed of *waqf* lands and
lands reclaimed by various governmental organizations, were
scheduled by the Ministry of Agrarian Reform for assignment in
full ownership to landless peasants. In fact in 1960 97,000 feddans
were distributed in full ownership and under tenancy status to
35,000 holders; this raised the area distributed by all state agencies
since 1952 to 430,852 feddans held by 162,773 owners and tenants.

The area finally transferred from big landowners to small landowners as a result of the 1952 and 1961 measures was probably
much more important than revealed by official figures pertaining

[5] S. Marei, *Agrarian Reform in Egypt* (1957), p. 247.

to expropriation and distribution during that period. The explanation of this is that many landowners sold the estates they were legally entitled to keep through fear of a subsequent reduction of the limit on residual holdings, or of more drastic tenancy laws.

TABLE 5

Area Distributed to Smallholders by Various State Agencies During 1953–60

(*feddans*)

Lands supervised by	Total area	Area distributed	No. of smallholders	Area scheduled for distribution	Area unfit for distribution[1]
Agr. Ref. authority	478,008	310,893	119,282	37,182	120,933
Ex-Mortmains	104,311	81,594	29,731	3,373	19,344
Nile lands[2]	10,058	10,058	6,582		
EARIS	13,860	13,860	2,772		
Permanent Organization for Land Reclamation	4,347	4,347	1,156		
Land reclamation companies[3]	6,000	6,000	1,450		
Ministry of Agriculture[4]	4,100	4,100	1,800		
Total	620,684	430,852	162,773	40,555	149,277

[1] Includes lands supposed to be either insufficiently productive or subject to legal disputes; a large part of these lands are tenanted.
[2] Strips of land accruing to lands bordering on the Nile banks; these strips are distributed to compensate landowners on the banks of the Nile who have lost part of their property through erosion by the river waters.
[3] Lands purchased from land reclamation companies at the end of 1959 for distribution to smallholders, in accordance with land reclamation legislation (see Ch. XI).
[4] Lands owned by the Ministry and distributed to smallholders.
Source: Agrarian Reform in Nine Years (1961).

Most of those who thus disposed of their property were foreigners, who in 1954 held 2·63 per cent of the owned area, i.e. nearly 160,000 feddans.[6] The greater part of this (70 per cent) lay in the Delta in the provinces of Daqahliya, Gharbiya, Sharqiya, Kafr al-Shaikh, and Buhaira. The estates sold by jittery foreign landowners were generally purchased in lots of 20–100 feddans by farmers who either kept them or broke them up further and sold them to smaller farmers in lots of 5 feddans. These massive sales increased after the Suez affair. The area affected by these transactions is likely to be considerable, especially if it is recalled that large tracts of land, mainly concentrated in the Northern Delta, were possessed by Egyptian subjects of foreign descent (Lebanese, Syrian, Greek) who during the period 1954–62 have received no better treatment than the specifically foreign community.

Claims advanced by responsible Egyptian officials in December 1961, that 141,151 feddans were still owned by foreigners (not

[6] Exactly 158,808 feddans, with an average area per foreign landowner of 50·4, as against 357,192 feddans in 1946, and an average area of 82 feddans.

including Egyptian subjects of foreign descent) do not seem realistic, nor do they conform to the trend of sales of foreign-owned lands as observed during the period 1946–54, when conditions for foreigners were far more favourable than from 1954–62. It would indeed be strange if during the period 1946–54 foreigners should have sold 200,000 feddans, i.e. more than half their property, while from 1954–62 they should have sold only 19,000 feddans.[7] One explanation of this discrepancy that has been put forward is that, despite the importance of sales during 1954–62, only a small part of these were registered, to evade currency control. Another more plausible explanation is that buyers were slow in settling the purchase price of their lands, so delaying registration formalities. These were carried out in most cases only after full payment of the purchase price.

ORGANIZATION AND OPERATION PENDING DISTRIBUTION IN FULL OWNERSHIP

The implementation of the expropriation measures decreed by the Agrarian Reform Law required the setting up of a highly efficient administrative organization to operate the requisitioned estates pending their redistribution in full ownership. In fact as soon as the Agrarian Reform was set in motion, these requisitioned estates were consolidated by the authorities into several regional administrative districts (also known as *mantiqat*) scattered all over Egypt. Each district covered an area of 10,000–15,000 feddans. It remained under the supervision of an Agrarian Reform regional administrative centre (*mantiqa*) headed by a *mandub* (delegate) who was first appointed by the Agrarian Reform authorities and after 1957 by the Ministry of Agrarian Reform. By 1959 the ministry controlled 43 *mantiqat*, the majority in Lower Egypt. These *mantiqat* were in charge of 480 *zira'at* (operational units) covering an area of approximately 1,000 feddans each, most of which were consolidated in large blocks of 200–1,000 feddans. In every *mantiqa* a *mandub*, supported by a large staff of agronomists, accountants, storekeepers, mechanics, foremen, and *ghufara'* (field wardens), was made the effective manager of the estates under his supervision, and it was he who initiated decisions, issued orders connected with farm management, agricultural credit, disposal of crops, &c., and who, generally speaking, was the mentor and guide of the small farmers living on the estates. Each *zira'a* of a *mantiqa* was considered as an administrative entity, at the head of which was appointed a *nazir al-zira'a* (agronomist) who was put in

---

[7] Including lands confiscated in 1956 from their British and French owners (13,010 feddans).

charge of the organization of cultivation and the use of the requisitioned lands. Assisted by a small staff of accountants, treasury clerks, storekeepers, and *ghufara'*, themselves quite often members of the expropriated landowner's staff, the *nazir al-zira'a* was in a position effectively to control agricultural production in the estates. Through him were channelled all funds provided by the Agrarian Reform authorities for agricultural credit, as well as seeds, fertilizers, and other items necessary for the operation of the lands.[8] He was also empowered to grant provisional tenancy status to peasants living in villages on the expropriated estates or in the vicinity whenever the lands supervised by him were previously owner-operated. He was entrusted with the collection of rentals due by these and other tenants, and to ensure that this proceeded smoothly, he was assigned the task of disposing of crops, through Agrarian Reform channels as far as possible. He was further in daily contact with the *mandub*, his administrative chief, who co-ordinated the activities of all the Agrarian Reform personnel. In fact, during the transitional period between the requisitioning of an estate and its assignment in full ownership, the *mandub* was the main link between the central Agrarian Reform administration in Cairo and the regional administration operating the expropriated lands.

In each *zira'a* the small farmers previously occupying the lands were allowed to continue as tenants under the supervision of the new administrative organization set up by the authorities. Big operators who had sub-leased the lands from the expropriated owners were automatically eliminated. Side by side with these 'old' tenants, were new tenants allowed to occupy that part of the lands which had been owner-operated. Both categories enjoyed the same status of tenancy, and were thus subjected during the interim period pending distribution in full ownership to the general principles laid down in the Agrarian Reform tenancy legislation[9] which granted security of tenure and pegged rents at a level equivalent to seven times the basic land tax assessed for a given plot.

Within the various operational units included in a *mantiqa* (in the sense of district) were lands which remained owner-operated (*ard 'ala'l-zimma*) by the Agrarian Reform authorities during the interim period and even after redistribution of most of the lands. In 1959 these extended over an area of 9,000 feddans (2 per cent of the area requisitioned from private individuals) and comprised lands not productive enough to be distributed in full ownership or under tenancy status. They also included lands which were

[8] See below, pp. 81–100.
[9] Arts. 31–37 of law no. 178 issued in Sept. 1952. See below, Ch. IX.

retained to feed the draught cattle owned by the newly established Agrarian Reform co-operatives and maintained by them as a reserve of draught power for unforeseen contingencies. These owner-operated lands were without doubt one of the least successful and most costly ventures entered upon by the authorities.

The expropriated orchards provided a vivid illustration of the difficulties encountered by attempts to owner-operate lands under the supervision of state employees. The orchards totalled 4,280 feddans;[10] they had not been distributed to smallholders, as the law of September 1952 specified expressly (Art. 10) that they could only be assigned to bearers of diplomas awarded by agricultural institutes. Total ownership was not to exceed 10 feddans, while the size of holdings planted as orchards and made available for distribution was not to exceed 20 feddans. In compliance with the law, distribution of orchards had been started on a very small scale in the *mantiqa* of Inshas (Sharqiya province) in 1955. But despite the selection of candidates the experiment turned out to be a failure, as most of the beneficiaries ended up by living in towns in exactly the same way as absentee landlords. Distribution of holdings planted in orchards was therefore discontinued, so that most of the expropriated orchards remained owner-operated under the supervision of the Agrarian Reform authorities, the income from them being credited to the co-operatives within whose boundaries they lay. In general, the condition of these orchards was fair.[11] Agrarian Reform publications claimed an increase in income of nearly 100 per cent,[12] but this claim was over-optimistic, for the increase had been calculated relative to 1954, i.e. two years after the expropriation of the orchards, when the level of production had already fallen as a result of the change in management. Moreover, prices of fruit had risen appreciably since 1952, thus masking reductions in output. In some orchards where output had in fact risen since expropriation, this was due to the natural development of trees which had reached maturity and thus become fully productive.

THE CONSOLIDATED TRIENNIAL CROP ROTATION

Most of the expropriated estates were in consolidated blocks and they remained so after requisitioning; further, many medium-sized expropriated estates were joined to larger ones adjacent to

[10] It was not possible for the author to discover whether this area was included in the figure of 9,000 feddans of owner-operated lands, but this is doubtful.

[11] In some areas (Fayyum, Marg) it was very poor, a situation which after much delay attracted the attention of the highest ranking Agrarian Reform officials in 1961 (see *al-Ta'awun*, Dec. 1961).

[12] *Agrarian Reform in Seven Years*.

them already expropriated or requisitioned. As the Agrarian Reform authorities completed the requisitioning of expropriated estates, they introduced in them a consolidated triennial crop rotation to preserve the fertility of the land. This was necessary because fertility had often been reduced by the more soil-exhausting biennial crop rotation with cotton predominating, which had been popular with large operators during the 1947–52 cotton boom. This triennial rotation, which had already been systematically applied by some diligent ex-landlords, was made standard practice in *mantiqat*, the only exceptions being the sugar-cane zones of Upper Egypt and the market-gardening zones in Giza province and in Buhaira province outside Alexandria. The lands of each of the separate villages of *mantiqat* were thus divided in three big consolidated blocks, each being assigned annually to one of three main groups of crops. A village such as al-Manyal, Damira *mantiqa* (Daqahliya province), with a total area of 1,262 feddans, was divided into three blocks of *circa* 420 feddans each; the first year one block was reserved for cotton, another for wheat and rice, and the last for clover and maize, but the second and third years the crops were rotated from one block to another in the following manner:

Consolidated Triennial Crop Rotation in the Co-operative of al-Manyal, Damira Mantiqa
Total area: 1,262 feddans

	420 feddans	420 feddans	420 feddans
First year	Clover (Permanent)	Clover snatch crop and seed-bed preparation for cotton	Wheat and barley or beans
	Maize	Cotton	Rice*
Second year	Clover snatch crop and seedbed preparation for cotton	Wheat and barley or beans	Clover (Permanent)
	Cotton	Rice*	Maize
Third year	Wheat and barley or beans	Clover (Permanent)	Clover snatch crop and seed-bed preparation for cotton
	Rice*	Maize	Cotton

* In other regions when no rice was planted this part of the land was planted in maize.

A tenant's holding was divided into three equal plots, each situated within the area allotted to one of the three main groups of crops in the triennial crop rotation. This pattern, which was rigorously followed throughout the expropriated villages, precluded the introduction of crops other than those mentioned above and tenants were requested to comply with it strictly. Exceptionally certain vegetable crops such as potatoes or tomatoes were permitted, on condition that they did not disrupt the rotations. The tomato summer crop (*nili*), for example, was planted by certain farmers instead of the maize crop; this did not interfere with the rhythm of irrigation of the other crops, since the requirements and the time of planting of both crops were nearly the same (in mid-July).

By cultivating a single crop over the entire area of such a consolidated block of holdings, according to an established rotation, it was possible to regulate the irrigation and drainage of Agrarian Reform lands, and wastage of water and superfluous drainage were thus partly avoided. Mechanical ploughing remained possible, while the control of the various agricultural operations, including pest control by the Agrarian Reform agronomists, was greatly facilitated. In addition, this system of crop consolidation constituted an essential element of the new system of supervised credit.[13]

PROCEDURE BEFORE DISTRIBUTION

The procedure regulating the distribution of holdings was evolved in compliance with the provisions of the Agrarian Reform Law.[14] Article 9 of the 1952 law had specified that expropriated land, with the exception of orchards, was to be distributed to farmers in holdings of 2–5 feddans subject to the following conditions:

1. The beneficiaries must be adult Egyptians without any criminal convictions.
2. They must be actually engaged in agricultural activities.
3. The total ownership of a beneficiary must be under 5 feddans at the time of distribution.

Priority was to be given to those farmers who actually cultivated the land, whether as full tenants, sharecroppers, or farm labourers; thereafter to the inhabitants of the village with the largest families and to the poorer inhabitants, and finally to farmers living in the vicinity. Strict conditions were laid down by the authorities to ensure that distribution conformed to the broader aims of the legislation. The number of tenants occupying the lands was checked when possible from the registers of the expropriated estates, after which they were divided into two groups:

1. Tenants occupying the lands before 1952, including those

[13] See below, Ch. VI.
[14] See also Marei, *Agrarian Reform* and AR publications on the estates of Damira, Za'faran, &c. (p. 224 below).

who had rented not from landlords but from intermediaries. Both were to benefit from distribution provided that it could be established that they were permanent cultivators and that the plots they farmed had long been recognized as the ones they worked on.

2. Tenants occupying the lands after September 1952[15] and those who had farmed the new expropriated lands before that date but who, due to some accident (illness, death, military service, or expulsion) had been compelled to forgo actual occupation. The former were entitled to benefit immediately from redistribution while the latter had to undergo a long period of probation. Assimilated to these—who were referred to by Agrarian Reform officials as *al-musta'jirin al-mu'alliqin* (tenants on probation)—were the following:

1. Those whose fathers were dead and who were still minors, who had to wait until they came of age, the land being leased meanwhile to their legal guardian.

2. Those with a criminal record who had to wait until it was clearly established that they had reformed. Meanwhile they were leased land in accordance with the basic distribution procedure.

3. Those owning smaller areas of land outside the expropriated estates than they might be allocated by the law. If they wished to benefit they had to sign a statement making over this property to the Agrarian Reform authorities and for a certain period they remained tenants on probation.

4. Those engaged in other trades who rented land at the same time were in principle precluded from benefiting, but since it was soon obvious that many tenants had been forced to combine various forms of employment to make a living and that strict application of this condition would have debarred a large number from becoming landowners, it was found necessary to qualify it in practice. Whenever a trade took up most of a tenant's time he was disqualified, but if it only occupied him part-time and provided him with a reasonable income, he was allowed full ownership after the deduction of an important share of the area that would otherwise have been his due. It was considered that the combination of a rural trade (grocer, butcher, carpenter, grain broker, &c.) and the possession of a reduced holding would provide enough to meet a family's expenses. Tenants engaged in jobs at a fixed salary, such as *ghufara'*[16] or road maintenance workers, were

---

[15] Priority among these tenants depended upon the date their occupation of the land started. Tenants of the year 1952/3 had priority over those of the year 1953/4, &c.

[16] *Ghufara'* are part of the institutional set-up of Egyptian agriculture; they were employed in large estates in Egypt, to prevent the pilfering and theft of crops, to safeguard the flow of water in the main irrigation channels, and in general to protect property from encroachment. In estates where share-cropping

allowed to rent their holdings for one to two years, undertaking in writing to resign from their jobs at the end of this period in order to become exclusively farming landowners, but tenants temporarily engaged in non-agricultural activities were not prevented from full ownership. This provision aimed at encouraging tenants to intensify agricultural production and at giving other unemployed rural inhabitants the opportunity of obtaining gainful employment.

Lists of the names of tenants were drawn up and carefully checked by the Agrarian Reform staff with the help of the employees of the ex-landowners and of the *'umda* and elders (*mashayikh al-balad*). A census of agricultural labourers working on requisitioned land was also carried out as these were eligible to become beneficiaries when the area to be distributed exceeded the ascertained needs of former tenants.

Assisted by specialized social workers, the Agrarian Reform staff also carried out systematic surveys to determine the social and economic status of each would-be beneficiary. The investigation recorded on printed forms particulars about the candidate and each member of his family, including the date of occupancy of the land, all property owned or rented and its location inside or outside the requisitioned area, housing conditions, annual income, &c. The social workers added their comments, and the forms were then examined and checked by one of the social and economic research committees, members of which included a social research worker as chairman, the *'umda*, two of the elders, the marriage registrar (*mazun*), the village tax-collector (*sarraf*), and the *mushrif ta'awuni* (co-operative supervisor).[17] The definition of a family adopted by the committees was 'a group of individuals gaining their livelihood from one and the same source on the land, no matter whether the members of the group resided in one or more places'. At this stage an estimate of the net income per feddan was thought necessary: this was established on the basis of the compulsory application of the triennial crop rotation taking into account the following points:

　　1. Gross income per feddan was assessed on the basis of the

---

or tenancy prevailed, they were appointed by the landowners to arbitrate the daily disputes between the occupants of the lands and arising in connexion with irrigation, drainage, pest control. They were also entrusted with safeguarding the rights of landowners when tenants attempted to move off their crops without prior payment of the rentals due; in such cases they could forbid the removal of crops, if necessary by force, until full payment of rentals was made.

[17] To ensure that answers given to the social research workers are true and to prevent fraud, since December 1961 the questionnaires have been classed as official documents; people giving false information to investigators have thus become liable to penalties for forgery of official documents.

average yields of the different crops and the market prices during the preceding seasons. The average yields of preceding seasons were available in the registers of a number of the expropriated landowners, but the estimates carried out by the land tax committees were sometimes set aside as they did not always correspond to the actual productivity of the land.

2. Net income per feddan was assessed by deducting from gross income the various expenses incurred (irrigation, upkeep of drainage, boundaries, land tax (*al-mal*), and the annual instalment plus interest) during one agricultural year.

3. Valuations took place in the fields set aside for redistribution and in the presence of the would-be beneficiaries, but the data they provided was accepted with caution.

4. It was presumed that each beneficiary would carry out all the manual agricultural operations exclusively with the help of members of his family; as such, manual work was not reckoned as additional expenditure.

To redistribute the lands equitably, the actual sources of income of the would-be beneficiaries' families and their size were studied, as well as the index of the cost of living in the various villages. By taking these variables into account and by determining the real productivity of the plots assigned to each beneficiary, the pattern of redistribution was made to fit in as closely as possible with the actual requirements of the rural communities. To accomplish this, sample surveys of the average cost of living for different-sized tenant families and of the different sources of family income were conducted. Visits to farmers' houses by the research personnel were said to have been undertaken to create an atmosphere of mutual understanding and good faith; this was generally followed up by a vigorous checking of answers to questions on annual tenant family consumption habits.

The size of the holdings allotted was calculated to give each beneficiary and his family an annual income exceeding bare subsistence expenses by 10 per cent: this margin was supposed to allow for price fluctuations or errors in the initial estimates and valuations. The minimum target figure aimed at per individual in Damira, for example, was an annual income of £E18, which was higher than the national average per rural inhabitant (£E14·5) as measured by government statistics in 1953–4.[18]

The yardstick used in adapting the size of distributed holdings to the families of candidates was the unit of land, the area of which

[18] Net income from agriculture in 1953/4 was approx. £E2621 m. (see NBE, *Econ. B.*, 1960, no. 1). But from this sum some £E60 m. had to be deducted in payment of rentals to absentee landlords. The residual approx. £E200 m. was shared by more than 14 m. rural inhabitants.

was related in every village to the fertility of its soil.[19] In turn, the number of land units allocated to a family was related to its age structure. Adults received 1 unit, and heads of families 1¼ units. Children under 5 received one-quarter of a unit, one-half being reserved for those between the ages of 5 and 13, and three-quarters for those between the ages of 13 and 21.

The provision limiting the size of the distributed holdings to 5 feddans precluded large families from obtaining their rightful share of land. To overcome this the Agrarian Reform officials divided families along the lines of their natural structure; thus the eldest married son and his family were considered as a separate entity, and this sub-family was given the right to receive a holding slightly smaller than that assigned to the original family. It was necessary to differentiate between the status granted to original families and that granted to sub-families to prevent large families so divided from obtaining holdings bigger than those assigned to average families. In consequence, sub-families were all allotted holdings half a feddan smaller than those granted to the original families. This procedure was claimed to be fair, for annual expenses per unit member of a large family were proportionately lower.

OCCUPATION OF THE NEW HOLDINGS

Once the preliminary procedures for redistribution according to the Agrarian Reform legislation had been completed, it remained to move tenants and other candidates to the lands they were to occupy, to assign them full ownership rights, and to deliver to them the legal titles. To conclude this last phase of the operation the fields had to be divided up to fit in with the pattern of re-distributed holdings. This was left to the Engineering Department of the Agrarian Reform administration. Maps were specially drawn on a scale of 1/5000, and the fields to be divided up were examined to determine their levels, the flow of irrigation water and drainage, the condition of the irrigation and drainage networks, the internal road networks, &c. All this information was noted on the maps, which were then checked by field studies. Crop rotations were planned and the holdings carved into three equal parts in order to continue the system of consolidated triennial crop rotation introduced during the interim period preceding redistribution. The maps were sent to the government Survey Department for final endorsement and registration; this department in turn appointed members of its regional staff in the various urban

---

[19] The unit of land varied from 10 *kirats* (10/24 of a feddan) in the fertile regions of Upper Egypt to 18 *kirats* (18/24 of a feddan) in the poorer regions of the Northern Delta.

centres to fix the iron stakes marking the boundaries of each plot. But the size of the plots assigned to candidates was less than that marked on their title-deeds because the land occupied by main irrigation, drainage, and internal roads was deducted from the area allotted *pro rata* to the size of the holdings. The area actually farmed by the new owners was thus slightly less than the area they owned; in the Northern Delta, where open-air drainage ditches occupied a high percentage of the land, this meant that holdings were sometimes over 12 per cent less than in the title-deeds. But it must be stressed that all beneficiaries enjoyed owner-ship rights over these networks, which were mentioned in the title deeds, and were proportionate to the size of the holdings.

The following precautions were taken before the final delimita-tion of individual holdings.

1. The three plots forming each holding were to be no more than 0·5 km. from each other.

2. The plots were to be as close as possible to the dwellings of beneficiaries.

3. The plots allocated to beneficiaries of very small holdings were to be given priority as far as nearness to dwellings was con-cerned.

4. Special attention was given to ensure the preservation of homogeneity of neighbourhood. The position of each plot of a beneficiary relative to that of his neighbours' plots was in addition the same in each of the three big blocks of the triennial crop rotation.

5. Each plot in each of the three big blocks of the crop rotation was clearly marked off from that of the neighbouring beneficiary by a tertiary drainage ditch.

6. In anticipation of future housing expansion, areas of land around the villages were withdrawn from the redistribution operation.

In practice, it appeared that despite these precautions, a large number of peasants were compelled to cover long distances daily, as their houses were from 1 to 3 km. distant from their holdings.[20] Though the distances separating houses from holdings were greater than was stated in Agrarian Reform publications, those separating the three plots (each located within the three con-solidated blocks of the triennial crop rotation) of each holding were smaller and averaged 0·25 km.

---

[20] In some *mantiqat* operators lived even farther from their holdings. In the *mantiqa* of Nabaruh (Bahut) (13,200 feddans), for example, a group of highly skilled peasants was allocated holdings at al-Manshia Qism Thani, 4 km. away from their houses in Bahut village.

LEGAL ASSIGNMENT OF OWNERSHIP

After completion of the above procedure, the beneficiaries received their title-deeds; included with the latter were the applications which they had filled in. On each title-deed were registered:

(a) the name of the applicant to whom the holding was legally assigned, i.e. that of the head of the family unit surveyed, as well as the names of those persons (adults or minors) considered by the social research committees as forming an integral part of the family unit, and who as such had been noted on the candidate's application;

(b) all particulars relevant to the size of the holding assigned, its division in three separate plots for the triennial crop rotation, its exact location, and the obligations of the new owner.

The most frequent size of holdings distributed was 3·5 feddans in the Northern Delta, and between 2 and 2·5 feddans in Central and Upper Egypt (the average for the whole of the area redistributed being 2·8 feddans in 1959). This was very low by European standards, but in Egypt it was considered quite substantial, especially if the potential returns from intensified agricultural production were taken into account.

In many estates of the Buhaira and Kafr al-Shaikh provinces (Idfina, Itay al-Barud, Za'faran), which had previously been part tenanted and part owner-operated through under-population, the Agrarian Reform authorities had to persuade peasants from overcrowded neighbouring villages to settle in the lands available for distribution. Even after allocating holdings to those living on the estates and in the vicinity, considerable tracts of land were often left over for further distribution. As landless peasants in neighbouring villages could only with great difficulty be coaxed into settling on these estates, the areas exceeding immediate distribution needs were rented to those smallholders who had benefited from distribution in full ownership but who were considered by the Agrarian Reform staff to be capable of farming larger holdings.[21] This procedure was adopted to keep the size of holdings allotted in full ownership within the legal limit; it was unusual, as the shortage of eligible candidates could have been remedied by immigration from overcrowded regions had there not been a lack

[21] At the star co-operative of al-Za'faran, for example, 1,219 feddans, i.e. 25 per cent of the area supervised by the co-operative, were rented, and nearly a third of the landowning beneficiaries were operating holdings part owned and part tenanted as late as 1959. A similar situation was to be found in the Itay al-Barud region, where in one of the co-operatives, Meliha, 240 feddans were rented to 22 tenants.

of housing facilities.[22] The same roundabout stratagem was applied in the fertile regions of Central and Upper Egypt to comply with the minimum limit set by the Agrarian Reform Law. Tenancy status instead of ownership status was granted to smallholders whenever the density of population on the estates was very high and the area available for distribution insufficient to carve out holdings of at least 2 feddans per beneficiary.

SMALL DISPERSED HOLDINGS (*Al-Mutana'thir*)

The distribution of smallholdings of under 200 feddans expropriated from medium-sized or large landowners and not directly adjacent to big Agrarian Reform estates was a permanent headache for the authorities. This was particularly true of holdings of under 50 feddans; because of their small area and their isolated position, these could not easily be supervised and controlled by the Agrarian Reform staff or submitted to the customary crop consolidation and the triennial crop rotation, even when their holders were included in an Agrarian Reform co-operative. In some cases[23] where the lands expropriated were very limited in area and not easily accessible to direct supervision, it was found necessary to sell them to peasants. Preliminary social studies were first conducted in compliance with standard Agrarian Reform regulations in order to allocate these isolated holdings fairly. The beneficiaries were often granted full ownership on conditions slightly different from the usual ones, and they were not forced to join any co-operative organizations. In doing this the Agrarian Reform authorities availed themselves of the option allowed by Article 10 of the 1952 law. In 1959 the area of dispersed holdings thus disposed of totalled 5,854 feddans sold to 5,589 beneficiaries; another 7,709 feddans were scheduled for sale in the near future.

FINANCIAL OBLIGATIONS OF THE NEW OWNERS

The purchase price of the land distributed to the beneficiaries was established on the same basis as that for the valuation of the

[22] Itself a sign of faulty planning seven years after the requisitioning of some of the estates. See below, Ch. V.
[23] A case observed by the author in 1960, and a particularly interesting example of the difficulties encountered by the Agrarian Reform authorities was that of a smallholding of approx. 30 feddans expropriated at the village of Tukh, Qalyubiya province, from a landowner possessing 230 feddans before the reform. The surplus 30 feddans were requisitioned in 1955, but since the *mantiqa* of Qalyubiya was unable to supervise this small isolated holding, it distributed it to small tenants, entrusting the expropriated landowner with the collection of the rentals, assessed at seven times the land tax. The subsequent remittal of the collected rentals to the Qalyubiya *mantiqa* was also made the responsibility of the ex-landowner.

compensation to be paid to the expropriated landowners. Bare land was thus valued at 70 times the basic land tax, an amount equivalent to 40–50 per cent of its market value before 1952. The price of existing buildings, fixed installations (pumps, &c.), and trees was added *pro rata* to the area distributed. These buildings and fixed installations were estimated by the valuation committees at the low figure of £E3·85 million;[24] their total value in all *mantiqat* was therefore estimated at the low figure of £E3·85 million, approximately 5 per cent of the estimated value of the bare lands.

The method of valuation sometimes led to gross injustice, as the land tax on some particularly poor lands was often claimed by the beneficiaries to have been assessed at too high a rate. This was a valid objection, for the land valuation committees who had carried out their assignment back in 1947 had now and again fixed rates after taking into consideration the average productivity of a big block of 30–100 feddans, within which some plots might well have been relatively infertile. To remedy this, and to satisfy the beneficiaries whose holdings had been overestimated, special committees were dispatched by the authorities to examine all complaints relating to the productivity of distributed lands. The committees were empowered to readjust the basic land tax so as to reduce the purchase price of holdings. By 1959 a reduction of the land tax previously assessed on an area of 15,000 feddans (5 per cent of distributed holdings in 1959) was decided upon by these special committees. However, in a number of cases the discrepancy between the estimate of productivity by the land tax committees in 1947 and that established after 1952 by the Agrarian Reform special committees, was more likely to have been caused by a recent fall in productivity than by faulty assessment in 1947.[25]

As a result of these reductions, the total purchase price to be paid by some of the beneficiaries was less than the compensation due to the expropriated landowners. From 1953–8 the difference was made good by increasing the land tax and therefore the annual instalments on neighbouring high-productivity lands. These decreases on some lands and increases on others were supposed to be an illustration of the co-operative spirit inspiring Agrarian Reform, and were called co-operative decreases (*takhfidh ta'awun*) or co-operative increases (*ziyada ta'awuniya*). The latter

24 See below, p. 200.
25 In May 1961 it was reported in the Egyptian press that another revision of the tax assessment on an area of 14,000 feddans was impending. This revision which was likely to bring about a reduction of annuities on redistributed holdings affected some 5,000 families in al-Mansura, Mahallat, Damira, Za'faran, Nabaruh, Simbilawain, and Dakarnas estates, all of which were located in Daqahliya province.

were highly unpopular. The system was abandoned in 1958 and the difference debited to the Central Fund of the Ministry of Agrarian Reform.[26]

The 1952 Agrarian Reform Law specified that 15 per cent was to be added to the price of the distributed holdings to cover costs of requisitioning, administration, and distribution. The total sum thus due by a beneficiary was to be repaid in thirty years plus interest at 3 per cent per annum. In 1958, to counteract the effect of the continuous fall in cotton prices, a new law[27] was promulgated, reducing the financial obligations of the beneficiaries; as in the case of compensation to landlords, the price of the distributed holdings was to be redeemed in forty annual instalments, at an annual interest rate not exceeding 1·5 per cent. The additional sum to meet the cost of requisitioning, &c. was reduced from 15 to 10 per cent.

In view of the changes brought about by the 1958 law, it is necessary to differentiate between the periods 1952–9 and 1959–61 fully to understand the payment system applied to the beneficiaries. During the first period, the total sum to be paid by a landowning beneficiary included the instalment on the purchase price of his holdings, the land tax and supplementary taxes normally paid by all Egyptian landowners, and so-called 'voluntary contribution' (*iradat al-gam'iya*) to Agrarian Reform co-operative administrative expenses. This contribution was made in conformity with a resolution 'endorsed' by members of all the Agrarian Reform co-operatives at the time of their establishment. The actual breakdown of these various payments was as follows.

The annual instalment due by a landowning beneficiary for the purchase of his holding plus costs of requisitioning and redistribution was equivalent to 3 921 times the basic land tax,[28] assuming a redemption of the purchase price in thirty years at 3 per cent interest per annum. To this was added the sum due for the basic land tax and the supplementary taxes (the latter being equivalent to 0·110 times the basic land tax). The total sum to be paid by landowning beneficiaries was therefore equivalent to five times the basic land tax ($3·921+1t+0·110t$), plus the *iradat al-gam'iya* (equivalent to the value of the basic land tax), the total payment thus being six times the basic land tax, i.e. 20 per cent

[26] Law no. 168, issued in 1958.   [27] Law no. 168.

[28] This calculation of the annuity (A) has been established by assuming a purchase price of C equivalent to 70 times the basic land tax (t) redeemable in 30 years at 3 per cent interest per annum + 15 per cent of the purchase price (without interest) for the requisition and distribution costs.

As such $C = t \times 70 + t \times 70 \times 0·15$

and $A = t \times 70 \times \dfrac{0·3 \ (1·03)^{30}}{(1·03)^{30}-1} + \dfrac{t \times 70 \times 0·15}{30} = 3·57t+ \quad = 3·92t.$

more than the amount specified by law. In fact during the first
two years (1953/4 and 1954/5) immediately after redistribution
of the first group of broken-up estates, landowning beneficiaries
were debited with 3·921 times the land tax, plus the basic land
tax and supplementary taxes, plus the 'voluntary contribution',
which was equivalent to 0·969 times the basic land tax, i.e. a total
of six times the basic land tax. In numerous regions peasants were
debited with an additional sum, equivalent to the basic land tax,
for the purchase of savings certificates (*sanadat al-iddikhar*) issued
by the Agrarian Reform co-operatives, and which were supposed
to be convertible into cash if pressing need arose. These nominal
savings certificates ranged between £E1 and £E5; they could
only be cashed if a written demand by the holder was approved
by the Board of Directors of the co-operative and by the *mushrif*.
The demand was rarely made unless in very exceptional circumstances (marriage, death, illness, indebtedness to the co-operative).
Peasants were thus in practice paying a total equivalent to seven
times the basic land tax for the occupation of their holdings (i.e.
the cost of the savings certificates added to the other costs). But
after 1955 the issuing of savings certificates was apparently discontinued in most regions, and payments by landowning beneficiaries for their holdings from 1955/6–1958/9 (not inclusive)
were equivalent to six times the basic land tax (instead of five
times, as specified by the 1952 law). It must, moreover, be stressed
that all these payments did not include the sums due by the
beneficiaries for loans in kind, cash, or services provided by
Agrarian Reform co-operative organizations during the agricultural
year to help them to operate their holdings.[29]

The reduction in annual instalment brought about by the
lengthening of the redemption period, the lower interest rate, and
the cut in the costs of expropriation and redistribution decreed in
1958 was intended to alleviate the financial obligations of the
beneficiaries at a time when cotton prices had fallen to their lowest
level since 1952.[30] This reduction, which had been decided on in
1958, was put into practice during 1958–9 in the various *mantiqat*.

[29] Miss Warriner (*Land Reform*, p. 36) states that the annual payment per
acre in the ex-royal estate of al-Faruqiya, Sharqiya province, was £E18, including the cost of seed, fertilizers, and services provided by the co-operative.
This error seems to have been attributable to defective information; in fact the
payment of £E18 (instalment + land tax + voluntary contributions) was equivalent to six times the basic land tax which in al-Faruqiya was £E3 per feddan,
i.e. £E18 not including the cost of seeds, fertilizers, and services. For the latter
an additional payment was made.

[30] 'If the annuity is calculated as six times the land tax, the margin between the
maximum fixed for rents and the annual payments of a landowning beneficiary
will be narrower and in poor seasons make payment of the annual instalment
difficult' (Darling, *YB. Agric. Co-op. 1956*, p. 15).

According to the accounting methods of the authorities,[31] the total annual amount due by a landowning beneficiary for the purchase price plus the basic land tax and supplementary taxes should thereafter have been equivalent to four times the land tax (instalment 2·890+basic land tax+supplementary taxes 0·110). In fact the beneficiaries were debited from 1958–9 with an amount equivalent to five times the basic land tax, the difference (equivalent to the land tax) being debited to them as 'voluntary contributions' to co-operative administrative expenses. Payments due for loans in cash and in kind and other services (*khadamat*) provided by the co-operative organizations to which beneficiaries were affiliated were added to this amount.

The direct consequence of the alterations in the redemption period and in the rates of interest, &c. was that many landowning beneficiaries assigned ownership before the enactment of the 1958 legislation felt frustrated, since new beneficiaries were now likely to receive land under more favourable terms. To counter this a law was decreed at the end of 1959[32] granting a refund to all landowning beneficiaries who had been debited with an annual instalment calculated on the old basis (i.e. redemption in 30 years at 3 per cent. interest per annum). This refund was in some regions quite important, and though it was supposed to have been applicable as from the date of assignment of full ownership to beneficiaries, it had still not been credited to them as late as the spring of 1960.[33]

It has already been mentioned that the payments by beneficiaries were equivalent to six times the land tax from 1953–4 to 1958–9. Land assessed at £E4 per feddan was thus rated at £E24. Such land was commonly rented at £E35–40 before the Agrarian Reform. The percentage decrease in payments for the occupation of holdings therefore ranged between 35 and 40 per cent if compared with rents previously charged to tenants. But starting from 1958–9 landowning beneficiaries were debited with the equivalent of five times

---

[31] After the reduction decided in 1958 the total instalment was equivalent, according to our calculations, to 2·5 times the land tax. This calculation of the annuity (A) has been established by assuming a purchase price (C) equivalent to 70 times the basic land tax (t), redeemable in 40 years at 1·5 per cent. interest + 10 per cent of the purchase price (without interest) for the requisition and distribution costs.

As such $C = t \times 70 + t \times 70 \times 0.15$

and $A = t \times 70 \times \dfrac{0.015 \times (1.015)^{40}}{(1.015)^{40} - 1} + \dfrac{t \times 70 \times 0.10}{40}$

$= 2.3387\,t + 0.175t = 2.5137t.$

[32] Law no. 205, 1959.

[33] In the regions of Damira, Nabaruh, Balqas, Sharbin, Dakarnas, Mansura, and Simbilawain the total refund was the equivalent of four times the value of the basic land tax. No wonder that the beneficiaries on these estates should have been clamouring loudly (in an open letter to the Agrarian Reform newspaper *al-Ta'awun*, 1 Mar. 1960) for the immediate application of law no. 205 of 1959.

the basic land tax, so that the percentage reduction relative to the period immediately preceding Agrarian Reform now ranged between 50 and 55 per cent.

The 1952 law specified that the maximum rent paid by all tenants (inside or outside Agrarian Reform areas) was not to exceed seven times the basic land tax. Payments by landowning beneficiaries from 1953–4 to 1958–9 (according to the above-mentioned rates) were thus 14 per cent lower than those made by tenants to landowners complying with Agrarian Reform tenancy regulations (six times the land tax instead of seven);[34] from 1958–9 onwards they were 28 per cent. lower (five times the land tax instead of seven). But the majority of landowners disobeyed Agrarian Reform regulations[35] and by 1958–9 rents extorted by them were back to their pre-1952 level. It can therefore safely be said that after 1958–9 Agrarian Reform landowning beneficiaries were paying 50 per cent less than they would have had to pay had they remained tenants of landowners disobeying the tenancy regulations. For a valid comparison of payments by beneficiaries and payment by tenants it should be borne in mind that part of the amount with which beneficiaries were debited was an annual instalment, payment of which would cease at the end of the 40-year redemption period.

FINANCIAL OBLIGATIONS OF THE TENANTS

Many farm operators were granted tenancy status on expropriated estates before their distribution in full ownership. Even after the distribution, a number of them continued to occupy holdings as tenants, either because they were tenants on probation or minors, or even because they were landowning beneficiaries who had been allowed to rent some extra lands not yet assigned in full ownership, &c. All the lands thus tenanted were rented annually during the period 1953–9 at a flat rate equivalent to seven times the land tax, regardless of the nature of the provisional tenure. In exceptional cases, where the assessment of the land tax was too high in relation to the productivity of the lands, rents were lowered, but in cases where the assessment was low, the level was raised. These variations in the assessment of rents were also called *takhfidh ta'awuni* and *ziyada ta'awuniya*.

With the lengthening of the period for the payment of compensation, &c., in 1958, the authorities reduced the rents paid by all Agrarian Reform tenants to the equivalent of six times the basic

[34] Agrarian Reform landowning beneficiaries paid at the rate of six times the and tax, while tenants of landowners complying with legislation paid at a rate of seven times the land tax.

[35] The highest percentage of landowners disobeying tenancy legislation was to be found among the class of small and medium-sized landowners (see below, Ch. IX).

land tax. This measure, applicable from the 1958/9 season, affected a considerable area already expropriated and still tenanted.[36] It was probably prompted by the desire to satisfy the numerous Agrarian Reform tenants who, though they were eligible for full landownership status, paid rents not deductible from the purchase price of a holding subsequently assigned to them in full ownership. A comparison of rents paid by Agrarian Reform tenants during 1953–9 with those paid before 1952 reveals that the former was 20–30 per cent lower, and this margin increased after 1958 to 30–40 per cent. There was, however, no difference between rents paid by Agrarian Reform tenants and rents paid by ordinary tenants of landowners complying with tenancy regulations until 1958/9, when Agrarian Reform rents were reduced by 14 per cent.[37] The situation of Agrarian Reform tenants was far more advantageous than that of the tenants of landowners disobeying tenancy regulations, their rents being 30–40 per cent lower.

OTHER OBLIGATIONS

The new occupants (landowning beneficiaries and tenants) of the expropriated estates were obliged to operate their holdings themselves, to maintain soil productivity, and to follow the technical advice offered by Agrarian Reform staff. These rules were enforced with a varying degree of success in all the *mantiqat* visited by the author. Most of the smallholders carried out their farm operations with the plentiful family labour available to them, and only resorted to hired labour exceptionally or at peak seasons, during the transplanting of rice seedlings in the Northern Delta, for example. The sub-letting of lands at a premium (of £E5–10 per feddan), though energetically repressed by the Agrarian Reform staff, was common, involving 5–10 per cent of the area distributed. This practice was undertaken for several reasons; some beneficiaries were gainfully employed elsewhere[38] and therefore unable to pay sufficient attention to their holdings; others found it more profitable to let them at a premium (*manfa'a*) to others in the vicinity; others, short of draught cattle, or even convinced of their inability successfully to operate their holdings, preferred to let them to more enterprising neighbours.[39] The obligation to maintain soil productivity and to follow the advice of the Agrarian Reform staff did not cause insuperable problems;

[36] More than 100,000 feddans, including the estates taken over from the *waqfs khairi* (*Agrarian Reform in Seven Years*, p. 102).

[37] Six times the basic land tax instead of seven.

[38] In particular *ghufara'*.

[39] For example, in the *mantiqa* of Bahut (province of Daqahliya) where the social research investigations had not been carried out with sufficient thoroughness, so that many beneficiaries were people who had never farmed previously.

as will be seen later, the agricultural instincts of the Egyptian peasant often made up for his low level of technical training, and the 1,000-year-old tradition of passivity to authority ensured acceptance of the leadership of the Agarian Reform staff in all the regions visited but one.[40]

The new occupants of the expropriated estates were also obliged to join the 'local' co-operative operating within the boundaries of the village where the holdings were situated. They were made to sign an undertaking agreeing to purchase from them all the requirements (seeds, fertilizers, insecticides, &c) for the operation of their holdings, and to dispose of all their produce through co-operative channels.

An additional obligation further restricting the freedom of action of the beneficiaries was that concerning the division of the income accruing to all members of their families, whose names had been supplied to the social research investigators and had thus been registered on the title-deeds. Whenever members of a family did not manage to agree on this among themselves, the matter was referred to the *Lagnat al-Musalahat* (Committee for the Settlement of Claims and Disputes)[41] of the relevant 'local' co-operative. If the committee found it impossible to arrive at a fair settlement, the Board of Directors of the 'local' co-operative intervened. The board was entitled to entrust the operation of the holdings to one or more members of the family, or even to rent the holdings to an outside operator, and then redistribute the income among the members of the family. To counter any further fragmentation of the distributed holdings and to prevent the disruption of the pattern of organization adopted in Agrarian Reform estates, the beneficiaries were also compelled to accept certain limitations on customary inheritance traditions. The distributed holdings were not allowed to be broken up and divided among the heirs of a beneficiary when he died. Instead, if all the heirs were adult, they were required to designate from among themselves the one to be entrusted with the operation of the holding of the deceased beneficiary, without affecting the division of the income of the holding among the other heirs according to normal legal procedure. Whenever agreement was not reached among the heirs, the Committee for the Settlement of Claims and Disputes stepped in. If it failed to arbitrate, the intervention of the Board of Directors of the 'local'

[40] The exception was the region of East Fayyum where peasants of nomadic Beduin stock proved difficult to handle; conditions in the neighbouring region of West Fayyum were slightly better.

[41] These committees were established in each of the 'local' co-operatives for the benefit of the new owners of the expropriated estates. Membership was confined to the directors of each 'local' cooperative, and powers covered the settlement of all disputes arising among beneficiaries.

co-operative was sought for, as in the preceding instance. If the heirs of the deceased beneficiary were minors, and if no responsible person could be found to operate the holding on their behalf, the board was entitled to recommend that the lands should be cultivated with the help of the staff of the Associated Co-operative Society.[42]

Another obligation further differentiating the legal status of an Agrarian Reform beneficiary from that of customary landowners was that he had to settle the entire purchase price of a holding (lands and buildings), as well as the interest due on it, before disposing of it by sale or mortgage.[43] To ensure the fulfilment of this obligation, which was also applicable to legal heirs, it was stipulated by law that no expropriation measures could be implemented by creditors of a beneficiary before the final settlement; an exception to this rule was, however, made in favour of the 'local' co-operative of which a beneficiary was member, as well as in favour of the Agricultural Credit Bank or the state itself, to enable them to implement expropriation measures whenever debts owed to them remained long outstanding.

In view of these obligations it is not surprising that the landowning beneficiaries should have become somewhat confused; they generally considered their condition of tenure similar to that of tenants enjoying long-term leases under favourable conditions, so much so that, when questioned about their annual payments, they spoke of *igar* (rent) rather than *qist* (instalment) and referred to other landowning colleagues as tenants (*al-musta'jirin*).

PENALTIES FOR DEFAULT

The very complexity of the status of the Agrarian Reform smallholders made it essential to impose sanctions on those evading their basic obligations. The authorities therefore imposed

---

[42] The Associated Co-operative Society took over the responsibilities of the *mantiqa*. See below, p. 57.

[43] It is doubtful whether a prosperous Agrarian Reform landowner would have been allowed to settle the debts contracted to purchase a holding and thus recover freedom of action, even if financially he had been in a position to do so. True, the statutes of the various local co-operatives were quite explicit on this point, but so many hurdles had to be cleared that in practice this alternative could not have existed. Art. 7 of the Statutes of the Damira local co-operatives, for example, precluded any disposal of the land redistributed to a peasant (whether by total or partial sale) except under the following conditions:

(a) Total payment of the purchase price of the new holdings.

(b) Sale to another member of the co-operatives, or to a peasant fulfilling the qualifications specified by the 1952 Agrarian Reform Law.

(c) Approval of the sale by the Co-operative Dept. at the Ministry of Agrarian Reform as well as by the General Co-operative Society grouping all Agrarian Reform co-operative societies (the General Co-operative Society being subject, in fact, to the direct supervision of the highest authorities in the Ministry of Agrarian Reform). See below, p. 59.

a number of sanctions ranging from censure to fines and even total eviction in an effort to induce peasants to fulfil their obligations and to enforce a minimum of discipline in the redistributed estates. But these sanctions were not applied rigorously, and the treatment meted out to even the most recalcitrant smallholder, though smacking of administrative bureaucracy, was neither harsh nor inhuman. The collection of money due to the co-operatives for the instalments, voluntary contributions, loans in kind and cash, services, &c. generally occurred without resorting to sanctions. Even in cases of gross negligence in the settlement of big outstanding liabilities such as those found in the regions of Bahut, Itay al-Barud, and Fayyum,[44] the authorities seem to have hesitated to initiate wholesale evictions which would have caused an uproar. To become effective, eviction had to be endorsed by a judicial committee,[45] after a thorough investigation, and after 1957 had to receive the final approval of the Minister of Agrarian Reform. No wonder, therefore, that eviction in the areas visited was reported to be a rare event, and, despite rumours to the contrary, the 1,339 cases (most of whom were tenants) admitted by official publications in 1959[46] are highly credible. Rumours commonly circulated about the high percentage of smallholders who relinquished their holdings because of their pitiful financial plight were on the whole unfounded, and stemmed mainly from the wishful thinking and fertile imagination of expropriated landowners. In reality, the percentage of smallholders who abandoned their holdings because of major financial difficulties was low, principally because of the lax treatment of the Agrarian Reform administrative machinery. It was rarely more than 15 per cent, the higher percentages being confined to regions in the Fayyum and in the Northern Delta, where productivity had fallen.

[44] See below, pp. 99–100.

[45] Amendment to Art. 14 of the 1952 law, enacted by law no. 454 issued in 1955. The Judicial Committee is composed of a magistrate from the State Council (*Maglis al-Dawla*) acting as President, and two other members having rank of directors of departments at the Ministry of Agrarian Reform.

[46] *Agrarian Reform in Seven Years*. In the star co-operative of Damira, for example, the number of persons evicted was seven out of a total of more than 5,000 smallholders.

IV

CO-OPERATIVE ORGANIZATIONS

A sound democracy depends heavily on the strength and number of institutions that stand between the individual and the national government, defending his individual rights in the process of defending institutional interests.

M. F. MILLIKAN and D. L. M. BLACKMER, eds., *The Emerging Nations* (1961)

THE 'LOCAL' CO-OPERATIVES

IMMEDIATELY after the completion of redistribution measures in a given *mantiqa* each of its *zira'at* came under the supervision of a 'local', i.e. a village, co-operative grouping all the peasants occupying lands within its boundaries. Very minute operational units (*al-aradi-al-mutana'thir*),[1] when dispersed among neighbouring villages, were grouped under a single co-operative sometimes extending over nearly 1,000 feddans.

As has been stated, membership of a 'local' co-operative was compulsory for all the occupants of Agrarian Reform estates,[2] which meant subscribing to its capital, the subscription being *pro rata* to the size of a holding, on the basis of one share valued at £E1 per feddan or part of a feddan. However, according to the 1952 Agrarian Reform Law, membership was not in principle exclusively reserved to Agrarian Reform smallholders; it was supposed to be open equally to owners of less than 5 feddans whose lands lay within the boundaries of villages affected by redistribution operations. In September 1959 a new law was issued extending the membership of the Agrarian Reform co-operatives to independent owners or tenants whenever they owned or operated holdings of less than 15 feddans which lay within the boundaries of adjacent villages. Nevertheless the only members of the Agrarian Reform local co-operatives until the spring of 1960 were the beneficiaries and tenants of the broken-up estates. The absence of independent farm operators, naturally loath to prejudice their freedom of action, was partly the result of the timid and inadequate efforts of the co-operative administration of the Ministry of Agrarian Reform, which failed to convince them of the advantages of

[1] These units had been formed to operate small or medium-sized expropriated holdings which were not adjacent to a big compact estate.
[2] i.e. all the beneficiaries and tenants, whether on probation or not.

membership. This was regrettable, for the presence of farmers not directly connected with Agrarian Reform organization and with no formal obligations to it might have been of the highest value.[3] It might have contributed on more than one occasion to a more constructive and dynamic attitude on the part of the boards of the co-operatives, whose members were too often completely subservient to the Agrarian Reform official members.

The 'local' co-operatives in the various *mantiqat* were primarily created to meet the day-to-day requirements of the new landowners and to help them to operate their holdings successfully. The services they provided included:

1. The provision of agricultural credit.

2. The supply to farmers of various types of equipment and help for the adequate cultivation of the expropriated estates. This consisted in the supply of selected seeds, fertilizers, insecticides, livestock and poultry, agricultural machinery, and storage facilities for crops.

3. The organization of efficient cultivation and land use, and in particular the introduction and enforcement of the consolidated triennial crop rotation, the supervision of farm operations and of the application of the fertilizers distributed, the maintenance of the buildings co-operatively owned, and the regular upkeep of the irrigation, drainage, and internal road networks.

4. The sale of the crops of members after deduction from the price (whenever necessary) of sums due for the purchase of the lands and the land taxes and for the settlement of the various loans in kind and in cash made by the co-operatives.

5. The undertaking of all other agricultural and social services required to benefit members.

The capital of each of the 'local' co-operative societies of a *mantiqa* was provided entirely by the shares of its members. The shares were nominative and indivisible, and no single member was allowed to own more than one-fifth of the paid-up capital. Whenever a society considered an increase in its capital would improve agricultural production, it was entitled to deduct annually a given sum from the dividend due on a member's shares, the same rate being applied equally to all other members of the co-operative. These deductions were made periodically, until the co-operative

[3] In 1957 in Italy membership of Agrarian Reform co-operatives was opened up by the authorities to include farmers operating lands not subject to Agrarian Reform, and, according to information obtained in October 1959, 10 per cent of the members of the Agrarian Reform co-operatives in the Maremma were then independent operators whose lands were not under Agrarian Reform supervision. The presence of these independent operators was reported to have brought about a more dynamic approach to co-operative problems. For further reference see G. Barbero, 'Riforma Fondiara', in *Annuario dell'agricoltura italiana*, p. 397.

had received the total sum which it estimated necessary to fulfil its purpose, and the repayment of the money was made in the same chronological order that it was deducted. The reserve funds of a co-operative were accumulated by an annual fixed deduction from profits, but in principle they could also be forthcoming from donations and testamentary provisions.

Management

The 'local' co-operative of a *mantiqa* was managed by the Board of Directors, under the supervision of a so-called *mushrif ta'awuni*, who was generally none other than the *nazir al-zira'a* appointed by the Agrarian Reform authorities during the transitional period preceding redistribution in full ownership. The members of each board were elected by all beneficiaries and tenants sitting in the General Assembly of their co-operative. Because the lands of a co-operative were divided up into three main blocks to comply with the triennial crop rotation, all the beneficiaries with land in each block elected a number of their colleagues to the Board of Directors. The number of elected board members differed according to the size of each co-operative. Each member always had a substitute who automatically took the former's place on the board if his seat became vacant for any reason (eviction from the board, death, &c.). The members of the board were given no special training in co-operative matters prior to their election.[4] Many of them were illiterate, sometimes as many as 50 per cent. This was not astonishing since the vast majority of the smallholders who had elected them were also illiterate, the percentage of illiteracy ranging between 75 and 80 per cent. But the illiteracy of board members was not to remain a permanent feature as the authorities encouraged as far as possible the election to office of younger men with a minimum of schooling, and the big drive to increase school attendance in rural areas was in the long run to lead to the emergence of a class of literate smallholders.

The *mushrifs ta'awuni* were appointed by the Board of Directors of each 'local' co-operative, acting on the suggestions of the *Idarat al-Ta'awun* (co-operative administration) set up by the Agrarian Reform authorities in Cairo.[5] A candidate could not be vetoed by

[4] Membership of a board was conditional on:
  (a) The purchase by the candidate's co-operative of 75 per cent of the value of the agricultural goods necessary to the operation of his holding.
  (b) Disposal through his co-operative of at least 75 per cent of the crops produced on his holding and which were generally retailed by the co-operative.
  (c) Promptness in repayment of loans by his co-operative.
  (d) Freedom from any business ties and connexions incompatible with a candidate's duties as a member of the board.
[5] After 1957, a department of the Min. AR. See below, pp. 63–64.

board members if he was supported by both the co-operative administration and the Agrarian Reform General Co-operative Society.[6] In practice, however, the appointment of the *mushrif ta'awuni* was left entirely to the *Idarat al-Ta'awun* in Cairo, which imposed its own choice on the co-operative board, which automatically approved. Candidates varying in age between 26 and 40 were generally agronomists with a minimum of technical training and a degree from one of the higher schools of agriculture or from a faculty of agriculture. A fairly high percentage of employees of the expropriated landlords were also kept in office and appointed as *mushrif ta'awuni*. Others were chosen from the personnel employed for the supervision of lands managed by the Ministry of Waqfs until 1959, the percentage of these increasing considerably after the requisition of the *waqf khairi* lands in 1959. Despite the urgent need for trained personnel no special training in agrarian reform problems was given to the *mushrif ta'awuni*[7] though they were supposed to have been recruited after passing an entrance examination in which one of the main subjects was rural co-operation. This disadvantage was partially offset by the presence in every *mantiqa* of an expert on co-operation (*mufattish al-ta'awun*), who directed the local *mushrif* on all matters pertaining to rural co-operation. Though the chairman[8] of the board, with a secretary and a treasurer, assumed in principle very extensive powers, it was in fact the *mushrif* who effectively managed a 'local' co-operative. In daily contact with the *mandub*, the *mushrif* had in most cases taken the place of the bailiffs of the ex-landlords.[9] Most of the time they were only concerned with the problem of obtaining as promptly as possible the settlement of the land taxes, annual instalments, and loans in kind or in cash due by the members.[10] Permanently on the alert to detect some new means of mopping up outstanding debts (often the result of the high level of instalments and rents), the efforts of the *mushrifs* therefore concentrated more on short-term objectives directly related to this rather than on the introduction of thorough and radical changes in the techniques and ways of life of the peasantry in their care. Active supervision of

---

[6] Created in 1957, it assumed part of the responsibilities which previously fell to the High Committee for Agrarian Reform. See below, p. 59.

[7] The general policy followed by the Agrarian Reform authorities was to send newly appointed agronomists to regions which were still in the transitional phase (i.e. after requisitioning but prior to redistribution), so that they should become acquainted with day-to-day agricultural problems. After this candidates were given the most complex responsibilities of the *mushrif ta'awuni* in redistributed lands.

[8] The chairmanship was assigned to members of the board in alphabetical order.

[9] In Damira, the best example of the Agrarian Reform co-operative structure, this was the case; how much more so therefore in the other *mantiqat*.

[10] See below, pp. 95–99.

agricultural operations was confined principally to the crops disposed of through co-operative channels since this provided an easy
way of collecting debts. The lack of confidence of the peasants
resulting from this approach was reinforced by the chilly, distant,
and slow reaction of the whole Agrarian Reform apparatus to
their demands and complaints (whether justified or not). But this
was not the only criticism that could be levelled at the *mushrifs*;
loath to reduce the annual profits of their respective co-operatives
and anxious to preserve the goodwill of the members (i.e. the smallholders), they were also apt to go slow on expenditure on the upkeep of the holdings (irrigation, drainage, road networks, buildings,
&c.). The ensuing laxity, of course, did great harm to the long-
term objectives of agrarian reform.

The dominance of the *mushrifs* in the management of the affairs
of the 'local' co-operatives was fully acknowledged by the Agrarian
Reform smallholders, who always referred to them as *nazir al-
zira'at*, the same term they had used in the past for the agents of
the ex-landlords. The *de facto* powers wielded by a *mushrif* over the
administrative and technical staff of a 'local' co-operative (about
12–15 people),[11] the fact that whenever differences of opinion arose
between him and the board, the dispute had to be arbitrated by the
Idarat al-Ta'awun in Cairo, and the fact that the board could not
discharge him without the former's consent, all contributed to this
dominance.

The *mushrifs* themselves were under the strict control of the
Agrarian Reform authorities and thus had to comply with the
instructions issued by the *Idarat al-Ta'awun*. Their salaries were
determined by the wage schedule laid down by the Agrarian Reform
authorities,[12] and the approval of the co-operative boards was
purely formal. The most usual salary was £E20 a month, to which
could be added an annual bonus of up to £E100 granted by the
Idarat al-Ta'awun and the respective Boards of Directors. The
financial rewards of the *mushrifs* (and for that matter of the members
of the boards) were inadequate. This seemed to be one of the causes
of the aloofness and often frequent turnover of Agrarian Reform
staff, who complained that their efforts to help the peasant communities entrusted to them went unnoticed and unrewarded. The
figures for bonuses given to the staff in the central administration
and in the various *mantiqat* seem to prove this point; in 1961, for
example, the total sum allocated amounted to only £E175,000 (less
than 0·75 of the value of the gross agricultural production of the

[11] The staff included the *mushrif*, his assistant (*mu'awin*), two or three field
supervisors (*mulahizen*), a foreman (*khawli*), a chief field warden (*shaikh ghafar*),
and *ghufara'* (3–5), mechanics for the irrigation pumps, an accountant (*katib*),
and a storekeeper (*makhzangi*).
[12] In 1959 identical with that currently in use at the Ministry of Agriculture.

expropriated estates) although some 8,000 people were employed by the 43 *mantiqat*. Co-operation assumes dedication on the part of those in charge of preaching its gospel, and no amount of financial reward can replace faith, but the very size of the programme of agrarian reform, the tremendous task involved in wresting a peasantry, downtrodden for centuries, from misery, squalor, endemic disease, and low productivity, had produced a demand for dedication that no free society could have satisfied unless it was determined to reward generously the efforts of those answering its call.

Size

By the end of 1959 312 'local' co-operatives were operating in the 43 *mantiqat* which supervised nearly 520,000 feddans (including *waqf khairi* lands). The co-operatives were therefore very large, the usual size being around 1,000 feddans, with a membership of about 300 per co-operative. Sir Malcolm Darling has already expressed grave doubts about the future of the societies;[13] it would probably have been more appropriate, from the angle of co-operation, to establish small co-operatives of 100 members, such as those set up in the Italian Maremma region[14] or the voluntary co-operatives in the Tuscan village of Borgo à Mozzano.[15] The opportunities in small or medium-sized co-operatives for members to get to know each other and learn to act together were certainly theoretically much greater. However, in Egypt the question of size was directly related to the problems of efficient farm operation and the rational disposal of crops, both of which could only be solved economically by dividing the lands wherever possible into operational units of about 1,000 feddans.[16] The complexity and intricacy of the irrigation and drainage networks, the imperative necessity for consolidated crop rotations, the vital importance of effective pest control, the provision of adequate agricultural credit, the collection of sums due to the co-operatives together with the rational disposal of crops by a centralized marketing agency are some of the arguments in favour of the large

[13] *YB Agric. Co-op., 1956*, pp. 20–21. Miss Warriner (*Land Reform*, p. 43) seems to have shared his doubts.

[14] By 1 January 1958 156 co-operative societies had been formed in the Maremma, with a total membership of 16,466. Their jurisdiction extended over an area of some 170,000 ha. (see Ente Maremma, *Land Reform in Maremma* (Rome, 1959)). The co-operative centre of Albinia, Orbetello Settlement Centre, visited by the author in the autumn of 1959, covered 8,000 ha. supervised by 7 co-operatives; 550 new farmers (podere) and 111 farmers, with additional plots of 3 ha. each, were members of these co-operatives.

[15] See below, p. 196, and for further reference, M. Tofani, *Borgo à Mozzano* (Univ. of Florence, 1956); and Shell Italiana's *Centro Studi Agricoli* (Genoa, 1960).

[16] Half the size of the Maremma units.

Egyptian Agrarian Reform co-operatives.[17] They are all the more convincing if it is borne in mind that it was not the actual area supervised by the co-operatives[18] that was in question, but rather the size of their membership. Further fragmentation of the 'local' co-operatives would have been of no use. The small dispersed co-operatives did not generally prove to be as efficient as the large ones, often because they were understaffed and sometimes because they were not important enough to engage the attention of the central authorities. The breaking up of the large co-operatives would have necessitated many more agronomists with a full knowledge of co-operative affairs, a practical impossibility in Egypt during the first seven years of Agrarian Reform since there was no adequate training programme for staff and since the ratio of trained technicians (for supervision and extension work) was already low: one for every 300–400 smallholders as against one for every 93 small holders in Italy, for example.[19]

Some solution could have been found for the problem of the size of the co-operatives by making the maximum use of forms of mutual self-help (*muzamala*), well adapted to Egyptian rural life. The purchase of farm equipment through partnership arrangements (such as at the co-operative of al-Manakhulla, Damira estate,[20] where members banded together in small groups to buy mobile irrigation pumps), deserved more energetic encouragement. The establishment of smaller co-operatives specializing in the mechanization of internal transport operations, in threshing grain crops, in cattle breeding, or in marketing poultry and livestock products could partially have balanced the big top-heavy Agrarian Reform 'local' co-operatives; though completely independent from the latter, there could have been some form of affiliation.

THE ASSOCIATED CO-OPERATIVE SOCIETIES (ACS)

During the transitional period between requisitioning of an estate and the assignment of ownership to beneficiaries, the *mandub* was the main link between the central Agrarian Reform authorities in Cairo and the *mantiqa*, which supervised the farmers operating the lands within its boundaries. After the assignment of

[17] See below, Chs. V–VII.
[18] In fact the area of the Agrarian Reform 'local' co-operatives was in 1959 relatively small if compared to the centralized units of production (sovkhozes and kolhkozes) current in Soviet agriculture. Of course, if the traditional cropping pattern now practised in the co-operatives is in the future replaced by highly intensive forms of production (orchards, flowers, market gardening, livestock), then the size, i.e. the area under the jurisdiction of a local co-operative, will appear large relatively to sovkhozes or kolkhozes because of the value produced and marketed per unit of area supervised.
[19] See Barbero, p. 396.   [20] See below, p. 106.

ownership, and as a result of the setting up of 'local' co-operatives, the supervision and control of a *mandub* was automatically slightly relaxed.

Since 1957 the trend has been to do away with the terms *mantiqa* and *mandub*. Immediately after assignment of ownership and the legal establishment of 'local' co-operatives in a given region, the responsibilities of the *mantiqa* were assumed by a regional Associated Co-operative Society (*al-Gam'iya al-Ta'awuniya al-Mushtaraka*), headed by a *mushrif al-ta'awuni al-'amm* (general co-operative supervisor) who was usually none other than the ex-*mandub*. This regional ACS grouped under its wing all the 'local' co-operatives operating within the boundaries of the dissolved *mantiqa*, and linked them exclusively to the newly established Agrarian Reform General Co-operative Society in Cairo,[21] which was supposed to take over a large part of the responsibilities of the Agrarian Reform authorities. The main functions of an ACS were:

1. The provision of agricultural credit for its local co-operatives.

2. The provision of the various types of equipment and commodities for adequate cultivation of the lands of the beneficiaries and tenants of the estates, including the bulk supply to the co-operatives of selected seeds, fertilizers, insecticides, livestock and poultry, agricultural machinery, and storage facilities for crops.

3. The overall organization of cultivation and use of the lands and the planning and co-ordination of the agricultural activities of the various 'local' co-operatives, and, last but not least, the control and upkeep of the main irrigation drainage and road networks.

4. The disposal by bulk sale of the crops of the members of the local co-operatives.

5. The settlement to the various government agencies of the outstanding balances due by the 'local' co-operatives for the purchase of the redistributed lands, for the government land taxes, and for the reimbursement of the various loans in kind and in cash made by the ACS to the 'local' co-operatives.

6. The provision of all other agricultural and social services required for the benefit of the members of the 'local' co-operatives.

7. The provision of a veterinary unit (*markaz ra'ayat al-hayawan*), the services of which were available to all members of the 'local' co-operatives.

Membership of an ACS was confined to the 'local' co-operatives operating in its area; its General Assembly was composed of all the members of their Boards of Directors, and its Board of Directors included their acting secretaries. The capital was subscribed mainly by the 'local' co-operatives, whose contribution (75 per

[21] See below, p. 59.

cent of the total) was paid out of their own capital. The remainder was provided by the General Co-operative Society.

The change in organization resulting from the creation of the ACS did not, however, have much effect. Although in 1959 the ACS were on the whole functioning according to plan, they were still commonly known to the Agrarian Reform staff, to the peasants and the general public, by the old denomination of *mantiqa*; the *mushrifs al-ta'awuni al-amm* themselves were still called *mandub*, and this confusion in terminology was a sure sign of failure to adapt to the new co-operative structure.

The administrative staff of an ACS consisted of a chief accountant, a cashier, several clerks, and a general storekeeper, his assistants, and a few ushers. Included among them were employees of the ex-landlords and of the Ministry of Waqfs, often comprising 40 per cent of the total staff. The technical staff included the *mushrif al-ta'awuni al-'amm* (ex-*mandub*), helped by an agricultural expert (*muffatish al-zira'a*) and a co-operative expert (*muffatish al-ta'awun*), who supervised the local *mushrifs ta'awuni*. In fifteen ACS a completely independent administrative unit, the veterinary unit,[22] had been created for livestock matters, under the direction of the *mushrif al-ta'awuni al-'amm*. A qualified vet was in charge of this unit, helped by several male assistants, a few semi-specialized workers operating poultry incubators, an agricultural engineer and his assistant. At a lower level, the technical staff of the ACS was reinforced by a mechanic in charge of its farm machinery pool,[23] who had several assistants, storekeepers, tractor drivers, and mechanics for the irrigation pumps.

THE GENERAL CO-OPERATIVE SOCIETY (GCS)

The co-operative organizations established at the village and the district levels were at first linked to the central administration in Cairo. But in November 1957 a new organization, the Agrarian Reform General Co-operative Society (*al-Gam'iya al-'Amma li'l-Islah al-Zira'i*), was created to relieve it of a large part of the responsibilities which it had assumed during the early phase of redistribution. The new co-operative was also supposed to enable the co-operatives at the village and the district levels to free themselves from the ties that had bound them so far to the purely administrative apparatus set up in Cairo. Membership of the GCS was in principle limited to the ACS, who were entitled to dispatch a delegate to the meetings of its General Assembly. But 'local' co-operatives not yet grouped in an ACS were exceptionally

---

[22] See below, pp. 114–17.   [23] See below, p. 105.

allowed to become members, all the 'local' co-operatives of one *mantiqa* electing one delegate to represent them at the General Assembly meetings. The main functions of the GCS were:

1. Catering for all the requirements of the Agrarian Reform co-operative societies. This included bulk supply of all agricultural goods (seeds, fertilizers, equipment, &c.), household goods and all other goods necessary for the normal economic, social, cultural, and sporting activities of the beneficiaries.

2. Supplying the co-operative societies with all forms of agricultural credit.

3. Obtaining loans from various sources, such as government agencies, banks, and other institutions, for productive projects and ventures under its own supervision or under that of its affiliated members.

4. Purchasing, selling, renting, or operating agricultural lands, and establishing model farms for livestock and poultry production, for the distribution of selected breeds, or for any other purpose, whether economic, social, cultural, or sporting, that might benefit the co-operatives or their members.[24]

5. Operating agricultural lands with the agreement of their owners, establishing co-operative societies to include the tenants and farm labourers of these lands in accordance with conditions to be determined between their owners and the Board of Directors of the GCS, and in such a manner as to protect the members of these co-operatives and to safeguard their interests; purchasing waste land for reclamation; selling reclaimed lands on an instalment basis under conditions to be laid down by the Board of Directors of the GCS; establishing co-operatives to include the peasants granted ownership of reclaimed lands by the board.

6. The production, manufacture, purchase, sale, and importation of all equipment, machinery, and goods, needed by the co-operatives and their members either for agricultural production or for household consumption. The exchange, trade, and hire of equipment, machinery, and goods, and establishment of industrial plant and repair shops for their upkeep.

7. The manufacture and production of various goods, meat, fish, dried and canned foodstuffs, furniture, pharmaceuticals, shoes, livestock and poultry feed concentrates and any other goods needed by the co-operatives and their members. Trading these goods through purchase or sale for the benefit of the co-operatives and their members.

8. Production, purchase, sale, transport, handling, grinding, storage, disposal, import and export of all goods of utility or im-

[24] This clause enabled the GCS to buy land owned by enemy subjects and sequestrated by the Egyptian Government in November 1956.

portance to the members of the co-operatives whether as producers
or as consumers.

9. Erection, purchase, sale, hire and renting of buildings or
houses for itself, for the co-operatives or their affiliated members.

10. Entering into contractual arrangements with various government agencies or with private establishments in so far as this was
beneficial for its members.

11. Supervision, inspection, control, direction, and provision of
advice for the co-operatives.

12. Establishment of a system of insurance giving full protection
to the agricultural and sanitary activities of the members of the
co-operatives.

13. Establishment of industrial plant and factories to facilitate the
disposal of the crops of its members; establishment of milk-
processing industries and of all other enterprises to augment the
income of members as a result of their agricultural activities.

14. Diffusion of agricultural knowledge and encouragement of
co-operative effort among members of the co-operatives and among
the rural communities in general, by organizing conferences and
cinema shows, by radio, by distributing books, pamphlets, written
studies, &c., and by any other practical methods of agricultural
extension work.

15. Acceptance of deposits from its members either on call or for
a fixed term, under conditions specified by the Board of Directors.

16. Issue of co-operative savings certificates to its members.

17. Execution of and participation in social projects initiated by
the GCS or by its member societies.

18. Undertaking all import–export operations.

19. Undertaking all other operations and providing all services
beneficial to members.

The capital of the GCS consisted of nominative indivisible
shares. The value of each share was worth £E4, which had to be
entirely paid up at the time of subscription. All members (whether
ACS or local co-operative societies) were made to subscribe half
the value of their paid-up capital. As in the case of the 'local' co-
operatives, reserve funds were supposed to be accumulated by an
annual fixed deduction from profits, though they could also be
forthcoming from donations and testamentary provisions. The
Board of Directors was entitled, whenever it found it useful for its
members, to increase the financial resources of the GCS by reducing
the percentage of distributed profits.

The GCS was managed by a Board of Directors of 15 members,
who were chosen according to the following procedure: 7 members
were elected by the General Assembly of the GCS from among the

delegates of the affiliated co-operatives; the president was elected
by a public vote of the General Assembly at the first meeting after
official registration of the co-operative; 7 members were to be
elected by the General Assembly from a list of candidates drawn up
by the president of the board, all of whom were to be members of
the Organization for Agrarian Reform.[25] The offices of vice-
president, general secretary, and treasurer were reserved for this
category of members.

The office of president ran for five years, but all other members
of the board were elected for an initial term of three years. Board
members received no salary, but a token fee for attendance was
paid as well as an annual bonus not exceeding 10 per cent of the
total net profits of the co-operative. A director-general of the co-
operative was appointed, but he could not be a member of the
Board of Directors, and though he attended meetings he could not
vote. On the other hand, the delegates of the member co-operative
societies took part in General Assembly meetings and voted. Each
delegate was entitled to one vote. The ACS usually appointed
their acting secretaries as their representatives. Some ACS, the
volume of whose annual transactions was more than the average
transactions of all the member co-operatives, enjoyed the privilege
of casting an extra vote and therefore appointed a second delegate
to attend General Assembly meetings. The ACS the volume of
whose annual transactions was double that of the average received
a second supplementary vote and therefore appointed a third
delegate.

The responsibilities of the General Assembly included the examination and approval of the various reports of the Board of Directors
—the annual balance sheet, the profit and loss accounts and distribution of profits—and the election of the Board of Directors
and its officers.

THE CENTRAL ADMINISTRATION IN CAIRO

The Agrarian Reform Central Administration in Cairo was the
outcome of a continuous evolution which had started in September
1952 with the creation of the High Committee for Agrarian Reform
(*al-Lagna al-Ulya li'l-Islah al-Zira'i*) which was established to
supervise the implementation of the programme initiated by the
1952 Agrarian Reform Law.[26] Presided over by the Minister of

---

[25] See below, p. 63.

[26] Arts. 12–13 of the law stipulated that: 'A committee shall be established
under the name of the "High Committee for Agrarian Reform". Its functions
shall include the implementation of the measures pertaining to the requisition,
the distribution and the management of the land requisitioned during the
period preceding distribution. The Committee shall be entitled to give directions

State for Agrarian Reform, it created an executive agency in Cairo
to handle all technical, administrative, and legislative affairs. Its
scope of action increased rapidly[27] and it was soon burdened with
a variety of responsibilities, some of which, such as land reclamation, had no direct connexion with the 1952 legislation. By 1957
it had become in principle an independent body, its name having
been changed to the General Organization for Agrarian Reform
(*al-Hay'a al-'Amma li'l-Islah al-Zira'i*), although in practice it was
virtually the same administration under a different name. Directly
attached to the Presidency of the Republic, it was managed by a
board of all the ministers in office, under the chairmanship of the
Minister of Agrarian Reform (the latter office having been created
in 1956). It was also supposed to have a separate budget and its
own rules of procedure for all budgetary, financial, and administrative matters.

In November 1957 further changes were introduced after the
establishment of the GCS, part of the executive agencies at its disposal being transferred to the latter. The Ministry of Agrarian
Reform was given new direct or indirect powers over all the various
bodies connected with the Organization for Agrarian Reform, the
GCS, and the Land Reclamation Organization. The ministry itself
was directed until 1961 by Mr Sayed Marei, who had been very
active since the beginning of Agrarian Reform and who had quickly
become the leading expert on agrarian reform problems; he was
assisted by two under-secretaries of state and a director-general of
the ministry.

By 1959 the administrative organization in Cairo operating under
the guidance of the Ministry of Agrarian Reform was as follows:

1. The Organization for Agrarian Reform, now limited to three
departments: (1) the Expropriation Department (*Idarat la Istiila*),
entrusted with implementing all legislation for the expropriation
of land, the staff of which had not decreased (a sure sign of developments still to come); (2) the Judicial Department (*al-Idarat
al-Qanuniya*), to handle all legal affairs; (3) the Distribution

to the Agrarian Reform co-operatives and to put them under its supervision
within the limits set by this law. It has the authority to approach all parties
concerned for the enactment of its delegation. It shall be presided over by the
Minister of State for Agrarian Reform and shall include the Minister of Agriculture, the President of the State Council, the under-secretaries of state for
agriculture, social affairs, public works, finance and economy, the Chancellor of
the Agrarian Reform legal department, the executive director of the Higher
Committee and five other members appointed by the President of the Republic.
The Committee comes under the Presidency of the Republic and the President
of the Republic shall be its supreme President. The Committee shall be autonomous and have a special budget, issued by the Committee itself. Such budget
shall be entered into the balance sheet of the Agrarian Reform Fund.'

[27] See above, p. 28.

Department (*Idarat al-Tawzi'*) entrusted with the redistribution of the expropriated estates to small farmers according to the laws enacted since September 1952.

2. The GCS, grouping all the ACS and all the 'local' co-operatives, included the following departments: (1) the Agricultural Department (*Idarat al-Zira'a*), entrusted with all the problems of crop rotation, varieties of crops, seeds, timing of agricultural operations, &c. in the redistributed estates; (2) the Irrigation Department (*Idarat al-Ray*) entrusted with all water problems; (3) the *Idarat al-Ta'awun*, entrusted with the supervision and control of all co-operative affairs; (4) the Engineering Department (*al-Idarat al-Mikanikiya*), responsible for all problems connected with machinery; (5) the Orchard Department (*Idarat al-Jana'in*), entrusted with the supervision and control of the orchards, expropriated but not distributed, and which remained in the meanwhile owner-operated by the local co-operatives; (6) the Livestock Department (*Idarat Tarbiat al-Hayawan*), entrusted with the problems of veterinary care, improvement of livestock, &c.; (7) the Projects and Statistics Department (*Idarat al-Buhuth wa'l-Ihsa'*), responsible for the initiation of certain schemes such as the poultry breeding scheme and for the collection and study of important data; (8) the Production Department (*Idarat al-Intag*); (9) the Waste Land Department (*Idarat al-Bur*), entrusted with the reclamation of land which had remained waste amidst cultivated expropriated lands, or lands whose productivity had so declined that they were not profitable enough to be operated by beneficiaries or tenants; (10) the Financial Department (*al-Idara al-Maliya*), entrusted with the supervision and control of all financial transactions.

3. The General Egyptian Organization for Land Reclamation (*al-Hay'a al-'Amma li Istislah al-Aradi*), entrusted with land reclamation projects outside the areas expropriated by the Agrarian Reform authorities. This body also supervised and controlled all land reclamation in Egypt, whether accomplished by private individuals or by special companies.[28]

4. The General Organization for Liberation province (*al-Hay'a al-'Amma li Mudiriyat al-Tahrir*), which until 1957 had been run as an autonomous body, but which was then placed under the guidance of the Ministry of Agrarian Reform.[29]

5. The General Organization for Desert Rehabilitation (*al-Hay'a al-'Amma li Ta'mir al-Sahari*), entrusted with reclamation in the desert, in particular in the Kharga and Dakhla oases, where the New Valley (*al-Wadi al-Jadid*) project was being undertaken.[30]

[28] See below, Ch. XI. [29] See below, Ch. XI.
[30] See below, Ch. XI.

6. Land reclamation schemes of the Egyptian–American Rural Improvement Society (EARIS) started in 1953 in Fayyum and Buhaira provinces, taken over in November 1956 and placed under the control of the Ministry of Agrarian Reform.[31]

CENTRALIZATION AND BUREAUCRACY

Despite the changes in organization and the drive to emphasize the co-operative character of the Agrarian Reform programme, the administrative machinery had become top-heavy and inflexible by 1959. The resulting procrastination was the cause of much frustration and dissatisfaction, not only among the smallholders, but also among the junior Agrarian Reform staff, who were often disappointed to find that their efforts to solve the daily problems of the estates entrusted to them were paralysed or strangled in a maze of red tape.

Much criticism was also voiced by the smallholders (and of course by the expropriated landlords) concerning the size of the staff employed by the 'local' and ACS and the central administration in Cairo which, in the eyes of the public and the smallholders, was the same as the Ministry of Agrarian Reform. Part of the criticism was due to lack of understanding of the real nature and scope of the work of Agrarian Reform staff, who were not only supposed to administer the expropriated estates, collect instalments, rents, taxes, &c., but also to alleviate the social and economic plight of thousands of peasants now farming smallholdings on the estates, by patient persuasion more than by blind dictatorship. The setting up of co-operatives, their management, the development of social welfare activities, &c., were all tasks which had never been attempted by the staff of the ex-landlords, but which were now squarely placed on the shoulders of the staff. And these new responsibilities were all the more difficult to carry out, not only because the training of the employees had been superficial, but also because many of them were formerly on the staff of the ex-landlords or of the Ministry of Waqfs, and could only with the utmost patience be made to understand the new objectives.

It was doubtful how useful a reduction in Agrarian Reform staff at the level of the 'local' and district co-operatives would have been. But it was clear that a higher degree of efficiency could have been attained, in particular by placing adequate transport at the disposal of the *nazirs al-zira'at*, vets, *mufattish al-ta'awun*, &c.[32]

---

[31] See below, p. 212.
[32] This obstacle has been surmounted in the Italian Maremma region by allowing every technician to own a car or motorbike, the Ente Maremma

At another level, greater co-ordination and more work could have been achieved by a smaller staff if the central administration in Cairo had been subdivided and its responsibilities gradually transferred to four or five separate and autonomous provincial units, each grouping under its wing several of the *mantiqat* (or Associated Co-operative Societies, as they were more recently named). The scope of these autonomous units could have been enlarged to include the cultural, social, and economic betterment of all the rural communities in *mantiqat* under its jurisdiction, and the *mandub* would thus be invested with wide powers to co-ordinate and control the various government agencies (public works, education, health, social affairs, agriculture) in their *mantiqat*.[33] Such a pattern of organization would have been more beneficial to the Agrarian Reform smallholders, better maintenance of government irrigation canals and drainage ditches would have probably resulted, and the problems encountered by the Rural Combined Centres (*Wihda Mugamma'a*)[34] would have been easier to solve.

But instead of decentralizing and concentrating in depth, the Agrarian Reform authorities chose a course which led to a vast, unwieldy co-operative organization. Every year they increased the scope and nature of their work, which by 1961 ranged from expropriation, redistribution of holdings, &c., to land reclamation.

Part of the disadvantages springing from the tentacular and ever increasing powers of the Agrarian Reform authorities could be traced back to the 1,000-year-old centralizing traditions of the Egyptian bureaucracy. A vivid example of this was to be found in the very strict control and constant checking by the authorities in Cairo over all financial operations and transactions involving the co-operative societies under their supervision, notwithstanding the

organization whenever necessary providing a credit for purchase; a daily allowance calculated on the basis of the schedule of work of a technician was then allotted to him to cover his transport costs.

---

[33] Similar suggestions were made in 1956 and 1959 by two leading experts on agrarian reform and community development projects (see M. R. Ghunaimi, *Hiazat al-aradi fi misr* (1956) and M. Santa Cruz, *FAO's Role in Social Welfare* (Rome, 1959), p. 37).

[34] The Rural Combined Centre was a form of community development project, the result of a concerted project between the four ministries of Social Affairs, Public Health, Education, and Agriculture. Each Centre was supposed to include a small hospital, a school, a social welfare centre, and a veterinary and agricultural extension centre. In 1959 200 Centres were in operation in different parts of Egypt, some of which were quite efficient while others were completely dormant. Despite the bitter criticisms often made of this project, which was in principle of the utmost value, plans for the establishment of some further 600 Centres by 1965 were to be implemented; the cost of this whole project was estimated at £E50 m., excluding annual running costs (see E. Garzouzi, *Old Ills and New Remedies in Egypt* (1958), p. 125). A slightly optimistic appraisal of the Centres may be found in Warriner, 'Land Reform and Community Development in the UAR', unpubl. report to UN, Apr. 1961, p. 51 and in her appendix, p. iv.

presence on their Boards of Directors of the *mushrifs* who in fact had been appointed by them. Thus all sums paid to the co-operatives were deposited in bank accounts opened in the name of the central Agrarian Reform authorities, while all financial decisions had to be endorsed by them before being executed, even when allocations from the Social Aid Fund of a co-operative were involved. Control was so stringent that the contribution of a co-operative to the funeral expenses of a deceased member was often remitted to his heirs several months after the event, and matters did not move faster when a co-operative board decided to help one of its sick members and attempted to pay his hospital bill.

The powers of the *mushrif al-taʿawuni* of an ACS, better known under his previous denomination of *mandub*, were themselves limited: purchases had to be made by inviting tenders and only exceptionally by mutual agreement. Tenders over £E2,000 in value had to obtain the prior approval of the Cairo authorities, and this was also the case when contracts other than by tender exceeded £E200. The total value of working capital placed at the disposal of an ACS was only £E1,000,[35] hardly enough to meet the needs of estates ranging in area from 8,000–10,000 feddans.

This rigid financial control of the activities of the co-operatives, though advantageous during the years immediately after their establishment in so far as it protected their assets, constituted a formidable obstacle to the efficient management of vast agricultural estates; moreover, it impeded the smooth functioning of the co-operative institutions in many ways, introducing routine in the day-to-day work and fostering the uninterrupted growth of the staff of the Agrarian Reform authorities in Cairo. Thus the enthusiasm characteristic of the first years of Agrarian Reform were gradually replaced by a bureaucratic aloofness and an impression of inhumanity inimical to the co-operative spirit and considerably reducing the psychological impact of co-operative effort.

To counter this, and to restore the necessary freedom of action and flexibility, the Agrarian Reform authorities started a new experiment during the summer of 1959 at the *mantiqat* of al-Zaʿfaran in Lower Egypt and of Burgaya in Upper Egypt, which allowed considerable financial autonomy to the co-operatives. Bank accounts were opened directly in their names to keep their accounts separate from those of the Agrarian Reform authorities, and all financial and administrative decisions endorsed by their

[35] In 1960 plans were said to have been drafted to increase the scope of the action of a *mushrif al-taʿawuni*. The limit on tenders was to be raised to £E5,000 and that on contracts by mutual agreement to £E500. A credit of £E20,000 was to be placed at the disposal of more than 10,000 feddans as working capital.

Boards of Directors could be executed without prior approval. Further, payments not exceeding £E50 from the Social Aid Fund[36] were permitted without consulting the *Idarat al-Ta'awun* in Cairo, subsequent notification being considered sufficient. But the experimental part of the new system was the transfer of the responsibility for collecting the money due to the co-operative from the *mushrif*. This responsibility was now given to the members of the co-operative Boards of Directors, who were thought to have a more intimate knowledge of the financial situation of each individual farm operator. In al-Za'faran this part of the experiment seems to have been successful, and within a few months outstanding debts of nearly £E90,000 owed by members were reported to have been settled without any pressure from the *mushrifs*, and without any seizure of crops or charges of embezzlement.[37] Debts settled amounted to more than 100 per cent. This achievement was mainly the result of the personal intervention of the members of the Boards of Directors, and it convinced the authorities that a more humane approach to co-operative problems was likely to yield striking results. Five new ACS were therefore due to be granted financial and administrative autonomy in 1960. The granting of this autonomous status did not imply, however, that the authorities were to relinquish their right of appointing the respective *mushrifs*.

The trend towards greater autonomy and independence for Agrarian Reform co-operative organizations was a promising sign. It might well have diminished the subservience of the board members of the 'local' co-operatives, thus narrowing the gap between the Egyptian (Agrarian Reform) conception of agricultural co-operation and that current in the Western hemisphere. More co-operative training for Agrarian Reform personnel, less illiteracy, and the provision of vocational agricultural training for board members and all the smallholders could in future greatly reinforce this trend towards autonomy, and thus rescue the co-operatives from the paternal but stifling embrace of the Ministry of Agrarian Reform. But it could doubtless be argued that it was not the supervision exercised by the ministry that was open to criticism but rather the rigidly bureaucratic manner in which it was carried out. In any case in the initial stages of Agrarian Reform, without some supervision it would have been impossible to maintain and sometimes improve crop yields in the expropriated estates; the problems of agricultural credit, irrigation, drainage, crop rotation, pest control, and marketing were too delicate to be left solely to the very individual-minded smallholders or to their representatives on the boards of their co-operatives. Greater

---

[36] See below, pp. 134–6.   [37] *al-Ta'awun*, 1960.

reliance on the personal initiative of the smallholders was desirable, but it was also risky, because of their lack of technical knowledge and in many cases (especially among former agricultural labourers) because it was difficult for them to assume the responsibilities involved in operating their newly acquired holdings at all quickly. It could not have been fully successful without a crash programme of agricultural vocational training. Such a programme had not, however, been contemplated.

V

PROBLEMS OF INFRASTRUCTURE

The question is how the farming operations of independent small-holdings can be promoted by co-operative methods without the formation of producers co-operatives, i.e. without taking the final step into joint or collective farming.

DR OTTO SCHILLER, in *Year Book of Agricultural Co-operation*,
1959

FARM BUILDING AND HOUSING PROBLEMS

MOST of the farm buildings, warehouses, sheds for fixed irrigation, pumps and farm machinery, cowsheds, offices, landowners' mansions, living quarters of administrative staff, &c., on the redistributed estates, had been erected before 1952.[1] They were taken over by the Agrarian Reform authorities during the transitional period preceding redistribution, and subsequently transferred to the 'local' co-operatives and ACS. Some farm buildings had, of course, been built under the auspices of the Agrarian Reform authorities, but very few, and in 1959 their total value did not exceed £E300,000,[2] far less than the amount calculated in 1959 by Agrarian Reform accountants as depreciation on expropriated farm buildings.[3]

All the warehouses, sheds, &c. were used either for storing the seeds, fertilizers, and insecticides to be distributed to the small-holders, or to stock the various crops marketed by bulk disposal through co-operative channels, or to house the machinery operated by the co-operatives. Offices previously reserved for the staff of the expropriated landowners were used by the employees of the co-operatives, and a special room was usually reserved for the meetings of board members. Most of the expropriated mansions and villas were inhabited by the *mandub* and senior Agrarian Reform officials, others of whom lived in neighbouring towns. Two-storeyed villas (concrete and brick) with modern sanitation and accommodation for two families (120 sq. metres per family) were also built by the authorities, to encourage staff to live on the lands

[1] See above, pp. 24–25 for compensation paid under the above heading.
[2] The exact figure was £E131,000 in 1957; this amount had probably doubled by 1959. For further reference see Marei, *Agrarian Reform*, p. 258.
[3] See balance sheet of the Agrarian Reform authorities in July 1958, below, p. 200.

entrusted to them. In villages where household branches of the local co-operatives were opened up to cater for the consumption needs of beneficiaries, a few single-storeyed buildings of 120 sq. metres each had been erected to provide the necessary premises. Despite the importance of the capital invested in all these farm buildings, however, their upkeep was neglected and they were slowly but surely falling into disrepair.

The housing problems of the beneficiaries of the redistributed holdings had hardly been tackled by the Agrarian Reform authorities as late as 1960. Several (hard) brick houses with concrete roofing had been designed by Agrarian Reform engineers and had been allocated to beneficiaries, most of them in the under-populated areas of the Northern Delta.[4] They cost about £E500 each, and the total purchase price, including land, was payable on an instalment basis on the same conditions as those applicable to the bare lands.[5] Each house covered an area of about 50 sq. metres and included two large rooms, an oven for baking bread, and a primitive toilet; at the back of each house was a large room used as a cowshed with its own entrance, so that the cattle owned by the occupants of the house went in and out of it from the back street. But manure pits had not been built close to the houses, and peasants piled up their manure on their doorsteps or on near-by communal lands before taking it into the fields by donkey. Houses were built in rows, facing each other along streets 5–10 metres wide. In some regions, such as Inshas (province of Sharqiya), they had been dispersed among the fields in small hamlets of 40–50 houses, to reduce the distance between the living quarters of beneficiaries and their holdings, this being one of the biggest obstacles to efficient production.[6] Running water and electricity were not available in these new houses, nor were they connected to any sewage system; their roofs were hidden under piles of cotton stalks, dry corn stalks, rice straw, &c. so that they looked neither tidier nor cleaner than the customary mud houses.

By 1957 1,160 houses had been built for the smallholders, and in 1959 it was claimed that this figure had doubled. The first batch of new houses thus built were distributed to the peasants of the ex-royal estate of Inshas, but it was very difficult to collect the annual instalments due for the purchase price of these houses, as beneficiaries complained they were unable to pay for the holdings and houses at the same time. This objection was fully valid, and the Agrarian Reform authorities were certainly to be

---

[4] See above, p. 40.
[5] i.e. thirty years at 3 per cent per annum, and after 1958 forty years at 1·5 per cent per annum.
[6] See below, p. 102 for more details on this very important point.

blamed for not having attempted to reduce construction costs by letting the beneficiaries help build them; the latter disposed of plenty of surplus labour which could easily have been put to use (with some psychological and material inducements).

Housing problems do not seem to have attracted much attention from the Agrarian Reform authorities, who ignored them until late in 1959.[7] Housing conditions in Agrarian Reform areas had therefore not improved since 1952, and the 130,000 odd smallholders (with their families over 500,000 people) were still living, in 1959, in overcrowded villages whose squalor, filth, and miserable appearance were indescribable and no better than that of other Egyptian villages. Their upkeep was deplorable, the streets were narrow, untidy, and dirty, and in the Delta on a rainy day, muddy and unfit for pedestrians and still less for cars; flies, vermin, and other pests were everywhere. The Committees for Street and House Cleanliness (*Lagnat al-Nazafa*), which came under the Boards of Directors of the local co-operatives, had been entrusted with the improvement of housing and sanitary conditions in the villages under their jurisdiction. But with the exception of some efforts to provide street lighting with kerosene lamps, they did nothing. However, in most villages, areas had been set aside for their future expansion, and sales of plots to smallholders were taking place on a long-term instalment basis at 1 per cent interest per annum, the houses being built of mud-bricks, according to the design and limited knowledge of their owners. One big achievement which struck a visitor was the availability of clean drinking water[8] in the vast majority of the Agrarian Reform villages. But this was not confined to these villages, since the establishment of a complete network of piped drinking water to 80 per cent of all villages of Egypt had been completed by 1960.[9]

The absence of any concerted plan and the half-hearted attempts to tackle housing and sanitary conditions, and to relieve the growing congestion in the overcrowded villages of the expropriated areas, could justifiably be considered a distressing phenomenon seven years after the enactment of the Agrarian Reform Law. Schemes have since been drafted within the framework of the second Five-Year Plan to cope with the housing problems of the Agrarian Reform regions, and 2,300 houses for landowning beneficiaries were to be erected during 1960–4 at a total

[7] In 1952–60, 820 houses were erected in areas occupied by some 31,548 families, according to publications of the Min. AR.

[8] In a number of regions defective installations deprived smallholders of access to clean drinking water as repairs were extremely slow (over 6 months in several cases), Agrarian Reform officials not being empowered to take any steps in this field.

[9] This percentage was scheduled to rise to 96 in 1964.

cost of £E1,800,000[10] (including 400 houses for Agrarian Reform staff and 800 other farm buildings). To implement this scheme, more active participation of the smallholders was said to be aimed at, and they are to join in building operations while contributing partial cash payments in advance. Nevertheless these plans are a mere drop in the ocean, and one form of mobilization[11] of the enormous manpower reserves in the Agrarian Reform villages should be put into operation. This should be accompanied by a drive to scatter the homes of the smallholders throughout the fields in small hamlets of 40–50 houses near their holdings, to reduce transport problems.

In this connexion it is important to point out that permission to plant orchards in the immediate surroundings of the new hamlets, by providing the necessary inducement, could probably generate the necessary enthusiasm for such a full-scale mobilization of manpower reserves, and it would also help to overcome the instincts of peasants traditionally opposed to abandoning their village dwellings however miserable they may be.

IRRIGATION AND DRAINAGE NETWORKS

In every *mantiqa* the distribution of irrigation water before the establishment of local co-operatives was the sole responsibility of the Agrarian Reform staff; after that it was assumed jointly by the regional ACS *mushrif ta'awuni* (ex-*mandub*) and its Board of Directors. It was also the *mushrif ta'awuni* who consulted the Ministry of Public Works engineer to decide with him the flow of water from the main government canals throughout the irrigation network of the expropriated estates. But in many cases, and in spite of considerable capital investment benefiting over 60,000 feddans,[12] the flow was not enough to cope with the requirements of smallholders, who complained that in the past water had been granted more generously by the Ministry's engineer to the ex-landlords. This was true, for after requisitioning, *mandubs* and *mushrifs* were less fortunate than the ex-landlords, as they did not

[10] Total investment on rural housing in the whole of Egypt was scheduled to rise to £E10 m. during the period 1960–4; of this £E1·8 m. was earmarked for housing in the Agrarian Reform areas (see *al-Magallat al-Zira'iyat*, Feb. & Mar. 1961).

[11] An example is to be found in Uttar Pradesh, India (see UN, *Community Development and Economic Development* (Bangkok, 1960), Pt IIA—a case study of the Ghosi Community Development Block, Uttar Pradesh).

[12] To solve the recurring complaint of water shortage during the early summer months and in some cases to provide additional irrigation facilities, the Agrarian Reform authorities had not hesitated to invest considerable capital in the improvement of existing irrigation networks, in the purchase of new irrigation pumps, and in the boring of artesian wells, the total area thus involved in the various *mantiqat* exceeding 60,000 feddans.

use the means of pressure and 'gentle' persuasion so often employed by the former. Some Agrarian Reform officials had excellent
personal relations with the local irrigation engineers, and thus
managed to overcome water shortage in the areas entrusted to
them; but in others they had been tied down by routine, &c.
Water shortage during the early summer was a standard complaint
in the rice-planting regions of Za'faran, Nabaruh, Bahut, Balqas,
Itay al-Barud, and Fayyum,[13] and smallholders often pointed out
that the ex-landlords had usually contrived by devious means to
keep them well supplied. It was, of course, difficult to convince
them that it was hardly feasible to resort to the feudal tactics of the
ex-landlords in a socialist co-operative society.

The distribution of the irrigation water within the boundaries
of the various villages of the expropriated estates was in turn
carried out jointly by the 'local' co-operative *mushrifs*[14] and boards.[15]
The day-to-day problems of irrigation involving the smallholders
were dealt with by the irrigation warden (*ghafar al-ray*), appointed
by the *mushrifs* and paid by the 'local' co-operatives. When necessary,
board members intervened to smooth out any major difficulties.

The upkeep of the main irrigation canals and drainage ditches
in the expropriated estates was also the sole responsibility of the
Agrarian Reform staff during the transitional period preceding the
setting up of co-operatives; after that it was assumed by the co-
operative organizations under the control of the *mushrifs* and their
agents. Co-operative labour gangs were supposed to do the rather
distasteful job of clearing the main irrigation canal and drainage
ditches by burning and cutting the brush and weeds blocking
them, to ensure a sufficient flow of water, and by clearing out the
mud silt at least once and often twice a year, to keep the canals

[13] In al-Za'faran, Kafr al-Shaikh province, priority in irrigation had always
been a privilege of the small tenants occupying lands owned by the ex-king; on
a lesser scale this was also true in the Nabaruh-Bahut region, Daqahliya province, owned by the Badrawi family or even in Sharq al-Fayyum. Frequent
irrigation was necessary in all these areas where some of the lands were saline
and therefore in need of repeated flooding.

[14] i.e. the ex-*nazir al-zira'a* in charge of the village lands. If these were over
1,000 feddans, they were divided into two separate units for the convenience of
operation, and an agronomist was appointed to help the *mushrif*; this aide
(*mu'awin al-zira'a*) assumed the direction of agricultural work, including
irrigation, in one of the two units.

[15] In a few regions the collaboration between the boards and their *mushrifs*
was quite good, and a big effort to overcome irrigation problems was made
jointly, sometimes by breaking the law if necessary. The *mushrif* of the Kafr
Damira Jadid 'local' co-operative, for example (one of the 'local' co-operatives
affiliated to the Damira ACS), rather than see the crops of the beneficiaries
shrivel up through lack of water, had surreptitiously given instructions to install
an additional irrigation opening to pump water from the Balqas main irrigation
canal, which passed through the Damira estates. A fine imposed on him by the
Ministry of Public Works was enthusiastically paid in June 1959 out of co-
operative funds on the proposal of the Board of Directors.

and drains at the right depth. The occupants of a given block of 30–100 feddans of the lands of a 'local' co-operative were asked to contribute to these work gangs a number of work-days (or workers) in proportion to the total size of their holdings and the size of their families. No payment in kind or in cash was due for this type of work, which was done under the guidance of the *mushrifs* and under the direct supervision of hired foremen, in order to prevent favouritism, as tenants and beneficiaries were not allowed to become foremen. The main advantage of this system of labour gangs was that the upkeep of the drainage and irrigation system was carried out without imposing unnecessary payments in cash upon the beneficiaries and tenants, who had plenty of time to spare for the work. The occupants of the lands who made only a partial contribution to the labour gangs had to pay for the necessary hired labour at a rate two or three times higher than the actual wage rate; this penalty, which did not seem to have been applied with sufficient severity, was inevitable if the narrow-mindedness and selfish ignorance of a small minority was not to imperil further co-operative efforts.[16]

Even so, the work accomplished by the labour gangs was not impressive, many beneficiaries and tenants were always absent, and the upkeep of drains and canals was extremely poor. Because of absenteeism and the slow deterioration of the irrigation and drainage networks, the Agrarian Reform authorities were more and more inclined to hand over the upkeep operations to contractors employing hired labour once or very occasionally twice a year,[17] costs being debited to the account of smallholders *pro rata* with the size of their holdings. Despite this, in practice the maintenance and upkeep of main canals and drains remained highly unsatisfactory; their appearance was untidy and their flow was far from full capacity. True, the main government drains to which the drainage system of the estates was linked were in a wretched condition, and in some cases drainage water flowed back from them, especially during early summer; the maintenance of these main drains was, as in the past, the responsibility of the irrigation engineers (*Muhandis al-ray*) of the Ministry of Public Works.

In reality the work done by the contractors was no better than that of the co-operative gangs. The performance of agricultural labourers employed by the contractors for the customary clearing of brush and weeds in winter was thoroughly unsatisfactory. Various tenants and beneficiaries, questioned about their reluctance

[16] See also below, p. 102.
[17] In Damira, the star example of co-operation, a decision was endorsed by the various boards of the 'local' co-operative society entrusting the upkeep of main drains and canals to contractors once every three years.

to join the co-operative gangs, emphasized the ignorance of some of their colleagues and the dishonesty of the contractors who tendered for the upkeep of main drains and canals. The general feeling among the peasants was that they were anyway being made to pay too much for the annual upkeep in relation to the service they were obtaining. Agrarian Reform officials pointed out, on the other hand, that proper and diligent upkeep of the main drainage ditches and irrigation canals was an expensive undertaking that might well have strained the limited resources of the co-operatives and their members; moreover, the members were already doing their utmost to limit all expenses with which they might be debited, even when these were fully justified.

The upkeep of the secondary and tertiary drains and irrigation canals was left to the beneficiaries and tenants, who on the whole did not pay much attention to them or to the drainage ditches separating their plots from those of their neighbours in the same block of crops. When questioned, smallholders explained that if they were to excavate the drainage ditches surrounding their fields to maintain them at the normal depth, water would flow back from the main drains where upkeep was bad. (This argument was not fully convincing.) Many peasants also accused their neighbours of gross negligence in the upkeep of the secondary drains which bordered their fields, thus affecting all farmers upstream, who, in despair at seeing the flow of their drainage water obstructed, themselves finally abandoned the upkeep of their drainage ditches. But the major cause of deficient upkeep appeared to be the complete ignorance of peasants of the detrimental long-term effects of poor drainage on crop yields. It is interesting to note that the upkeep of the secondary and tertiary irrigation canals was much better, as peasants were quick to understand that an adequate flow of irrigation water was a question of immediate life and death to their crops.

At the successful *mantiqa* of Shibin al-Kawm, Minufiya province, the *mushrifs* had attempted to promote better upkeep of the irrigation and drainage networks by rewarding the co-operative labour gangs; peasants fulfilling their obligations to these gangs were entitled to bigger cash payments from the surplus balances (*fa'id*) due to them by their co-operative after the sale of their cotton crops. As a result of this pragmatic approach, the drainage network of the lands of Shibin, though far from perfect, was in better condition than in other Agrarian Reform estates. This demonstrated that, given incentive, it was possible in the short run to enlist the co-operation of smallholders in improving drainage, even when the effects would only become apparent in the long run.

To sum up, it may be said that the improvement of drainage

conditions in Agrarian Reform lands was an urgent necessity and a top priority, and that if the majority of these lands had not been extremely fertile and healthy, a falling-off in yields would have occurred. It should also be stressed that if standards of upkeep of drainage networks had been closer to those prevailing in well-managed Egyptian farms, the increase in crop yields reported in certain *mantiqat* of the Delta[18] would have been more striking, especially after the large-scale introduction of potent insecticides; moreover, the failures in yield so frequent in the Northern Delta regions might also have been avoided.

When this criticism was made to Agrarian Reform officials, it was stated in reply that no effort had been spared to improve the irrigation and drainage networks, and that over 30,000 feddans (7·5 per cent of the area requisitioned) had already benefited from new drainage projects, and in 1958 alone £E200,000 had been spent on the maintenance and upkeep of existing drainage ditches and canals. It was argued, moreover, that drainage conditions would in any case improve as soon as the ten-year plan to introduce tiled underground drains throughout the Delta area was implemented.[19] But in view of the poor condition of the existing open-air drainage networks it is doubtful whether the underground drains, which were infinitely more delicate to maintain, would alone solve the drainage problems; it was just as necessary to set up an adequate organization for upkeep, as well as a thorough training programme.

INTERNAL ROAD NETWORKS

No major changes in the layout of the internal roads of the expropriated estates occurred after redistribution to the Agrarian Reform smallholders, but their maintenance and upkeep was often not as good as in the past, mainly because of a breakdown in discipline. Heaps of silt extracted from canals and drains and piles of farm manure accumulated by smallholders next to their plots obstructed the secondary and tertiary roads; movement on them by car, tractor, or bullock cart was perilous and troublesome. Agrarian Reform officials supervising the estates entrusted to them had great difficulty in travelling from one village to another except by the main highways, and were therefore considerably hampered in their extension service activities.

WINDBREAKS

In the majority of the estates casuarina and eucalyptus trees had been planted by the expropriated landlords to provide windbreaks

[18] Damira, al-Khazan, Simbilawain, Shibin al-Kawm, &c.
[19] See below, p. 170.

and to reinforce the banks of canals and drainage ditches bordering the main roads. Since the Agrarian Reform these trees had become the property of the various 'local' co-operatives, but in nine cases out of ten they were in a pitiful condition, as they were slowly but surely being lopped to mere stumps or cut down by the small-holders, despite the injunctions of their *mushrifs*. The loppings were used by the smallholders for fuel, but the felled trees were sold by the co-operatives to increase their income, this addition to their financial resources being budgeted as 'miscellaneous income'. The trees which escaped destruction were surreptitiously attacked by farmers whose plots they bordered, as their shade and roots projecting sometimes as far as 10 metres reduced yields over an important area. Worse still, no young trees had been planted to replace those already destroyed, nor had there been any effort to establish windbreaks in those estates which had none at the time of expropriation.

The passive attitude of the Agrarian Reform staff to this problem stemmed from their deep conviction that nothing could be done to prevent or check the vandalism of smallholders. The preservation of existing windbreaks and the development of new ones was highly important for agricultural, economic, and even aesthetic considerations. It could have been achieved at little cost by compensating farmers whose plots were bordered by trees through reducing the amount of the annual instalment due on their holdings, or the size of their holdings could have been increased proportionately to the area affected by these trees. In both cases farmers should have been made personally responsible for the protection of the trees. Moreover, by regularly cutting the mature trees and replacing them with saplings, it would have been possible to preserve existing windbreaks while at the same time providing a cheap source of timber for housing projects in Agrarian Reform areas. Even thinning, if conducted scientifically, could have made a valuable contribution to household fuel requirements.

THE SYSTEM OF CROP ROTATION

Despite the redistribution of the large estates to many small-holders, fragmentation was avoided thanks to the systematic application of the system of consolidated triennial crop rotation,[20] which remained in force after distribution in all *mantiqat* except those in sugar-cane[21] or market-gardening zones.[22]

The area of each of the three big blocks in which every small-holder had one of his three equal plots was equivalent to a third

---

[20] See above, p. 32.   [21] In Upper Egypt.
[22] In Giza province near Cairo and in Buhaira province outside Alexandria.

of the *zir'a* controlled by a 'local' co-operative, or to a third of several small *zira'at* not adjacent to one another. Each block was compulsorily sown with one crop. Thus all the advantages derived from the earlier introduction of the consolidated triennial crop rotation continued to be reaped. With the exception of the few operations supposedly accomplished by co-operative labour gangs,[23] the smallholders alone were responsible for manual work on their individual plots. This system had often been applied by the ex-landlords to their tenants and sharecroppers who had little objection; it was commonly accepted by the Agrarian Reform smallholders and never raised as a subject for complaint. Its only disadvantage, which could have been remedied by replacing draught animals with tractors and trailers, was that it increased transport problems for farm operators who in most cases lived 1–3 km. away from their holdings (these in turn, as has been pointed out, being divided into three plots separated by 200–500 metres). But the advantages from the compulsory application of the consolidated triennial crop rotation were such that they more than outweighed any disadvantage. Enforced with strict severity throughout Agrarian Reform estates, it was one of the specific features of the Egyptian Agrarian Reform, and stands out as one of the most positive contributions to the general theory of agrarian tenure. The Egyptian approach to the problem of fragmentation offered a practical solution not only for the consolidation of small holdings in areas where irrigation and drainage networks had to be entrusted to a centralizing agency, but also for regions or countries where the scale of farming in fragmented small holdings rendered operation of the latter uneconomic.

It has already been stated that the main advantage of consolidated crop rotation was that it allowed for a collective treatment of certain problems, such as pest control, which were extremely difficult to cope with individually by farmers of minute holdings. It also paved the way for the implementation of a generous policy of agricultural credit by making supervision infinitely easier. It did not prejudice or restrict the legal rights (as determined by the original grant) of smallholders on the plots assigned to them, and it avoided impersonalization of each holding by drowning it in a collective form of agrarian tenure. On the contrary, it preserved the individuality of farm operators, who were left free to carry out personally a majority of farm operations on their clearly demarcated plots so that all labour or material inputs were expended on their own private property rather than on property collectively owned or collectively operated. Personal incentive

[23] Labour could be hired, but as has already been pointed out, the smallholders were required to operate the holdings themselves.

was thus unrestricted, and if this individuality had been reinforced by literacy and adequate vocational training, the 'managerial' character of the land-distribution programme could well have been done away with. There was therefore nothing in common between the consolidation of crops as practised on Agrarian Reform estates up to 1961,[24] and collectivist patterns of agrarian tenure, such as the Russian kholkoz, the Israeli kibbutz, the collective *ejidos* of Mexico, or the self-managed farms of Ben Bella's Algeria.

FRUIT AND VEGETABLES

The system of crop rotation followed throughout the *mantiqat* of the Delta and Central Egypt up to Minia comprised snatch crops of clover or onions, then cotton, wheat, or barley, then rice or maize, permanent clover or beans, then maize. Though vegetable crops were permitted exceptionally, on conditions that they did not disrupt the rotation, the percentage of the cultivated area of the Agrarian Reform estates under vegetable crops was small (discounting the onion snatch crop). In the vicinity of the big cities of Alexandria and Cairo (*mantiqat* of Alexandria and Idfina and Qalyubiya and Giza) and in Minya (*mantiqa* of Minya, estate of Burgaya) vegetable crops occupied 10 per cent of the cultivated area; in all the other regions the percentage fluctuated between 1–1·5 per cent.[25] The low level of vegetable production was reported to be the result of the lack of marketing opportunities and sometimes of the isolated position of estates not effectively linked to main roads (such as in Za'faran, for example).[26] An attempt was made in 1958 to gear the *mantiqa* of Sabarbay (Gharbiya province) to export markets; special varieties of potatoes and carrots were planted by the smallholders on the advice of their *mushrifs*, but this important experiment, which met with success on the production side, failed miserably through lack of co-ordination with the contracting state agency entrusted with export operations.

[24] 'The status of landownership in Agrarian Reform areas is a limited landownership for each individual smallholder, whereby the organisation of farm operation is integrated in an overall co-operative frame. In other words, the fundamental axiom of Agrarian Reform farming is private ownership. Every person is entitled to his own plot of land, the entire production of which accrues to him personally. The Agrarian Reform co-operative society is established to help him in the operation of his holding' (statement to the press by S. Marei, Minister of Agrarian Reform, Study No. 45 of *Bureau des Documentations syriennes et arabes* Sept. 1957).

[25] In the *mantiqa* of Damira, supposedly a successful example of Agrarian Reform efforts, vegetable production covered hardly 1·5 per cent of the cultivated area in 1959.

[26] Asphalt roads connecting this region with the main highways were due to be made in 1960–2.

The unimportance of vegetable production in the *mantiqat* was matched only by that of other specialized crops. No summer forage crops for cattle, such as Sudan grass, sorghum, or green maize, were planted in the lands occupied by the smallholders, despite the contribution they could have made towards raising the level of livestock production. Fruit and flowers or medicinal crops, which could have doubled or trebled income per unit of land, were totally non-existent in the holdings of the beneficiaries, and no plans for their future production had been drafted. Some orchards were planned after 1956 in lands owner-operated by the Agrarian Reform authorities, and by 1959, 800 feddans of orchards had been added to the 4,280 of expropriated orchards. Moreover, despite the grave difficulties already encountered in administering these orchards,[27] the authorities had drafted plans to double the area during 1960–4.[28] If these plans are implemented, at the end of a total period of twelve years of Agrarian Reform guidance and supervision, 2·5 per cent of the lands expropriated from private individuals and *waqfs* will have been reserved for fruit production.[29] None of this will directly benefit smallholders, since orchards are not available for distribution to them.

[27] See above, p. 32.

[28] The original plan was, during 1960–4, to raise the acreage allotted to orchards by 2,500 feddans at a cost of £E150,750, i.e. an average of £E70 per feddan. In 1961 it was decided to increase the acreage by 8,500 feddans during 1960–5 (see *al-Magallat al-Zira'iyat*, Mar. 1961).

[29] On the potentialities of fruit production in Agrarian Reform regions see pp. 126–9.

VI

THE SYSTEM OF SUPERVISED AGRI-CULTURAL CREDIT

A group of medium-sized farmers co-operatively associated with one another for securing common services is the best hope for the success of an intensive agricultural development programme.
D. C. KARVE, at International Conference of Agricultural Economists, Cuernavaca, Mexico, August 1961

THE shortage of credit before the Agrarian Reform[1] was dealt with by the High Committee for Agrarian Reform in the early autumn of 1952 when it obtained, with a state guarantee, a credit of £E1 million at 3 per cent per annum from the Agricultural Credit Bank. These funds were placed at the disposal of the *mandubs* to satisfy the demand for agricultural credit from occupants of the expropriated estates before the establishment of the 'local' co-operatives. In accordance with a so-called supervised credit system, loans in kind and in cash were channelled to the various *zira'at* where they were allocated to smallholders against their undertaking to deliver their crops for bulk disposal by the Agrarian Reform authorities. But after the distribution of holdings started and 'local' co-operatives were established, it was exclusively through the latter that funds were made available. All loans in kind or in cash, whether short- or medium-term, were granted by the co-operatives to their members, who were obliged to deliver their crops to the co-operative warehouses for bulk sale. Rates of interest with which members were debited for the loans they received ranged between 3 and 5 per cent per annum, but whenever large reserve funds were accumulated by the co-operatives they were used to finance credit operations so as not to penalize unduly members owing interest to the Agricultural Credit Bank.

In principle, it was the Board of Directors of each co-operative who assumed, with its 'local' *mushrif* and his staff the responsibility for assessing all the requirements of affiliated members for the normal operation of their holdings; distributing to them the various loans in kind and in cash; ensuring that these loans were actually used for the purpose for which they were intended; enforcing the delivery of the crops to the co-operative warehouses;

[1] See above, p. 8.

disposing of the crops by sale on behalf of members; settling with them the value of the crops disposed of after deducting the sums due for (1) the annual instalment on the purchase price of the holdings, (2) the annual land tax, (3) the *iradat al-gam'iya*, (4) repayment of the loans in kind and in cash granted by the co-operative, (5) any other services provided by the co-operative.

In practice, however, and possibly as a result of habits formed during the period of transition which followed expropriation, it was the *mushrif* of each 'local' co-operative who assumed most of these responsibilities,[2] particularly so far as control of the loans and enforcement of the delivery of crops was concerned. He was helped in this by the *ghufara'* at his disposal, who immediately informed him when a beneficiary diverted to other purposes the loans with which he had been provided. In such cases the *mushrif* warned the culprit and referred the case to the co-operative board for more drastic action if necessary. Notwithstanding the control thus exercised by the *mushrifs*, it was rumoured that many loans to the smallholders were diverted to other purposes or consumed by their recipients. These rumours were substantiated by the fact that in many regions selected seeds, fertilizers, and insecticides distributed by the Agrarian Reform co-operatives could be purchased on the market at a discount. However, these rumours appeared to be a gross exaggeration. The percentage of loans diverted or consumed fluctuated on average between 5 and 10 per cent. It is interesting to note that this was most frequent in regions where peasants from the start had been very poor,[3] or where a high percentage of agricultural labourers had benefited from redistribution. Poor peasants lived on a hand-to-mouth basis, incapable of thrift, diverting to other purposes the loans made to them, to such an extent that they were often compelled to use bad seeds, little fertilizer, &c. This resulted in low crop yields and inevitably in an accumulation of big unsettled debts owed to their co-operative. Anxious to reduce these debts, the *mushrifs* cut down the loans,[4] so that indebted smallholders, swept along in a vicious circle, sunk more and more into debt and misery. Adequate vocational training, a more thorough control by board members, and the postponement and payment of outstanding debts by instalment were the only answer to this problem. The authorities seem of late to have adopted this policy, and instalment payment

[2] The only exception to this being the two co-operatives of Za'faran and Burgaya which were granted financial autonomy in 1959.
[3] In the *mantiqat* of Alexandria (co-operative of Kingi 'Uthman), Itay al-Barud, Balqas (near Mansura), Bahut, and East and West Fayyum, where the lands were none too fertile and the peasants less prosperous, the percentage of loans diverted ranged between 20 and 30 per cent.
[4] In the Itay al-Barud *mantiqa*.

on a five-to-ten-year basis was granted to smallholders with big outstanding debts in 1961.

LOANS IN KIND

These loans included selected seeds, fertilizers, and insecticides supplied to the 'local' co-operatives by their respective *mantiqat* or by their ACS. Both these bought the goods from the Agrarian Reform GCS or from the authorities in Cairo, who in turn obtained them from the Agricultural Credit Bank, the Ministry of Agriculture, &c. Before distribution to the members of a 'local' co-operative, the seeds, fertilizers, and insecticides were stored in its warehouses. Receipts were signed by the beneficiaries for goods and the value was debited to their accounts. The prices charged by the co-operatives were the same as paid by the Cairo authorities or the GCS, plus transport costs and a 3 per cent commission.

In most Agrarian Reform estates, selected seeds, fertilizers, and insecticides for wheat, cotton, rice, maize, and part of the other crops (potatoes, &c.) were regularly distributed in sufficient quantities.[5] Every member of a co-operative was given, at the appropriate season, the quantity of seeds required for the area he devoted to each crop; and whenever necessary supplementary quantities were made available for re-sowing. A weak point of this programme was the fact that no seeds for the clover crop were distributed and seeds for vegetable crops were only occasionally handled by the co-operatives.

Every member was also given chemical fertilizers for the area devoted to the wheat, cotton, rice, and maize crops. The quantities allotted (corresponding to those prescribed by normal agricultural practice) were enough to obtain average yields.[6] The *mushrifs* were reluctant to distribute any more on credit as they hesitated to increase the smallholders' debts, but in principle additional quantities could be purchased from a co-operative for

---

[5] Selected seeds, fertilizers, and insecticides distributed in Agrarian Reform areas in 1959:

Selected Seeds (ardebs)		Fertilizers (tons)		Insecticides (value, £E)
Wheat	52,500	Nitrogen	63,650	400,000
Cotton	63,750	Superphosphates	28,446	
Hybrid maize	15,000	Ammon. sulphates	7,500	
Rice	31,250	Ammon. nitro sulph.	2,912	

Source: Agrarian Reform publications.

[6] Quantities of fertilizers distributed per feddan for:

Wheat	75–100 kilos of calcium nitrate + 17–100 kilos of superphosphates
Cotton	100 kilos of sodium nitrate + 75–100 kilos of superphosphates
Rice	75–100 kilos of ammonium sulphate
Maize	75 kilos of calcium nitrate

cash. The *mushrifs* were also authorized to reduce the quantities of fertilizers distributed if dealing with recalcitrant, over-indebted peasants, and they seized on this pretext considerably to restrict the allocation on credit of superphosphates for the clover crop. When asked about the real cause of this gap in the agricultural credit programme, they explained that one of their main duties was to collect the sums due to the co-operatives from their members and to eliminate debts as much as possible; the distribution on credit of superphosphates for clover, by over-burdening peasants financially, was liable to run counter to this objective. This explanation contained some truth, but the net result was to increase debts of peasants who, instead, purchased their superphosphates on credit from local merchants. The shortage also indirectly increased the debts of peasants who did not purchase from local merchants and whose clover yields were poor through insufficient use of fertilizers.

Insecticides were mainly used against cotton pests in Agrarian Reform estates in Lower and Central Egypt. They were handled by squads of hired workmen who sprayed the cotton fields under the guidance of the *mushrifs* and their aides.[7] The operations were charged to the account of beneficiaries and did not involve any cash payments. Peasants anxious to combat cotton-leaf worm infesting newly sown fields of permanent and temporary clover were given insecticides on credit and were left free to choose the method of utilization; this procedure was not successful. Farmers rarely utilized the insecticides correctly and heavy attacks of cotton-leaf worm resulted. In most of the Northern Delta regions, for example, clover had to be resown in the late autumn of 1959, farmers thus incurring both additional expense and the loss of one cut of clover.

The distribution on credit of concentrate feeds for poultry and cattle was only rarely attempted in Agrarian Reform estates, despite the pressing need.[8] Officials justified this second gap in the agricultural credit programme by saying that smallholders were too often tempted to resell on the black market, at a considerable premium (50 per cent), the cotton-seed cake given them on credit for their cattle. To prevent this, poultry feed and cotton-seed

---

[7] See below, p. 103.

[8] Even in Za'faran, a star co-operative, cotton-seed cake was sold partly on a cash basis to beneficiaries who owned cattle covered by the health insurance system set up under the patronage of the veterinary unit. The quantities allotted per animal insured were delivered against a cash payment equivalent to 50 per cent of the value of the cotton-seed cake, the remainder being debited to the account of the owner of the cattle. In Itay al-Barud, where the only milk-collecting centre of all the Agrarian Reform regions had been established, the situation was worse and smallholders purchasing cotton-seed cake from their co-operatives were compelled to make 100 per cent cash payments.

cake were retailed in limited quantities[9] by the co-operatives but against cash payments; prices were the same as the official government price, plus transport costs and a 3 per cent sale commission.

Other loans included services (*khadamat*) extended by the co-operatives to their members, the cost of which was debited to their accounts, without their needing to pay cash. The various services covered a wide range, including irrigation with fixed and mobile motor pumps, upkeep of the irrigation and drainage networks, ploughing,[10] occasional threshing, pest control, &c., the total value of which had risen to £E1,630,000 in 1958 alone.[11]

The Agrarian Reform smallholders paid slightly more for these services than did the co-operatives, who retained a small margin of profit of 3-10 per cent (according to the type of service) to increase their income.[12] But the costs incurred by the co-operatives (or the Agrarian Reform authorities) due to the inefficiency of their staff were already over 10-30 per cent higher than the normal cost for similar types of work. Smallholders were not unaware of this; their complaints and loss of faith in the Agrarian Reform programme could have been prevented if the quality of the services had been improved and their cost reduced.

Another of the loans in kind provided by the co-operatives was the sale of 1-1½-year-old buffalo heifers to poor beneficiaries without cattle on an instalment basis. The animals sold were supplied to the co-operatives by the Projects Administration [13] of the GCS, and allotted for slighly less than their market value, i.e. about £E40 per head. A beneficiary benefiting from this type of medium-term credit undertook to repay the price of the heifer in five annual instalments without interest and to sell the co-operative the first female calf, delivery to take place when it was at least three months old. Fifty per cent of the sale price of the calf (determined by market prices) was to be deducted from the beneficiary's liabilities, the remainder being paid to him in cash. He also undertook not to dispose of the additional offspring of the heifer by sale, mortgage, or by entering into partnership, without the prior consent of his co-operative, for five years. In case of sale,

[9] The quantities of cattle feed allocated per annum (90 kilos per small herd of cattle and 180 kilos per large herd) against cash payments were hardly sufficient to obtain average yields from meat or milk cattle exclusively fed on wheat straw and a few leaves of corn stalks. On livestock production in Egypt see Saab, *Motorisation*, pp. 337 n. and 350 n.

[10] Included under this heading were payments for the utilization of tractors owned by the Agrarian Reform authorities or by the co-operatives, or hired by the co-operatives on behalf of their members.

[11] See *Agrarian Reform in Seven Years*, p. 157.

[12] The decision to do away with these profit margins for smallholders benefiting from the so-called *khadamat* was announced late in 1961. For further reference see *al-Ta'awun*, 21 Nov. 1961.

[13] *Idarat al-Mashru'at wa'l-Buhuth.*

his co-operative had first priority to purchase the offspring at market value. The beneficiary could dispose of the heifer by sale, mortgage, or by entering into partnership, without the written consent of his co-operative and after settlement of the remaining sum due on its purchase price. Pending full payment of the latter, the heifer remained in the hands of the beneficiary as a loan to him to facilitate the efficient operation of his holding. Any infringement of this obligation exposed the beneficiary to disciplinary action that might result in complete eviction. He had to have the heifer insured, and he had to make use of the co-operative veterinary unit either for artificial insemination or for the use of bulls certified by the beneficiary's co-operative. A co-operative was entitled to supervise the upkeep of the heifer and its health (by means of the veterinary unit), and retained the right to take back the animal if the beneficiary did not live up to his obligations, or if it considered that his chances of meeting his obligations were flimsy.

The instalment sale of cattle began in 1955 in various *mantiqat* and it was without doubt a considerable step forward, compared with the customary *shirq* (partnership) system[14] which had until then provided needy operators with the sole source of capital for the purchase of cattle. The scale of the programme was, however, small, and by 1960 had benefited hardly 5 per cent of all smallholders, with about 1,000 sales annually. In the course of the second five-year plan (1960–4) the sales were to continue at nearly the same rate,[15] the number of heifers to be disposed of totalling 4,165 head. A suggestion that sales should be increased to expand livestock production was brushed aside by Agrarian Reform officials, who hesitated to overburden beneficiaries and feared it

[14] In this form of partnership commonly practised in rural Egypt, the rights and obligations of partners in livestock production are fixed by custom. One of the partners, usually a prosperous village merchant, provides the capital necessary for the purchase of a cow or a female buffalo; the animal is entrusted to the care of his partner, a peasant, who becomes responsible for its complete upkeep (feed, housing, etc). In exchange for his services, and the food and shelter he supplies, the peasant is entitled to half the value of the milk products and to a 50 per cent share in the new-born calf (male or female). In case of sale, the partner, who provided the purchase price of the animal, recovers the full value originally paid, the remaining profit (if any) being divided up equally. If the animal dies accidentally, the merchant partner recovers from his peasant associate the original purchase price in full. The *shirq* system was popular before 1952 among big landowners in areas under reclamation; nowadays it has become one of the main forms of investment for the class of wealthy village capitalists and merchants; in some Egyptian villages over 50 per cent of the cattle are part-owned by a few merchant partners. A certain current of opinion (see *al-Ta'awun*, Nov. 1959) has advocated the complete prohibition of *shirq* agreements; a more liberal policy of agricultural credit, which would treat livestock production on a par with other agricultural activities, may well have the same effect.

[15] In 1958, for example, 1,000 heifers were disposed of to smallholders; in 1961 this figure rose to 1,491, including young calves.

might lead to an increase in the percentage (10–20 per cent) of surreptitious disposal by dishonest peasants. This (typically) overcautious attitude was unfair to the numerous hard-working beneficiaries who obtained high crop yields and therefore enjoyed a greater margin of solvency. A more aggressive livestock credit policy directed towards the latter would have been advisable, if only because of the large scope for developing forage resources; it would also have contributed to mobilize savings which meanwhile were being consumed.[16] Late in 1959 the Agrarian Reform authorities suddenly realized the advantages of intensified livestock production in the areas under their supervision. It was therefore decided to grant loans to beneficiaries for the fattening of beef calves during the winter season, and £E525,000 was allotted for the purchase of some 20,000 calves during 1960–4. The following procedure for the granting of this new type of short-term loan was laid down.

1. The applicant for a loan had to be a landowning beneficiary with no outstanding debts at his co-operative, with a good reputation, and with the necessary quantities of green fodder (i.e. clover).

2. The loan was made in kind, i.e. a male calf, 10–18 months old worth £E25–30 was bought at the neighbouring cattle market by the co-operative staff and handed over to a beneficiary for fattening on clover during the winter and spring. An additional £E1·2 was charged per animal to give it the cover of a health insurance policy.

3. In May, at the end of the clover season, the calf was to be returned to the co-operative; its value was to be estimated by a committee composed of a member of the staff of the ACS, the vet in charge of the veterinary unit, and co-operative board members. The difference between its purchase price and its estimated value was to be paid to the beneficiary. It was impossible, however, to find out on what basis this estimation was to be made, the Agrarian Reform officials being reluctant to provide information on this subject. Since the official price of meat on the hoof was 25 per cent below black-market prices, the profit accruing to a beneficiary from this venture depended in no small measure on the basis of estimation.[17]

4. The calves returned to the co-operatives after fattening were to be kept for an additional period of three or four months before

---

[16] See below, pp. 124–5.

[17] For the economics of meat production see Saab, *Motorisation*, pp. 348–53 and S. Saffa, 'Exploitation économique et agricole d'une domaine rural égyptien', *Ég. contemp.*, 1949, pp. 342–7. It is amusing to note that one of the reproaches made by the Butchers' Union to the Minister of Supply in 1961 was that the Agrarian Reform authorities were among the first to infringe the official price tariffs on meat.

being sold for slaughter. They were to be fed exclusively with concentrates under the supervision of the co-operative staff and at their expense. The profit of this last operation was to be credited to the account of the co-operatives and later redistributed to their members in addition to the normal annual profits from other co-operative activities.

It was difficult to assess the value of this project but experiments in fattening cattle under the exclusive supervision of the co-operatives or their technical staff had been previously attempted in many Agrarian Reform regions, and had met with only limited success.

The instalment sale of poultry was a scheme begun in 1955 by the Agrarian Reform Projects Administration. Since then selected strains of poultry have been regularly distributed by co-operatives to the smallholders in the fifteen *mantiqat* where veterinary units were established. A considerable quantity of poultry was supplied to the Agrarian Reform co-operatives, sometimes by the al-Marg Agrarian Reform incubating centre[18] and sometimes by the district veterinary unit. Hatching capacity available for this scheme rose to a total of nearly 500,000 chicks a year by 1960.[19] Annual production had averaged 300,000 chicks and in each of the *mantiqat* an average of 20,000 chicks had been annually sold on an instalment basis. The procedure adopted for this scheme was as follows: three-week-old Rhode Island chicks and pedigree cocks, all immunized against the various poultry diseases, were supplied to peasants who undertook to repay their value the following year at the rate of four eggs per chick received;[20] each peasant family was alloted 12 chicks. A contract embodying a number of obligations was signed by each recipient; the chicks were to be looked after and fed with the utmost care and according to the directions issued by the staff of the veterinary unit; they were to be submitted to the latter for immunization against contagious diseases at fixed dates. The recipient was to comply with any anti-pest measures enacted by the vet in charge of the unit, and when chicks died the carcasses were to be presented to him for post-mortem examination. To avoid cross-breeding, the recipient undertook not to keep cocks of any other breed and to get rid of any such cocks in his possession. Further, the recipient could not dispose of the chicks of the distributed birds without first submitting them for sale to his co-operative . The latter was entitled to withdraw the chicks distributed if a recipient failed

[18] Specially set up on the eastern outskirts of Cairo in the expropriated estate of al-Marg, Qaliyubiya *mantiqa*.
[19] Appropriations for this scheme during the second five-year plan totalled £E570,000.
[20] As from August 1959 this was changed to five eggs.

to take proper care of them, or if he failed to comply with the directives of the staff of the veterinary unit. The eggs repaid the following year were incubated under the supervision of the unit; the newly hatched chicks were later distributed.

The scheme seemed to have worked quite well, despite a very high rate of mortality among the distributed poultry (nearly 60 per cent according to the Agrarian Reform staff) and despite a considerable amount of loss from numerous dishonest and short-sighted peasants who immediately resold their chicks in the neighbourhood at a premium. Large numbers of Rhode Island poultry could be seen throughout the estates, and in Damira, for example, they must have represented at least 60 per cent of the total number possessed by the peasants. If breeding conditions had not been so bad, this percentage, notwithstanding outside leakage, would have been much higher; it was apparent anyway that the peasants were all convinced that the advantages of breeding the pedigree Rhode Island chick were nearly double that of the local breed, and their weight when slaughtered was 25–30 per cent more. As a result of this higher productivity, a surplus of eggs was now available in many *mantiqat* the disposal of which was left to the initiative of the beneficiaries. Peasants were, however, reluctant to pay back the four or five eggs per chick distributed as stipulated by their contracts with their co-operatives, and the latter were therefore compelled to penalize those not fulfilling their obligations. For each egg not delivered, peasants were charged £E0·025, but as this sum was not demanded in cash, the deterrent effect was completely lost.[21]

TABLE 6

Pedigree Poultry Distributed in Damira 1955–60

	Pedigree chicks distributed	No. of eggs received in return	No. of cocks distributed
1955	32,000	112,000	—
1956	14,500	29,391	1,300
1957	56,622	133,490	500
1958	86,450	..	395
1959	85,000	..	200
1960	55,033	..	
	329,605		

.. = not available.

Source: Information obtained from Damira *mantiqa*.

---

[21] This was even the case in Damira, as may be seen from Table 6.

CASH LOANS

Loans in cash were provided to help smallholders during peak seasons (e.g. before harvest), as their tight financial situation might have often led them to hire themselves out to independent local operators rather than cultivate their own holdings. In the relatively sparsely populated regions of the Northern Delta, these cash loans enabled smallholders to hire some seasonal labour. Three types of cash loans were provided by the co-operatives to their members (at the same time as loans in kind), the interest rate on them varying between 3 and 5 per cent per annum.

1. A loan[22] of £E4·5 per feddan of rice cultivated in the Delta was given to each beneficiary early in May to help him finance the transplanting of the rice crop from the nurseries to the flooded fields. This absorbed a considerable amount of manual labour over a relatively brief period and was often done by the beneficiaries helped by hired labour from the densely populated regions of Damietta and Mit Ghamr.

2. A loan[23] of £E3 per feddan of cotton cultivated was given to each beneficiary early in September to help him at the time of the cotton harvest.

3. A loan equal to 90 per cent of the value at current market prices of the cotton crop of a beneficiary was extended to him as soon as he delivered it to his co-operative's warehouses, if the price of the crop had not already been fixed by a sales agreement entered upon by the co-operative authorities.

No medium-term loans were made by the co-operatives to their members for the purchase of agricultural machinery, individually or in partnership. Yet such loans, granted at a low rate of interest, would certainly have accelerated the pace of mechanization in *mantiqat* and improved the condition of livestock production. Partnership agreements to purchase equipment offered scope for such a credit policy. A vivid example of this was to be found in the village of al-Manakhulla, Damira *mantiqa*, where many hard-working, fairly prosperous peasants had banded together and bought out of their own private liquid assets several 7–12 h.p. mobile irrigation pumps. The capital had been found from savings on expanding incomes. These savings were supplemented by credit facilities (12–18 months' credit) from farm-machinery dealers in the city of Mansura. Seventeen mobile irrigation pumps were bought by various groups of ten to fifteen peasants each. Each group hired a mechanic to run its pump, and running costs

---

[22] *Salafiyat shatl al-aruzz.*
[23] *Salafiat gany al-qutn.* From May 1961, in compliance with a decision of the GCS, peasants were relieved of the payment of the 5 per cent interest previously charged.

were shared in proportion to the size of the holdings of the partners. This spontaneous experiment was (still) running smoothly in 1960. In other co-operatives, where the financial situation of the beneficiaries was not as favourable, a medium-term credit policy carried out by the co-operatives would have done much to encourage similar initiative. Loans directly to groups of beneficiaries for the purchase of light, multi-purpose 7–12 h.p. tractors[24] for irrigation, furrowing, harrowing, threshing, and transport would have been of assistance and would have contributed to the investment of available savings.

TOTAL VALUE OF LOANS

From 1953 there was a considerable rise in the total short-term loans and services provided annually to the smallholders by the Agrarian Reform authorities or the 'local' co-operatives on the supervised credit system. This can be seen from the following table:

(£E 000)

1953	1,114	1957	2,890
1954	1,678	1958	3,150
1955	2,142	1959	3,721
1956	2,680	1960	4,351

Sources: Agrarian Reform in Seven Years; Agrarian Reform in Nine Years.

This rise was mainly due to the rapid growth of the area under Agrarian Reform jurisdiction, and to the increase in the number of landowning beneficiaries. The total value of these loans and services averaged nearly £E9 per feddan operated in 1959, when about 420,000 feddans were supervised by the Agrarian Reform authorities and occupied by beneficiaries. Agronomists were free to adjust the loans and services to beneficiaries in accordance with the productive capacity of their holdings and taking into account other factors such as manpower reserves, reputations, &c. In the relatively fertile and prosperous *mantiqa* of Damira, for example, the loans in kind, cash, and services totalled in 1959 £E14 per feddan operated.[25] A landowner operating a 3-feddan holding thus received, on average, about £E42 in loans and services; his debts (*al-matlub*), including all money he owed to his co-operative (instalment, land tax, voluntary contributions to co-operative expenses, and the loans and services) totalled about £E99 before the reduction in the annual instalment decreed in 1958,[26] i.e.

---

[24] See Saab, *Motorisation*, pp. 290–1.
[25] *al-Magallat al-Zira'iyat*, Nov. 1959, pp. 99–100. (Also Min. AR, *Agrarian Reform Co-operatives in Daqahliya Province* (1960)).
[26] See above, p. 43.

£E33 per feddan (assuming that no debts had been carried over from the preceding year). After the reduction, the debt on a 3-feddan holding decreased to about £E89, or slightly less than £E30 per feddan. At the very prosperous Mit al-Mawz co-operative, Shibin al-Kawm *mantiqa* (one of the most successful of all the *mantiqat*), the value of loans and services to landowning peasants averaged £E15 per feddan in 1959, and the total debt was about £E35 per feddan. At the other end of the scale, at the co-operative of Hugmin, East Fayyum *mantiqa* (one of the least successful), the value of loans and services to tenant operators averaged about £E7 and the debt totalled about £E15. In Damira the loans and services amounted to nearly 75 per cent of the running expenses incurred on a holding, excluding the value of the labour inputs of a farmer and his family, and of the instalment, land tax, and voluntary contribution. At Mit al-Mawz the ratio of loans and services to running expenses was equally high at 70 per cent; even in Hugmin it was not far from 50 per cent.

The contribution of the supervised credit programme to the fruitful operation of the distributed holdings was therefore considerable; it was also quite understandable that the authorities should have hesitated to burden smallholders with over-generous short-term credits, though there was a case for a more venture-some policy towards the least favoured of them, whatever the risks.

The success of the supervised credit system furthermore weakened the hold of usurers (money-lenders, grain and cotton brokers buying crops in advance with a big discount, &c.) which had been so strong before 1952. At Damira, where nearly half the tenant operators had been dealing with money-lenders before 1952, the percentage of operators resorting to their services was reported in 1959 to have fallen to 10 per cent. In the prosperous region of al-Khazan it fluctuated around 15–20 per cent, and even in the regions of Itay al-Barud, Bahut, and East and West Fayyum, it only rose above 30 per cent exceptionally. These variations in the importance of the part played by money-lenders in each of the *mantiqat* can be traced not only to a more generous agricultural credit policy pursued in some, but also to other factors such as increasing yields, expanding incomes, efficient co-operative organizations, better technical knowledge of small-holders, and a higher standard of living at the outset.

SMALLHOLDERS' ACCOUNTS

Each smallholder had been given an account book (*bataqa*) in which were written his name, the exact area of his holding, and all his financial transactions with the Agrarian Reform authorities

or his co-operative. On the credit side were entered all the payments in kind (i.e. the crops delivered for bulk disposal) and in
cash which an operator made to the authorities or to his 'local'
co-operative. On the debit side were entered all the loans and
services with which he was provided, as well as the money due for
the holding. The latter was called calculation of rent (*rabt igar*),
whether the occupant was a landowning beneficiary paying a lump-
sum including the instalment, land tax, and 'voluntary' contribution, or an ordinary tenant paying a straightforward rent. The
use of the same name for two different forms of land tenure added
to the confusion in the mind of the peasants as to the real nature
of their status. As well as these credit and debit items, peasants
received from the Agrarian Reform or co-operative accountants
and storekeepers receipts for all the money they paid or for the
crops they delivered; they were also given copies of the receipts
they themselves signed when they were provided with loans in cash
or in kind or with services.

From 1957 accounts were balanced at the end of June of each
year. Immediately afterwards outstanding debts were re-entered
in the book as well as the sums due for the occupation of holdings,
the basis of calculation of the latter being mentioned (i.e. the land
tax on each plot). This annual accounting was purely formal, and
as far as a peasant was concerned, the real accounting only took
place in October, once his cotton crop had been picked, weighed,
and stored in the co-operative warehouses and his account credited
with a loan equal to 90 per cent of the value as determined by
current prices, or with its full value if its price had already been
fixed by a sale contract with the Agrarian Reform authorities or his
co-operative (as was the case in the majority of *mantiqat* in 1959).[27]
It was then and then only that a peasant was allowed to cash any
surplus (commonly referred to as cotton surplus, *fa'id al-qutn*) in
his favour. When the prices of the cotton crop were fixed at a
later date, the difference between the loan made on the basis of
current market prices and the value of the cotton as fixed by
subsequent sale was credited to the operator's account and a cash
payment followed. In Damira, for example, a very high percentage of smallholders enjoyed the privilege of these cash payments,
which usually occurred between October and November and
proceeded regularly. The same was true of Shibin al-Kawm[28]
where in 1959 smallholders received as surplus from cotton an
average of £E10 per feddan operated, half of which was paid be-

[27] See below, pp. 117–18.
[28] At the record-breaking co-operative of Mit al-Mawz, Shibin *mantiqa*,
smallholders received in 1959 an average £E20 per feddan operated as surplus
from cotton.

fore the sale of the crop and the other half just afterwards early in January. But with the exception of a few well-administered *mantiqat* delay in accounting and in the payment of surpluses from cotton was the rule; and peasants frequently complained that they could not follow up on their accounts, and that surpluses were only paid to them after several months' delay.[29]

COLLECTION OF SMALLHOLDERS' DEBTS

It has already been stated[30] that in compliance with the system of supervised credit the only guarantee or collateral demanded by the co-operatives for loans in kind and in cash was an undertaking by their members to deliver their crops to the co-operative warehouses for sale. It was not easy to secure compliance with this undertaking, even though the crops marketed by the co-operatives often fetched far more than those obtained by direct sales by the beneficiaries and tenants. Many of the latter were reluctant to pay their debts and settle their accounts, as they seemed to consider that whatever they had received had been given by a government agency (i.e. the Agrarian Reform authorities of the co-operatives), and that as such there was no special reason to hurry up and repay. The fact that money owed for the occupation of the holdings was debited to the same account as that of the loans or services was doubtless influential, and the more so since the calculation of the annual instalment or the annual rent differed from year to year.[31] Delay in drawing up the accounts of the beneficiaries and tenants and the ensuing confusion in their minds were also partly responsible for this attitude, which was typical of the Egyptian peasantry, and showed that the new landowners, who had been insufficiently indoctrinated, still distrusted the new co-operative structures.[32] To cope with this, and to ensure that the delivery of the crops to the co-operatives was punctually enforced, a number of measures were enacted by the *nazir zira'at* and the *mushrif*. These varied according to the crops, and according to the degree of indebtedness of the members of the co-operatives.

With cotton, on average the gross returns fluctuated, in Damira, for example, between £E75 and £E100 per feddan, bearing in mind average yields and according to current prices. The returns were higher than those of any other single crop and normally were

[29] See *al-Ta'awun*, 23 Mar. 1959.
[30] Above, p. 82.   [31] See above, pp. 41–47.
[32] A similar attitude was noted in 1961 by the author in Syria when surveying Agrarian Reform co-operatives in Ghazlaniya (Damascus region) and in Humaimat (Aleppo region). See also F. Kuhnen, *Case Study of the Effects of Syrian Agrarian Reform* (Berlin, Inst. für Ausländische Landwirtschaft, 1963).

sufficient to settle all outstanding debts; the cotton crop was therefore considered by the Agrarian Reform staff as the main guarantee for the loans made by the co-operatives and as the only tangible collateral for money due to them by their members. In consequence, picking of this crop was subject to the prior consent of the *mushrifs*, who never allowed the peasants to enter the cotton fields until a complete block of 30–50 feddans was fully ripe. Enforcement of this rule was left to the *ghafir*. At the co-operative of Hawasliya, Minya Province, Upper Egypt, only one picking of the cotton took place instead of the customary two practised by Egyptian farmers who aimed at high-grade fibres. According to the Agrarian Reform officials, a considerable amount of leakage in the delivery of the crop to the co-operative would have occurred if the peasants had been allowed to harvest their cotton in the customary manner; this would have given them the opportunity to take away part of their crops surreptitiously. Surreptitious picking would have been hardly noticeable and therefore difficult to prevent if the cotton were first picked when some of the bolls reached maturity and a second time when the remaining bolls ripened; it might easily have occurred at night between the two pickings and would have provided dishonest peasants with a unique occasion to move off the crop and avoid or delay settlement of their debts to the co-operatives. Notwithstanding all these precautions, and possibly as a result of the laxity of the *ghufara'*, on average peasants in the different *mantiqat* managed to make off secretly with a third to a half of a kantar of cotton per feddan, i.e. approximately 5 per cent of their crop in Damira but slightly more than 10 per cent in regions where crop yields averaged 3–4 kantars.

The delivery of the cotton to the warehouses of a local co-operative was supervised by a board member. He controlled the sifting in the fields to ensure the cleanliness of the crop, and directed weighing jointly with the *mushrif* and the storekeeper. As soon as these operations were completed, 90 per cent of the value of the cotton at current market prices (or 100 per cent if the price was already fixed by a sale) was credited to the account of the beneficiaries; in the case of a peasant operating a 3-feddan holding and planting 1 feddan of cotton (assuming his yields were equal to the Damira average) this amounted to £E65–100, according to the cotton prices. If no other cash payment had been made during the year by the peasant, or if no other crop had been delivered by him to his co-operative for sale, his account would not have balanced and his debt would be carried over during the following year; until 1959 this averaged around £E100 a year, not including outstanding debts carried over. To prevent large debts being carried over, cash payments, or the delivery of other crops than cotton, were demanded from smallholders, their volume depending on the fertility of the various *mantiqat* and the degree of their indebtedness. This was standard practice in the regions of the Northern Delta, where crop yields were relatively low and subject to fluctuation, especially during 1954–9 when the beneficiaries were being debited with an instalment price calculated on the basis of a redemption in thirty years at 3 per cent interest per annum. The reduction of the instalment, of the interest rate, and of administration costs[33] reduced the debts of the smallholders. Consequently as from 1960 the importance of cash payments during the year, or of the delivery of crops other than cotton dwindled except in the case of very low yields, gross negligence, or dishonesty of peasants.

The average gross returns of the wheat crop in Damira, for example, did not exceed £E25–30. In view of this low figure the disposal of this crop was generally left to the discretion of smallholders, who consumed part of it and sold the rest to the Agricultural Credit Bank and to wheat merchants. Some skilful peasants with high-quality wheat crops sold them through co-operative channels at a premium to the Ministry of Agriculture who redistributed them after grading as selected seeds. But to reduce the risk of indebtedness at the end of the year partial payments on account were demanded from beneficiaries as soon as the wheat crop reached maturity. These payments could be made in cash or kind and varied according to the state of a peasant's account, the condition of his holding, and his reputation. Usually they varied between £E5–10 or 1–2 ardebs of grain (15–30 per cent of the crop) per feddan of wheat. To safeguard the interests of the co-operatives and to make the collection of outstanding debts easier, the *mushrif* prohibited the harvesting of the crop until these payments in cash or in kind were made; the *ghufara'* were made responsible for this. It was not very difficult to collect these interim payments from the relatively prosperous Damira peasants, and by mid-June 1959 nearly all the fields had been cleared of their crops. Only a few isolated fields of unharvested wheat were observed throughout the Damira estates, whereas they were very frequent in the neighbouring Balqas-Bahut, Sharbin, and in Alexandria, Itay al-Barud, and even Za'faran *mantiqat*, where the *mushrifs* had no other choice but to delay the harvest to obtain the interim payments from numerous recalcitrant peasants. However, this did considerable harm to the yields both of their wheat crop and of the subsequent rice crop; substantial quantities of wheat grain were lost and many peasants, from fear of missing the planting season and to make up for the time lost, broadcast (*badar*)

---

[33] Above, p. 43.

their rice seeds, rather than use the more productive method of transplanting (*shatl*) rice seedlings.

The authorities or the co-operatives only rarely demanded partial payments from smallholders during the winter season, when the clover (*barsim*) was grown. Sometimes, if a peasant was really slow in settling his liabilities, his *mushrif* was entitled to ask him for a partial payment of £E5–10 before he fed the second or third cut of clover to his animals; if this was not forthcoming the *ghufara'* were asked to prevent any removal of the crop from the fields, a measure often resorted to in the less prosperous regions. The rice and maize crops, which matured after the cotton crop, were left to the beneficiaries and tenants for their own personal consumption or for sale, but in extreme cases of insolvency, the *mushrif* issued orders to the *ghufara'* to delay harvesting until settlement was forthcoming. Peasants planting vegetables were more prosperous than the average and were therefore not late in settling their accounts, so that the disposal of their vegetable crops was left to their own initiative.

When peasants showed signs of unwillingness to settle their accounts with their co-operatives, or if they repeatedly attempted to dispose of their crops secretly so as to avoid payments demanded of them, the Agrarian Reform agronomists or *mushrifs* had the right to open judicial proceedings for the seizure of their crops. The peasants were made the custodians of their own crops and a written report (*mahdar hagz*) signed by the local village *sarraf* was drawn up to establish the responsibilities of the custodian; peasants removing their seized crops without a court writ exposed themselves to charges of embezzlement (*mahdar tabdid*), which could land them in jail. In the Damira region charges of embezzlement were drawn up against hardly 5 per cent of the smallholders because, as they were relatively well off, they were not likely to expose themselves to such rigorous treatment. In other regions (in neighbouring Bahut, for example) the proportion was very much higher, though Agrarian Reform agronomists and *mushrifs* were generally reluctant to initiate judicial proceedings for the seizure of crops, as their recurrence would have proved to their superiors that they themselves had not been sufficiently active in convincing smallholders of the necessity of fulfilling their duties as members of the new Agrarian Reform communities. Outstanding debts, the illiteracy of the vast majority of the smallholders, who found it difficult fully to grasp the accounting system, and delay in drawing up accounts were the main obstacles to a smooth and rapid settlement of outstanding liabilities. In spite of this, they were not on the whole very large except for a few regions in the Northern Delta and Fayyum province.

Year	Per cent collected of total sums due in all regions	Year	Per cent collected of total sums due in all regions
1953/4	98	1956/7	90
1954/5	93	1957/8	93
1955/6	89		

Source: Agrarian Reform in Seven Years.

These figures seem credible, for though certain regions were heavily indebted and the percentage collected of sums due was relatively low (such as in Itay al-Barud, Simbilawain,[34] or in the two Fayyum *mantiqat*), this was compensated by the high percentage (sometimes as high as 30 per cent) of collection in regions such as Shibin al-Kawm, or the Upper Egypt *mantiqat*. It must also be remembered that substantial reductions (*takhfidhat*) (following the reassessment of the basic land tax on a holding) of the total amount due for the occupation of a holding affected some 15,000 feddans: these diminished the volume of outstanding liabilities.

In Damira (15,169 feddans, 5,060 smallholders) the outstanding debts (*muta'akhirat al-mantiqa*) of some 500 smallholders were reported to have totalled about £E100,000 in 1959; if spread over the whole area operated, they averaged £E7 per feddan, the equivalent of more than twice the basic land tax of £E3·22 per feddan. In Za'faran co-operative (4,891 feddans, 1,462 smallholders) they totalled £E43,000 in 1958, but decreased the following year to £E23,000, i.e. twice the basic land tax of £E2·4 per feddan. In the region of Shibin al-Kawm (7,300 feddans, 3,946 smallholders), outstanding debts were down to £E5,196 in 1959, averaging £E0·7 per feddan, i.e. less than 0·3 times the land tax of £E3 feddan. In most of the Upper Egypt regions the situation was nearly as favourable. In sharp contrast to these, outstanding debts of the members of the Bahut Nabaruh *mantiqa* (13,312 feddans, 5,000 smallholders) were extremely large in 1959, totalling nearly £E400,000 and averaging £30 per feddan, about ten times the basic land tax. At the co-operative of Kafr Bahut (1,550 feddans, 580 smallholders), Bahut Nabaruh *mantiqa*, these debts were enormous, as much as £E40,000 at the end of 1959, averaging £E27 per feddan, i.e. nine times the average land tax of £E3. At another of the Bahut co-operatives, Kafr Katta (1,050 feddans, 370 smallholders), debts were proportionately even higher, totalling £E35,000, an average of £E35 per feddan. The situation was not much better in some other Northern Delta

[34] In Simbilawain the percentage of collection improved considerably in 1959 (128 per cent).

regions such as the Itay al-Barud–Gabaris region (20,446 feddans, 5,000 smallholders), where outstanding debts were over £E500,000 in 1959, averaging over £E25 per feddan. The two *mantiqat* of East and West Fayyum (Fayyum province) shared the record of being the most indebted of all the *mantiqat*: at the co-operative of al-Aziziyat (2,000 feddans, not including waste lands, 582 smallholders), East Fayyum, outstanding debts totalled £E65,000 in 1959, despite reductions of £E10,000.

VII

PRODUCTION AND MARKETING IN THE DISTRIBUTED ESTATES

Before creating consumers, the Revolution should create producers.
R. DUMONT, *Cuba ou la Réforme Agraire* (1961)

APPLICATION OF ORGANIC MANURE

THE customary stabling practices prevailing in Egypt were followed by all Agrarian Reform smallholders without exception: the litter, consisting of dry mud silt extracted from the main and subsidiary canals close to their houses, was changed every ten to fifteen days. The farm manure thus produced was supplemented with human excreta and household refuse, which were all piled up in the open next to the farmers' houses or on near-by communal lands. Three or four months later it was taken by donkey to the fields to be fertilized and accumulated on a near-by drain or canal bank or on a road; the work thus involved was painstaking and time-consuming, for the fertilization of fields required 15–20 tons of farm manure per feddan, which had to be carried by donkeys with a maximum load of 50–60 kilos. Because of the primitive methods of production, storage, and handling of manure, its quality was extremely poor and the loss of nitrogen considerable. If the smallholders had been encouraged to build concrete manure pits, and to use their dried cotton and corn stalks as litter instead of burning them, these disadvantages might have been avoided.[1]

Agrarian Reform staff claimed that the stable tenure enjoyed since 1952 by the operators of the estates gave them greater incentive to cultivate their lands carefully and that, as a result, more organic manure was being spread on the fields. At the same time they underlined that the number of cattle had increased since 1952; in prosperous regions, such as Damira, Shibin al-Kawm, and Minya they estimated this at roughly 15–20 per cent and sometimes more. Attributed to the cumulative growth of income, the increase in the number of cattle was said to have brought about a heavier use of organic manure. But though this was certainly

[1] Experiments conducted in Sirsal-Layan, Minufiya province, by Thedorovich have established that by using dried corn stalks as litter and by constructing cement manure pits, it is possible to treble the fertilizing value of Egyptian farm manure (see *al-Magallat al-Zira'iyat*, July 1959, pp. 113–26).

true in many cases, in others the distance from the houses and cowsheds of smallholders to their lands and the lack of mechanized transport remained formidable obstacles to a satisfactory level of organic fertilization. To overcome this a few prosperous farmers in Damira and Shibin al-Kawm, for example, recently erected in a corner of their holdings small open-air cowsheds to house three or four head of cattle; built with mud bricks and roofed with branches and reeds, these cowsheds spared farmers the considerable time and effort which would otherwise have been lost in the transport of fodder and manure.

USE OF MANPOWER

Operations such as spreading organic manure or chemical fertilizer, sowing, planting, hoeing, weeding, transplanting, harvesting, threshing, and the upkeep of tertiary drains and subsidiary canals were carried out individually by the Agrarian Reform smallholders, who used their own primitive equipment—hoes (*fa's*), Archimedes screws, sickles, *nawrags* (threshing-carts), &c.,— as in the past. As previously explained,[2] in a few regions, such as Damira and Za'faran, some farm operations (upkeep of main and secondary canals and drains, pest control, cotton picking) were done with the help of co-operative labour gangs, when the occupants of a given block of 30–100 feddans of land were asked to contribute workers. Successful promotion of these gangs was rare and manual operations, such as cotton picking and sifting, were accomplished individually by smallholders, whereas the more delicate pest-control operations were undertaken with hired agricultural labour. In May and early June, during the first phase of the fight against the cotton-leaf worm (*prodenia litura*), pest-control operations were left to the initiative of the smallholders, who used the customary manual method of leaf picking with the help of their families. As soon as a heavy increase in eggs laid by the butterflies was observed, special parties were sent out on the orders of *nazir zira'at* or *mushrifs* to scour the fields and complete the work. These parties, in all Agrarian Reform estates (except Za'faran and part of Damira) were composed of hired workmen under the control of foremen, and their wages were charged to the account of smallholders. Efforts to spare the latter these costs and carry out the pest control with co-operative labour gangs had failed; smallholders, some of whom were not rich, preferred to offer their available labour for hire outside the Agrarian Reform estates, or even in neighbouring Agrarian Reform estates, for a daily wage, paying later for the

[2] Above, p. 74.

work accomplished (often inadequately) in their own fields by pest-control parties recruited by the Agrarian Reform authorities.

Pest control with insecticides was entrusted to relatively trained hired workers who were recruited and supervised by the *nazirs* and *mushrifs*, and who sprayed cotton fields with low- and high-pressure hand sprayers. Spraying was often irregular because of inefficient workers, who walked through the fields too fast. Even in the Damira estates, complaints about the manner of spraying were to be heard, for fields sprayed a few days previously were soon reinfested by cotton-leaf worm, while in other fields apparently just sprayed entire furrows had been left unsprayed. The limited success of the pest-control programme was attributed by peasants to the lax supervision of the pest-control squads, who were insufficiently trained and unaware of their responsibilities, and who, moreover, were equipped with many sprayers in poor condition. Smallholders were generally of the opinion that the cost of pest control was too high[3] in relation to the quality of the service. But they acknowledged that since the introduction of potent insecticides pest control was much more effective than previously with the customary method of leaf picking.

USE OF DRAUGHT POWER

In the Damira *mantiqa* most peasants only possessed one head of fully mature draught animals, generally a buffalo cow; the poorer peasants had cows and nearly all beneficiaries had a donkey.[4] Several farm operations needed two fully grown animals, and the peasants to meet this difficulty used the traditional mutual-help system (*muzamala*); they would lend their animals to neighbours who in return lent their animals when necessary. About 6,000 head (including horses, donkeys, and cattle)[5] were owned by the Damira beneficiaries, most of which served a dual purpose. Their milk yields were very low (about 1,000 kilos a year). The total number of mature animals available for draught purposes far exceeded the actual requirements of an area of 15,000 feddans; 3,000 animals would have been more than enough,[6] assuming that no mechanical draught power was used at all; but this was not the case.

[3] Complaints voiced by peasants in various regions were also to be found in the Agrarian Reform press; for complaints in the Itay al-Barud region, for example, where costs for pest control totalled £E7 per feddan of cotton in 1957/8 and £E12 in 1958/9, see *al-Ta'awun*, 22 Mar. 1960.

[4] See App. VI for figures of livestock owned by the Damira landowning beneficiaries.

[5] Assuming that 10 donkeys = one mature head of cattle.

[6] Normal requirements of draught power for a 5-feddan holding have been estimated in Egypt at one head of mature dual-purpose cattle. For further details see Saab, *Motorisation*, pp. 64 n. and 260–1.

Farm operations undertaken by draught animals—owned, borrowed, or rented—by occupants of the Damira estates were as follows:

1. Levelling dry land (*taqsib*) or levelling land flooded for the cultivation of clover or rice (*talwit*); in both of these animal draught power was used exclusively.

2. Ploughing (*harth*) and harrowing (*tazhif*). The use of draught cattle varied according to the crop: wheat and rice 50 per cent minimum, maize nearly 100 per cent; cotton 10–20 minimum as farmers were convinced that mechanical ploughing at a depth of 25–30 cm. was good for cotton seed-bed preparation and quicker. In fact tractors were essential in ploughing for cotton in view of the prevailing habit among the smallholders of trying to increase their forage resources by growing a snatch clover crop in the cotton fields until early February. Planting would have been delayed until after mid-March if draught cattle had been used exclusively and as a result of late planting the yields of the cotton crop would not have been as high. There was a general delay throughout the Damira estates in clearing the clover snatch crop, as in all other Northern Delta Agrarian Reform regions, at the end of January 1960, whereas on most large farms in the vicinity the cotton seed-beds had long been completed. This delay in clearing the clover fields excluded the utilization of draught cattle, which was too slow.

3. Furrowing (*takhtit*); nearly 100 per cent of the furrowing for cotton was done with draught animals.

4. Transport. All transport was by draught animals. Donkeys were used as pack animals for manure, clover, &c. as well as for transporting persons; camels were also used as pack animals to carry the wheat and rice crops; horse-drawn carts were sometimes used by peasants taking their crops to Mansura.

5. Threshing. A very high percentage was done with draught animals (nearly 90 per cent) attached to *nawrags*.

6. Irrigation. More than 60 per cent of the lifting of irrigation water by water wheels (*saqias*) was done with draught animals and was a common sight on the Damira estates where the water lift was only one or two metres.[7]

The following farm operations were undertaken with mechanical draught power:

1. *Ploughing and Harrowing*

As mentioned above, ploughing and harrowing the   cotton

---

[7] Some 30 fixed irrigation units were removed by the Min. AR during the early stages of expropriation and dispatched to other areas where they were urgently needed; these motor pumps were replaced by *saqias*, driven by draught animals.

seed-bed was nearly always done with tractors on the Damira estates, as being faster and more effective. Tractors were obtained either from the ACS machine pool[8] (that is the machine pool of Damira *mantiqa*) or from local contractors, but usually if tractors were available at the co-operative they were called upon. Ploughing twice, plus harrowing during the cotton seed-bed preparation, cost the Damira beneficiary a total of £E1·40 (inclusive of the wage of the driver). Actual operating costs were slightly less, the difference going to the co-operative as profit. If it had not been for the high maintenance and repair costs and the low utilization rates of the tractors (500–600 hours a year), the co-operative would have made a handsome profit,[9] since the compulsory application of the triennial crop rotation and the crop consolidation provided ideal conditions for farm machinery.

It was up to the Damira occupants to decide whether to plough with their own draught animals or with tractors belonging to the co-operative, or hired from local contractors; exceptions to this were when preparing lands for the cotton crop or when peasants were late in preparing for other crops. In the former case, in view of the importance of the cotton crop, the decision would be made by the co-operative directors acting either on their own initiative or on a suggestion by the *mushrif*. The scarcity of equipment available at the farm machinery pool prompted each individual co-operative to call in contractors nine times out of ten. They were invited to tender according to specifications laid down by the board, who then accepted the lowest bid. The contractors were paid by the co-operative after completion of the required work, and not before obtaining from the peasants concerned satisfactory evidence that the work had been accomplished in compliance with the specifications of the tender; the latter were extremely chary of giving their approval. A 5 per cent commission for the co-operative was added to the price paid to contractors, the total cost per feddan being charged to the account of the smallholders in proportion to the ploughed area of their holding. The consolidation of crops enabled the contractors to tender at low prices averaging £E1·40 (plus the 5 per cent commission). This was not excessive compared with the prevailing prices of local contractors, especially since operating costs considerably increased after 1956. On the other hand, some peasants had their fields ploughed by contractors on their own account. The price paid per

---

[8] Equipment available consisted of 7 wheel tractors capable of 281 h.p., 3 caterpillar tractors capable of 126 h.p., 21 fixed and mobile irrigation units capable of 352 h.p., 2 tractor-powered *saqias*, 3 cars, 1 jeep, and 3 trucks.

[9] For full details on costs of operating tractors in Egypt see Saab, *Motorisation*, pp. 130–53. The general upkeep of the equipment available at the Damira farm machinery pool was fair.

feddan (£E1·45–1·5 for cotton and £0·8–0·9 for wheat, rice, or maize) was equivalent to those in Daqahliya province for similar work.

2. *Transport*

It has already been pointed out that the various transport operations in Damira and other Agrarian Reform estates were done exclusively with draught animals, despite the considerable distance often separating holdings from the peasant's house in an over-crowded village. Small tractors (7–12 h.p.) with trailers could have solved these transport problems; they could have been bought on a co-operative or partnership basis and also used for irrigation and threshing to shorten the period of amortization.

3. *Threshing*

To thresh their crops a few smallholders individually, without any intervention from the co-operative, hired tractors pulling *nawrags*. The cost per hour normally varied between £E0·30 and £E0·40. Smallholders whose crops had been seized for delay in settling their accounts (rare in the prosperous estates of Damira) were charged 30 piastres per ardeb of wheat threshed mechanically under Agrarian Reform supervision, a price equivalent to that generally demanded by large farmers renting their threshers to sharecroppers.

4. *Irrigation*

The banding together of peasants in al-Manakhulla village to buy 17 mobile pumps was exceptional, and there was an unusually high percentage (about 60 per cent) of mechanical water-lifting there. In other villages it was the draught animals who bore the brunt of the operation. Irrigation with motor pumps (fixed and mobile) owned by the Damira ACS was rare and the number of available machines limited. The cost of irrigation with machines supplied by the machine pool was charged to smallholders and assessed according to actual operation costs plus a 5 per cent commission for the co-operatives.

The abundance of dual-purpose cattle, the low price of milk, the shortage of credit for the purchase of agricultural machinery, and the high costs of operation of farm machinery were the main obstacles to the development of mechanization; obsolete agricultural techniques (such as those for the maize seed-bed preparation[10]

[10] Maize seed-beds in the Damira estates were prepared according to the *hirathi* technique; after harvesting the last cut of clover the land is left unirrigated for about a month. The surface dries up and large cracks, 60–70 cm. deep, are formed. During this period operators accumulate and spread out the necessary organic manure. As soon as the Nile flood begins (early in July) the land is heavily irrigated. After a week or so, when the land is still very damp, it is ploughed with the customary wooden *baladi* (cattle-drawn) plough; women and

or for levelling in flooded land for rice),[11] and the difficulty of moving large tractors on muddy roads during the rainy season can be counted among the secondary obstacles to mechanization. Rather than incur costs with which they would later be charged, the peasants, who were sceptical of the advantages of mechanization, preferred to use their cattle even if this meant reducing milk and meat production.

Prices of fresh milk were low (a maximum of 1–1·2 piastres per *rotl* of buffalo milk with 5 per cent fats), and peasants who thought it dishonourable to sell milk generally consumed their products. Any left over was turned into clarified butter or cheese by the women using primitive methods for skimming, churning, &c. Marketing methods were archaic, as most sales were made locally and in neighbouring Mansura. Milk and beef yields of the Damira cattle were low since up-grading had only been attempted very recently. On the other hand, if yields had risen as a result of the animals being spared draught work, a glut of milk products would have ensued, because of the absence of a co-operative marketing organization for milk and other livestock products.[12]

Draught power problems were tackled in all the *mantiqat* along lines similar to those followed in Damira, although Agrarian Reform publications frequently claimed that a complete mechanization of farm operations (i.e. the replacement of animal draught power by mechanical draught power supplied by tractors and fixed or mobile irrigation pumps) was not far off on Agrarian Reform estates. This was hardly the case in 1959. Animal power was extensively used, as the smallholders relied mainly on the dual-purpose cattle they or their neighbours owned to farm their holdings. Even the co-operative of al-Za'faran (4,891 feddans), supposedly one of the most mechanized estates,[13] spent hardly £E6,000 in 1957/8 on ploughing and threshing, i.e. £E1·2 per feddan.[14] In the whole of the Itay al-Barud region (10,000 feddans),

children then sow the maize seeds, after which the land is harrowed to cover the seeds. The *hirathi* technique is typical of archaic production methods for the maize crop in Damira and in nearly all the Northern Delta. It is highly detrimental to yields and should not be used when planting high-yielding hybrid maize or American Badri seeds.

---

[11] The habit of levelling flooded land for rice is one of the main factors compelling farmers in the rice-cultivating regions of the Delta to retain dual-purpose draught animals (see Saab, *Motorisation*, pp. 45–47).

[12] No milk-processing plants existed anywhere around Damira, but a pasteurizing factory, with a daily capacity of 20 tons, was supposed to start operating in Mansura in 1962 under the supervision of the state Five-Year Plan Commission.

[13] Six caterpillar tractors (Int. Harv. T.D.9) had been bought in 1955, and nearly 12 tractors (not all running) had been taken over at the time of expropriation.

[14] Costs for tractors used on large estates varied between £E1·9 and £E4·2 per feddan operated, according to investigations by the author in 1955. A survey

where the only Agrarian Reform milk-collecting centre had been established, expenditure on ploughing did not exceed £E4,083 in 1957/8, despite the presence of 17 tractors owned by the farm machinery pool. At the Abis EARIS land-reclamation project (460 feddans distributed since 1953), in spite of the over-abundance of farm machinery,[15] most agricultural operations were done by draught cattle as late as 1959. Even at Shibin al-Kawm (7,300 feddans) the co-operatives spent only £E2,020 on plough-ing in 1957/8. In the two Fayyum regions (nearly 30,000 feddans), mechanization had made less progress, and it was only partial in the Minya *mantiqa* (10,000 feddans), and mainly concerned the cotton crop, tillage operations often being accomplished with hired tractors. The percentage of mechanical equipment used on estates was roughly as follows: levelling nil; transport nil; irriga-tion 50 per cent; tillage operations 30 per cent; threshing 10–20 per cent.

The low rate of mechanization was disappointing, especially if it is borne in mind that since 1952 the Agrarian Reform autho-rities and co-operatives had been provided with pumps, tractors, threshers, &c., some of which had been requisitioned from the expropriated landowners and others purchased. This equipment was considerable by the end of 1959 as yearly allocations had been very substantial.[16] It included 437 fixed irrigation pumps, 219 irrigation pumps for artesian wells, 364 mobile irrigation pumps, 154 caterpillar tractors, 390 wheel tractors, 409 ploughs, 118 threshers (3·5 to 4·5 metres), and 4 combine harvesters. In theory the tractors, irrigation pumps, and threshers owned by the Agrarian Reform authorities and their co-operatives, if adequately handled, could have been enough for the complete mechanization of all draught operations (irrigation, tillage, transport, threshing) in 20 per cent (approximately 100,000 feddans) of the requisitioned area. But in 1959 many tractors were out of order, and some could not be repaired through shortage of spare parts.[17] The equipment operated by the Agrarian Reform authorities and the co-operatives carried out jointly by an FAO expert and the Ministry of Agriculture in Daqah-liya province in 1956 revealed that, in 1956, costs per feddan in estates of over 50 feddans ranged between £E1·5 and £E4·9 per feddan operated (see Saab, *Motorisation*, pp. 131–221).

[15] Some 247 tractors.

[16] e.g. in 1956 £E750,000; in 1958 £E1,042,000; in 1960–4 expenditure scheduled for repairs and the purchase of new stock was £E2,140,000.

[17] No figure was available for the percentage of machines out of action in 1959, but according to a statement of the Ministry of Agrarian Reform, 40 per cent of the tractors owned by two state agencies (the Organization for Liberation Province and the Permanent Organization for Land Reclamation) were out of order. There was little reason to believe that the condition of the equipment operated by the Agrarian Reform authorities and their co-operatives was any better (see 'Sectors Unemployed', *al-Magallat al-Ziraʻiyat*, Aug. 1959, p. 14).

was expensive to use. The criticisms voiced in Italy against mechanization[18] were fully applicable to the Egyptian Agrarian Reform mechanization schemes, and dumps for mechanical equipment, similar to that of Civitavecchia in the Italian Maremma region, were the rule in several Agrarian Reform regions. Had it not been for the help of contractors, who were employed by the co-operatives or by individual smallholders to undertake farm operations such as tillage, the rate of mechanization would have been much lower; it was in fact astonishing that more encouragement was not given to solve all the draught-power problems of Agrarian Reform areas by resorting extensively to the services of contractors, since crop consolidation allowed them to tender at very reasonable prices. But the whole programme of mechanization and its interrelationship with livestock production and marketing and agricultural credit, despite its fundamental importance, received little attention from the Agrarian Reform authorities. Smallholders, who anyway could not find a profitable outlet for their livestock products,[19] continued to use their cattle for draught operations, convinced that this was cheaper than the machines operated by the Agrarian Reform authorities, the co-operatives, or even the contractors.

PRODUCTIVITY

In sharp contrast to other countries where Agrarian Reform was initiated to break up extensively cultivated large estates, which were far below their potential productivity, the Egyptian legislation aimed at redistributing large estates most of which (approximately 85 per cent) were highly productive at the time of requisitioning.[20] This fact played an important part in ensuring the success of the redistribution programme, and in maintaining and often raising the level of crop yields.

It was said on the eve of the Agrarian Reform that the redistribution of the expropriated estates would lead to a fall in crop yields, but on the whole this did not happen. True, crop yields fell sharply during the transitional phase in many estates owner-operated before 1952 which had been distributed to agricultural labourers formerly employed on them since they were inexperienced and often incapable of immediately assuming the responsibilities inherent in the operation of a holding. Examples of this could be found even in some of the very fertile lands of Middle Egypt,

[18] See Barbero, 'Riforma Fondiaria', pp. 417–18.
[19] See below, p. 209. See also Saab, *Motorisation*, pp. 165–75 and 334–87.
[20] The area of poor and waste lands requisitioned was 66,382 feddans; 20,262 feddans were poor lands, 3,836 feddans of which were improved by 1959, and 46,120 feddans were waste lands, of which 6,770 were in the process of being reclaimed (see *Agrarian Reform in Seven Years*, p. 92).

such as Taftish al-Gafadun, Fashn Bani Suwaif *mantiqa*, where the previously owner-operated 2,000-feddan estate was distributed to 1,000 beneficiaries, nearly all of whom had been agricultural labourers until 1952. In this estate, which was requisitioned in the autumn of 1952 and distributed in full ownership in 1955, cotton yields dropped from 7 to 3 kantars after expropriation; but as a result of strict Agrarian Reform supervision this downward trend was reversed in 1956, and by 1958 yields were back to their 1952 level. Despite such temporary falls in productivity the crop yields of smallholders in previously owner-operated fertile lands were in 1959 generally at the same level as those of the evicted landowners, if not slightly higher.

On estates which were tenanted before expropriation, the average crop yields of Agrarian Reform smallholders were higher than those of the small tenants and sharecroppers of the evicted landowners. In the Damira *mantiqa*, for example, average yields[21] had increased, according to calculations made by the author, by about 16 per cent by 1959: cotton yields, which averaged 4·25 kantars during 1949/50, 1950/1, and 1951/2, had risen to 5·45 kantars (including surreptitious picking) during 1956/7, 1957/8, and 1958/9, i.e. an increase of nearly 30 per cent. Yields of wheat were estimated to have risen by 20 per cent, rice by 25 per cent, and maize by 5 per cent, but clover yields remained stationary. These yields were 10–15 per cent higher than those of the average neighbouring small independent (not subject to Agrarian Reform control) landowners and tenants, but were 10–20 per cent lower than those of some well-organized big farms of over 50 feddans on land of equal quality near Damira. The same was true in most of the *mantiqat* visited, and yields of the Agrarian Reform smallholders on large consolidated estates were nearly always equal to those of small independent farmers operating neighbouring (fragmented) holdings of under 5 feddans. In many instances they were better than those of small independent farmers, some of whom had recently bought land from people disposing of their property under Article 4 of the 1952 Agrarian Reform Law.

But the average yields of Agrarian Reform smallholders were nearly always lower than those of large operators (of over 50 and up to 500 or 600 feddans) who had increased their productivity by 25–40 per cent since 1952, principally by a judicious combination of selected seeds, fertilizers, and insecticides. At Taftish al-Lawandi, Aga district, near Mansura, on a 683-feddan owner-operated farm[22] reduced to 500 feddans by the Agrarian Reform, cotton yields, for example, which averaged 6·5 kantars of

[21] Of cotton, wheat, rice, maize, and clover.
[22] Owned by several members of the same family.

Karnak cotton before 1952, varied between 8 and 9 kantars in 1959. Cotton yields of Agrarian Reform smallholders on the adjacent area of 183 feddans expropriated and joined to the Aga local co-operative, Simbilawain *mantiqa*, fluctuated in 1955 around 6 kantars, rising to 7·25 kantars in 1959. The difference in yields between the large owner-operated holding and the expropriated area was mainly due to a bigger outlay on chemical fertilizers and insecticides[23] in the former, thanks to the very ample financial resources at the owner's disposal as well as to sound management. Cotton yields in the surrounding Simbilawain *mantiqa* (10,919 feddans, 3,876 members) were 4·19 kantars in 1957, 4·45 kantars in 1958, and 6·2 kantars in 1959. At Taftish al-Muqattam, Dasuq *mantiqa* (6,500 feddans, 2,145 members), where cotton yields in the residual holdings of the landlords rose from 3·49 kantars in 1952 to 5·25 kantars in 1959, yields of the Agrarian Reform landowners and tenants on an adjacent area of 150 feddans, expropriated in 1955, remained at the 1952 level (3.5 kantars in 1958 and 3·75 in 1959). Similar examples were found in other Delta regions and in Central and Upper Egypt.

Nevertheless, striking increases in cotton yields, compared with 1952, were achieved in a number of *mantiqat* such as al-Khazan, Shibin al-Kawm,[24] and Burgaya, most of which occurred after 1956/7 as a result of the enforcement of the consolidated crop rotation, the combined use of selected seeds, fertilizers, and insecticides, and sometimes the introduction of highly productive varieties of cotton.[25] In these regions the Agrarian Reform authorities claimed increases in yields of up to 100 per cent. But if a considerable effort had been made to maintain and improve cotton, wheat, and rice yields in these and other *mantiqat*, it was not equally true of other crops, in particular maize and clover. The quantities of hybrid maize seeds distributed in 1959 were hardly sufficient to cover the needs of one-third of the area devoted to the maize crop[26] while cultivation techniques remained primitive,

---

[23] Outlay on insecticides in 1958/9 in the owner-operated holding: £E12 per feddan (12 applications); in expropriated area: £E3 per feddan (three applications) plus reliance on hand-picking of cotton-leaf worm by smallholders. As late as mid-June 1959 the cotton of the large holding had been sprayed five times, while that of the Agrarian Reform smallholders was receiving its first application. But as only two sprayers were available for an area of 61 feddans, cotton-leaf worm eggs were already hatched and young worms were spreading in the Agrarian Reform fields.

[24] In Shibin al-Kawm cotton yields increased from 3 kantars in 1955, when distribution operations started, to 6·46 kantars in 1959. Figures for 1952 were not available, but it seemed highly probable that if the percentage increase in 1959 had been calculated relatively to 1952 (i.e. the period preceding expropriation), it would have been less favourable than that claimed by Agrarian Reform publications.

[25] e.g. Bahtim cotton in Burgaya.   [26] Above, p. 84.

especially in the Northern Delta. As for clover, no selected seeds were ever distributed, superphosphates were only rarely made available, and pest control was practically non-existent.[27]

It has recently been reported[28] that

a weighted average calculated from official data[29] for the area under cotton and total cotton output in supervised co-operatives in 16 districts shows that the yields per acre rose by 45 per cent between the pre-requisition period and 1959. During 1952–1959 the incease in the average cotton yield for Egypt was 15 per cent. Although the statistical data do not permit comparison of the rate of increase of total agricultural production in the supervised co-operatives and in Egypt, the fact that their increase in cotton yields has been so much above the average would indicate that their overall production increase had been higher, though certainly not in the same proportion as for cotton.

This statement probably reflects the situation in so far as the sixteen *mantiqat* are concerned, but it can only be accepted with caution as far as the remaining twenty-seven *mantiqat* not covered by the published statistical data are concerned. Crop yields in the naturally fertile lands of the Central Delta and Middle and Upper Egypt (about 70 per cent of the expropriated areas) were doubtless good and 15–20 per cent higher than the 1952 levels. But crop yields in the Northern Delta (Alexandria, Buhaira, Kafr al-Shaikh) and in the two Fayyum *mantiqat* (i.e. about 30 per cent of the expropriated areas) were not always satisfactory, and at best equalled the 1952 level. Had it not been for the technological changes (better seeds, balanced fertilization, improved pest control) introduced since 1952, the unsatisfactory upkeep of the drainage networks might well have affected the crop yields more noticeably.

It was furthermore clear, in all the *mantiqat* visited, that the highest yields were obtained on average by smallholders who had previously been tenants or sharecroppers, or by farmers who, though owning some land, had benefited from distribution. The lowest yields were to be found among former agricultural labourers or people not previously occupied in agriculture who were financially irresponsible and unable to balance expenditure and income.[30]

[27] In early January 1960, for example, the growth of both the permanent clover crop (*bersim mustadim*) and the clover snatch crop (*bersim kalb*) was behind-hand in nearly all *mantiqat* 100 km. from Cairo. Both these crops had been re-sown, as a result of heavy attacks of cotton-leaf worm in mid-October which had not been combated by appropriate pest-control measures, so that farmers incurred additional expenses and the loss of one cut of clover in both the permanent (i.e. 20 per cent of the crop) and the snatch clover fields (i.e. 40 per cent of the crop).

[28] Warriner, 'Land Reform and Community Development', unpublished report to UN, Apr. 1961.

[29] Min AR, *Information and Statistics relating to Agrarian Reform in the Southern Region* (1960).   [30] See above, pp. 69, 83, 110.

Similar difficulties have arisen in India whenever land distribution benefited former agricultural labourers. In Italy they were partially overcome by improving the technical knowledge of candidate beneficiaries through vocational training.[31] In Egypt, however, they were not very important, since the vast majority of the expropriated estates had been cultivated in some form or another by tenants and sharecroppers who had at least a minimum knowledge of the responsibilities involved. This may well change if the ceilings on landownership and farm operation are again lowered,[32] and if the proportion of beneficiaries from the class of landless agricultural labourers increases. It may also change in land-reclamation areas if distribution is to be exclusively reserved to former agricultural labourers. Failures in crop yields will be more likely in both cases, unless a thorough programme of vocational training is instituted.

Since 1958/9 determined efforts have been made to reward Agrarian Reform smallholders who obtain high yields by giving them special prizes in money or in kind (cattle grants, radio sets, &c.) which totalled £E100,000 in 1960.[33] These inducements to hardworking smallholders were most welcome. In the Sabarbay *mantiqa* (Gharbiya province), for example, where a number of transistor radio sets were given to successful beneficiaries, farmers could be seen in January heavily manuring their cotton fields, and enthusiastically competing with one another.

LIVESTOCK AND POULTRY PRODUCTION

The expansion in money incomes through improved crop yields resulted in an increase in the cattle owned by smallholders in several prosperous *mantiqat*. But the standard of livestock production had not progressed substantially. There were too many dual-purpose cattle in all *mantiqat* except the Fayyum, these cattle had hardly been improved, conditions of nutrition had not changed, forage production in winter and in summer had not been increased, and silage was not used. No effort had been made to provide vocational training or to ensure an adequate flow of short- and medium-term credit for livestock production.

[31] For difficulties of this sort in Italy, see C. Barberis, 'Durra; una società rurale alla vigilia della irrigazione', in *Centro Studi della Cassa per il Mezzogiorno*, no. 40 (Rome, 1961). Also by the same author, 'Problèmes sociologiques de la réforme foncière face a l'irrigation', in Bull. Inst. of Rural Economics, *Lectures on Agrarian Tenure and Agricultural Co-operation in the Mediterranean Basin* (Beirut, 1962).
[32] As they were in 1961 (see below, p. 181).
[33] This was deducted from the annual profits of the co-operatives and from the refunds due by the Egyptian Cotton Commission after the disposal of the 1958/9 cotton crop. See below, p. 117.

Since 1955 a comprehensive scheme has been carried out in several *mantiqat* for the establishment of centres for the improvement of livestock, veterinary care, the provision of insurance for cattle, and the distribution of selected strains of poultry. By 1959 these veterinary units (which had to overcome numerous obstacles), were operating in fifteen *mantiqat*.[34] Cattle insured totalled about 10,000 head,[35] i.e. about 17 per cent of the total owned by the smallholders. As has been seen, the scheme for distributing pedigree chicks on credit[36] under the auspices of the veterinary unit, in spite of high mortality rates, was also running satisfactorily and helping to increase farmers' incomes.

The Damira veterinary unit, which was established early in 1956, was typical of those in other areas. The staff consisted of a vet, an agricultural engineer and his assistant, 7 male nurses, and 3 semi-specialized workers operating poultry incubators. The unit was entrusted with the care of the livestock and poultry owned by the farmers of the Damira estates and was installed in the main administrative buildings of the Damira ACS. It was equipped with medicines and instruments. The services provided included:

1. The treatment of all sick animals and poultry, eradication of cattle parasites (particularly liver fluke, which was very frequent but, according to the vet, was decreasing), preventive treatment of cattle against toxaemia and of poultry against Newcastle disease, plague and white diarrhoea of chicks, spraying cattle with insecticides against external parasites and farmers' houses to protect their poultry.

2. The supervision of animals sold on credit or distributed for fattening and of the poultry distributed on credit.

3. Supervision of the pedigree buffalo bulls and Holstein Friesian bulls distributed to the co-operatives, which could be used for artificial insemination or breeding. There were two bulls to each co-operative; 10 piastres were charged for mating if the cow was not covered by insurance and 2 piastres if it was.

4. The implementation, supervision, and control of the livestock insurance scheme initiated in Damira to protect farmers against the total loss of their livestock through epidemics, disease, or illness. Only cows, calves, buffalo cows and calves, bulls and buffalo bulls over 3 months and not more than 15 years old could be covered by policies. Animals to be insured were examined by a committee consisting of the vet, the *'umda*, and the secretary of

[34] By 1959 these units were functioning in the *mantiqat* of Damira, Bahut Nabaruh, Simbilawain, Za'faran, al-Khazan, Kafr al-Dawar, Idfina, Abis, Itay al-Barud, Inshas, al-Mata'ana, al-Minya, &c.

[35] Animals insured by the veterinary units established by the Agrarian Reform authorities totalled 11,500 in 1961.

[36] See above, p. 89.

the co-operative of the member who wanted the policy. After examination the animal was registered in the books of the veterinary unit and a number clipped on its ear. The committee also valued the animal annually with the help of a representative of the Agrarian Reform Projects Department and the *mushrif ta'awuni*. An insurance policy cost 120 piastres for a cow or buffalo cow and 60 for a calf, or 120 for a heifer, as soon as it was mated. The cost of insurance was low on the average; a fully grown buffalo heifer was worth £E50–60 and a year-old calf £E20, while the risks were considerable.

The insurance was paid in two instalments, in July and November. It was charged to the account of the owner and collected as soon as he had made his first payment to the co-operative after the annual accounting in June. The veterinary unit gave preferential treatment to insured animals, and owners received all kinds of veterinary assistance free of charge. In principle the milk yields of their animals were recorded. Owners of uninsured animals had to pay for veterinary assistance and for drugs and medicines provided.

If an insured animal died the owner received compensation equal to 75 per cent of its most recently assessed value. If it was slaughtered and the meat sold, the price was deducted from the compensation due. In order to claim compensation, the owner had to report to the centre any illness as soon as it appeared by informing either the secretary of the local co-operative or the main office of the Damira ACS. In emergencies if the animal was slaughtered before the arrival of the vet, he would carry out a post-mortem examination to establish the cause of death. Compensation was also subject to the approval of the local co-operative board. A total of 1,711 animals were insured on the Damira estates in May 1959 and negotiations to insure another 500 were going on. The proportion of animals insured was about 30 per cent of the cows, buffaloes, and calves owned by the Damira beneficiaries,[37] a lower percentage than on the al-Za'faran estate where it was reported to be nearly 40 per cent.[38]

There were certain obstacles in the way of accelerating the livestock insurance scheme. Many farmers owned cattle jointly, according to the *shirq* system[39] and their 'sleeping' partners objected strongly to participation in the scheme in case it weakened their claims. They even spread rumours that the scheme was the first step to expropriation of the insured cattle by the Agrarian Reform authorities.

Moreover, the transport facilities at the disposal of the vet in

[37] 6,302 cows, buffaloes, and calves.
[38] 750 animals out of about 1,600.   [39] See above, p. 87, n. 14.

charge were inadequate. The jeep supposedly reserved for his use was in bad condition and often used by senior officials of the ACS. No fast transport was provided for his assistants. In an area of 15,000 feddans, this was a serious obstacle to the smooth running of the scheme because of the distance between one village and another, particularly since the vet was also supposed to be in charge of the veterinary unit in the neighbouring Nabaruh, Bahut (13,200 feddans). Peasants resented the consequent importance given to the testimony of the local co-operative secretary about a sick or dying animal, as they believed the secretaries often abused their powers. A final obstacle was that payment of compensation was often delayed.

Other livestock schemes were initiated by the Agrarian Reform authorities and operated under their own supervision and control; they had a wide range and included the improvement of large imported Simmental herds in Idfina, Idqu, Alexandria region, Abis, Marg, al-Wadi, and al-Mu'tamadiya (in the Northern and Central Delta), the fattening of calves in Damira and the Itay al-Barud *mantiqat*, for example; the improvement of a herd of 550 local-breed 'Baladi', cows crossing with Friesian bulls in Za'faran ('Abadiya Hamul'), and milk production with a large imported Friesian herd in Liberation province. These schemes[40] had cost a considerable amount of money and effort, but had met with only limited success. Despite this, and despite the disappointing results of nearly all government-sponsored and operated cattle-breeding projects to date,[41] they were being expanded at a high cost. Yet the smallholders would probably have benefited more if the human and capital investment involved had been used to boost the short- and medium-term agricultural credit programme for livestock, to develop forage resources, to establish vocational training centres for livestock and poultry production, or to help in the co-operative disposal of livestock and poultry products.

Some effort to avoid the difficulties encountered in the earlier state-sponsored ventures seems to have been made in the so-called 'Nasir' cattle-distribution project, which was decided upon in July 1959 to meet the demands of landless peasant families (agricultural labourers, tenants, sharecroppers) outside Agrarian Reform regions who had not benefited from land-distribution measures because of the shortage of land available. Buffalo heifers, bought on the village markets or bred in Agrarian Reform studs specially set up for the purpose[42] were to be distributed to

---

[40] See App. VIII, p. 206; for plans during 1960–4 see below, p. 139.

[41] One notable exception was the recently established Holstein Friesian stud operated by the Council for Social Services in al-Qanatir Qalyubiya province.

[42] One was established in Abis, Buhaira province, in 1960.

destitute peasants on a five-year instalment basis, without interest. A specially created fund, with a capital of £E0·5 million loaned by the Agricultural Credit Bank, was set up to finance the scheme, and 2,000 heifers were scheduled to be distributed in the over-populated provinces of Minufiya and Minya during the first years. Of these 1,936 had already been distributed in January 1961.

THE DISPOSAL OF FARM PRODUCTS

It has been seen[43] that the cotton crop was disposed of through Agrarian Reform or co-operative channels; until 1960, with the exception of a small number of sugar-cane plantations in Upper Egypt, it was the only crop marketed in this way[44] (nearly 90 per cent of total production). Other crops, such as wheat or rice, were rarely marketed through co-operative channels (15–20 per cent of total production) unless they were delivered to the special state agencies as selected seeds, or when they were seized and sold on behalf of the Agrarian Reform authorities in settlement of big outstanding debts. All attempts to overcome the hesitation of smallholders were concentrated on inducing them to deliver up their cotton for bulk disposal under Agrarian Reform auspices, because it was the principal collateral for loans in kind and in cash and for their other financial obligations, and because the 3–5 per cent commission on bulk sales retained by the co-operatives provided their most important source of income. When it was delivered to the Agrarian Reform or co-operative warehouses, the crop was immediately fully insured against destruction by fire and a premium equal to 0·5 per cent of its value was deducted from the sale price to meet insurance costs. Special public auction sales were organized in the Cairo headquarters of the Agrarian Reform authorities which were attended by all the big cotton merchants. The smallholders' cotton was sold in the presence of two or more delegates of the respective co-operatives, at prices on average 10–15 per cent higher per kantar than those paid by village brokers to small farmers disposing of their crops piecemeal. In spite of the co-operatives' commission, a substantial margin remained. Since 1958, however, most of the cotton crop has been marketed under contracts between the Agrarian Reform authorities

---

[43] See above, pp. 95–97.
[44] Quantities marketed through AR or co-operative channels were as follows (kantars):

1952/3	27,000	1955/6	237,000	1958/9	403,541
1953/4	84,800	1956/7	311,137	1959/60	454,849
1954/5	162,700	1957/8	369,008		

See *Agrarian Reform in Nine Years*.

and the state-sponsored Egyptian Cotton Commission.[45] The co-operatives were required 'voluntarily' to endorse these sales, which often fetched lower prices than those the smallholders imagined they could have obtained by auction. Ill feeling among the latter and among their *mushrif ta'awuni* was reinforced by the attitude of the Cotton Commission, who showed little eagerness to fulfil the profit-sharing clauses stipulated in the contracts.[46] By the spring of 1960 a number of co-operatives were protesting loudly.[47]

Since 1959 considerable encouragement has been given to Agrarian Reform co-operatives to dispose of their cotton crop after ginning instead of marketing it raw. Numerous resolutions in favour of doing so have been endorsed by the boards of many of them, but few have been put into practice, even though the additional profits resulting from ginning were said to be around 20 per cent at the Shibin al-Kawm co-operatives, for example.[48]

No co-operative marketing was organized for other farm products, such as vegetables, animal and poultry products, &c., with the exception of a half-hearted effort to set up a milk-collecting centre in the Itay al-Barud *mantiqa*.[49] Six milk-cooling plants, set up under the auspices of the Social Services Council, remained idle in various combined centres for nearly two years. Plans were subsequently drafted to establish six milk-processing plants by 1965, with a capacity of 10–20 tons of milk each. These were to be operated by the Agrarian Reform co-operatives.

[45] Regulations issued in 1958 specified that all Egyptian farmers receiving selected cotton seeds from the Ministry of Agriculture were to proceed with the ginning of their cotton before 31 December of each year. The co-operatives of the Agrarian Reform estates who had been allocated selected seeds were therefore required to comply with these regulations and sell their cotton in November so that ginning was completed by the prescribed date. The purchase of this cotton by the Egyptian Cotton Commission was arranged to avoid massive sales on the stock market by the Agrarian Reform co-operatives and thus to avoid depressing market prices. In October 1959, on the proposal of the executive committee of the GCS, the Boards of Directors of the various Damira local co-operatives, for example, endorsed a resolution approving the sale of the newly picked cotton crop, to the Cotton Commission at an average price of £E16·2. When the crop was delivered this price was approximately £E0·70 to £E1 more than prevailing stock market prices for cotton of equal quality, though subsequently prices rose considerably.

[46] In Damira the agreement with the Cotton Commission stipulated that if an increase of cotton prices occurred on the stock market before 31 December 1959, the resulting profit would be shared on an equal basis between the Commission and the Damira 'local' co-operatives on behalf of their members. A 20 per cent share of the profits from the ginning of the cotton was to be reserved for the co-operatives on behalf of their members.

[47] See *al-Ta'awun*, Mar. 1960.

[48] See ibid. 10 Jan. 1961.

[49] See App. VIII, p. 207.

VIII

ECONOMIC, SOCIAL, AND FINANCIAL ASPECTS OF THE LAND-DISTRIBUTION PROGRAMME

The peasants at first attempted to remedy the loss of vitality, and above all of sexual virility caused by diseases, by taking hashish. When this was cut off they replaced it by tea, total consumption of which has increased severalfold since 1914—a condition reminiscent of England during the Hungry Thirties and Forties.

C. ISSAWI, *Egypt at Mid-Century* (1945), p. 65

THE land-distribution programme of the 1952 Agrarian Reform had three main objectives: the satisfaction of the land hunger of the landless rural community living on the large expropriated estates or in their immediate neighbourhood, the improvement of their living conditions, and the raising of productive capacity. The success or failure of the programme set in motion in 1952 can, therefore, be gauged with a certain degree of accuracy by observing how nearly it fulfilled its objectives by 1961. As has been seen, the first objective was achieved with most success in sparsely populated regions of the Delta, and this as soon as the allocation of ownership titles took place. The fact that the exercise of the ownership rights was to some extent restricted did not really detract from this aspect of the programme. Moreover, peasants occupying Agrarian Reform lands on a tenancy basis, though not fully satisfied, were in any case very much happier and more secure than they would have been in the old days, with short-term leases and the threat of eviction constantly hanging over their heads, or than tenants or sharecroppers on land not subject to expropriation but supposedly protected by the tenancy regulations of the 1952 law and subsequent legislation.[1]

The fulfilment of the second objective, the improvement of the living conditions of the peasants, was more difficult to achieve, for it depended to a large extent on increasing their annual net income through reducing costs of production (inclusive of the cost of the land factor) and stabilizing or increasing gross returns (price increases or improved yields). But it depended also on the use to which such an increment in income was put.

[1] See Ch. IX below.

INCOME OF THE BENEFICIARIES[2]

The fact that beneficiaries of the land-distribution programme paid a lower price (in the form of instalments or rentals) for the holdings they occupied than they had paid in the past, and the fact that crop yields remained relatively stable and had sometimes improved, had brought about a considerable increase in net income. According to estimates made by the author, based on field surveys,[3] the beneficiaries, whose status throughout 1953–8 had fluctuated between tenancy and landownership, had obtained an average annual net income (i.e. after payment of all sums due to the authorities and co-operatives and of all operating expenses) of £E25–30 per feddan operated during this period. This figure was inclusive of the value of livestock production.[4] Farmers operating holdings of 3 feddans thus netted £E75–90 annually. In 1958/9, as a result of increases in crop yields, higher cotton prices, and the reduction of instalment payments and rents, the average net income per feddan improved by about 10–15 per cent. In the low-quality lands of the Northern Delta and in the Fayyum province, where good drainage was of prime importance, the average was well below these figures, while in the fertile lands of the Central Delta, Middle Egypt, and in the sugar-cane area of Upper Egypt, the average was well above this. During that period the average net income per feddan in various *mantiqat* was as follows: Itay al-Barud and Bahut about £E15–20; Fayyum about £E10–15; Damira about £E40 (£E37 during 1953–9). Average net income in a co-operative of the Central Delta, Mit al-Mawz (447

---

[2] A sample survey of the Agrarian Reform estates of Damira, Za'faran, Mansura, and of the neighbouring Ministry of Waqfs' estates of Shawa, Byala, and Saft Khalid was carried out during 1956–64 by S. M. Gadalla. According to him, during the period of the survey farm income was 20 per cent higher in the Agrarian Reform holdings than in the estates managed by the Ministry of Waqfs (£E96·30 in the Agrarian Reform holdings as against £E80 in the waqf holdings. See *Land Reform in relation to Social Development in Egypt* (1962)).

[3] The estimates of income of the Agrarian Reform beneficiaries were made by the author

   (a) By obtaining when possible the official records of production and the sale prices, &c., on the estates visited. Figures relative to the period preceding the Agrarian Reform were also scrutinized.

   (b) By checking the figures thus obtained with Agrarian Reform officials and beneficiaries, and by analysing the account books of beneficiaries—and by adding when necessary all other items of expenditure pertaining to farm operation.

   (c) Extensive field visits were carried out to ascertain the yield of the crops on the estates visited and to check the information obtained from individual operators.

[4] Figures quoted in Saab, 'Rationalization of Agriculture and Land Tenure Problems in Egypt', *ME Econ. Papers, 1960*, p. 76, were exclusive of the value of livestock production.

feddans, 180 smallholders—the most successful of all the co-operatives of the Shibin al-Kawm region) was about £E50. In Upper Egypt, Hawaslya co-operative (Minya *mantiqa*) it was about £E30, in Burgaya, also Minya *mantiqa*, it was about £E50.

Net money income per feddan was 40–50 per cent higher in 1958/9 than in 1951/2 in most of the *mantiqat* visited, partly because of the higher prices of the various crops in 1959 (in particular cotton) compared with 1952. But even in the Damira *mantiqa*, comparing 1953/9 with 1947/52, when cotton prices were at an unprecedented maximum because of the post-war boom followed by the Korean war, the difference in favour of the former was still 33 per cent. Miss Warriner[5] expresses the belief that the increase in the income of smallholders was '50 per cent above the pre-reform level', a view which is entirely accurate if by 'the pre-reform level' is meant the year 1951/2. In reality, however, the percentage increase in purchasing power was lower, mainly as a result of the rise in prices of certain basic commodities (maize, sugar, tea, tobacco, fuel) since 1952, the reduction in the purchasing power of the Egyptian pound ranging between 10 and 15 per cent.[6]

The percentage increase in the income of individual members of smallholding families was also slightly less than that per feddan, partly because of the reduction in employment opportunities and partly because of the big population increases in Agrarian Reform areas since 1952.[7] Even so, the average income per individual

---

[5] See her report to UN, May 1961, p. 25.

[6]

Indices of costs
(pre-war = 100)

	1952	*1959*
Cost of living	298	324
„ „ textiles	467	485
„ „ fertilizers	366	436

Prices of Main Commodities (£E)

	1952	*1959*
Maize (per ardeb)	3	3·5
Tobacco (per oke)	3·94	6·05
Tea (per oke)	0·90	1·13
Coffee (per kantar)	28·64	36·00
Sugar (per kantar)	2·50	4·16
Fuel (kerosene, 4 galls)	0·19	0·26
Cotton-seed cake (per ton)	6·65	7·50

Source: NBE, *Econ. B.*, xiii/1–2, 1959.

[7] A study of population trends carried out at the co-operative of Mit Khalaf, Shibin al-Kawm *mantiqa* (Minufiya province) reveals that an increase in population was taking place at the rate of 2·5 per cent per annum (see H. al-Shenawani, *al-Ahram*, 20 Feb. 1960). Figures provided in the 1960 population census indicate that in Daqahliya province the rate of increase has been higher still (population in 1947, 1,413,905; in 1960, 2,016,000).

member of a smallholder's family, though higher than the peak year 1951/2 of the period 1947–52, was still very small by western standards. An average of 2·8 feddans was distributed in full ownership by 1959 and there were six members in an average family, so that the individual's average income from the operation of a holding was not more than £E14–16. Additional income from poultry production, agricultural employment, or co-operative profits in some cases added 5–10 per cent, but never more.

It must be noted that some of the smallholders who before 1952 had tenanted or sharecropped bigger holdings than those allotted to them after redistribution were worse off, but these were a very small minority. Although it was not possible to obtain figures in all the regions visited it was obvious that they did not amount to more than 5 per cent of the Agrarian Reform smallholders. Such cases were most frequent in the Northern Delta, on the estates of Idfina, Alexandria, Za'faran, and Itay al-Barud. Some small-holders already owning land near large expropriated estates com-plained because they had been allotted holdings smaller than those they had tenanted in addition to their own property in the past; they agreed that they had suffered since the Agrarian Reform, even though they were in fact paying lower instalments on the reduced holdings allotted to them than they had previously paid in rent.

INCOME OF AGRICULTURAL LABOURERS ON OR NEAR EXPROPRIATED ESTATES

The financial status of agricultural labourers who had worked on the expropriated estates before Agrarian Reform and had not benefited from redistribution had deteriorated because of the fall in the purchasing power of the pound in all the regions visited, to-gether with very steep rises[8] in the price of maize utilized for the preparation of bread. The rise in prices was most acutely felt by these landless peasants, who were apt to complain bitterly about it and about the fewer opportunities of employment since 1952.

The reduction in employment opportunities has been reported by various writers[9] studying the Egyptian Agrarian Reform. It had affected an average of 5–10 per cent of the tenants and agri-cultural labourers formerly employed on the expropriated estates and not benefiting from redistribution. There were several causes:

---

[8] On the average 50 per cent and in certain areas slightly more.

[9] Darling, *YB Agric. Co-op. 1956*; Warriner, *Land Reform*; Thweatt, *M.E. Econ. Papers 1956*; Money-Kyrle; Garzouzi; P. Pissot, 'La réforme agraire en Égypte', *Bull. soc. française d'écon. rurale*, Oct. 1959.

the new beneficiaries employed less hired farm labour than the ex-landowners because they did all farm operations with family labour and because the upkeep of the drainage and irrigation networks was less vigorous than in the past. There was also a general drop in the rate of agricultural investment by medium and large-scale farmers (100–300 feddans) not directly affected by Agrarian Reform measures in 1952. Thereafter many of the latter slackened the pace of certain agricultural activities, such as the upkeep of the irrigation and drainage networks, the erection of new farm buildings, the upkeep of old ones, cattle-breeding projects, the establishment of orchards, &c. Suddenly realizing the immensity of the social problems confronting rural Egypt, these farmers alternated periodically between bouts of optimism and pessimism. Many even preferred to break up their holdings and sell out to small farmers, who were reported to be employing less hired labour than previously. No doubt too the Agrarian Reform had induced some of the big landlords, who had surrendered part of their estates, to owner-operate their residual holdings and farm them intensively. Medium-sized landowners, who had hoped to increase their holdings, were now faced with the ceilings of the new legislation and had also taken to intensification. The doubling of the rate of increase of orchards since 1952, as reported in official publications,[10] was certainly one of the proofs of this intensification. It was, therefore, difficult to assess whether intensified farming by some landowners made up for the lack of investment by others. Conflicting opinions on this have been advanced.

Whatever the cause, the low level of agricultural wages in the sparsely populated regions of the Delta throughout the period 1952–61 and despite the changes in the price index, seemed to bear out the complaints of the landless peasants so far as reduced employment opportunities were concerned. Some of the consequent hardship was alleviated by charity payments made by the prosperous Agrarian Reform co-operatives from their Social Aid Funds (*al-Maʿuna al-Igtimaʿiya*), but even in the richest co-operatives, such as those of Damira where less than 500 families were reported to be landless, the total sum allocated under this heading was ridiculously small and did not exceed £E3,000 during the whole of the period 1954–9. The tithe (*zakat*) due by all good Muslims as a contribution to their poorer brethren, and collected and distributed under Agrarian Reform auspices, hardly amounted to £E75 a year in a region such as Damira (15,169 feddans) where Agrarian Reform smallholders paid £E0·005 a year of *zakat* per feddan operated.

[10] See NBE, *Econ. B.*, 1955–61.

USES OF ADDITIONAL INCOME

In all the regions visited most smallholders spent the additional income on consumption and only a thin trickle found its way into investment.[11]

The marriage rate increased. For instance, in Damira peasants with higher incomes were apt to allow their children to marry younger. Cases of peasants divorcing and taking a second wife were reported, though this was said to be rare and polygamy seemed exceptional. Officials, when asked about the rise in income of peasants after Agrarian Reform, were inclined to give the increase in the marriage rate as an example. This was common in other prosperous *mantiqat* such as Shibin al-Kawm and al-Khazan.[12] A typical example of the tendency of averagely prosperous peasants to remarry was that of a successful peasant of Bahut, Nabaruh, who occupied a holding of 4 feddans. This man had a family of 16 dependants[13] living off his holding; despite this, he was about to take a second wife on the pretext that she could read and write whereas his first wife could not. He complained bitterly of the smallness of his holding (despite another 5-feddan holding surreptitiously owned in Kafr al-Shaikh province), but still could not understand that the second marriage would increase his expenses, and probably his troubles!

There was also a rise in the consumption of foodstuffs and clothing (textiles and shoes). In all the prosperous regions the consumption of sugar soared sky-high, meat was being eaten once or twice a week instead of once a month and sometimes less, more cattle were slaughtered, and therefore butchers were doing a brisk trade. The use of textiles in Damira was said to have grown tremendously. Agrarian Reform officials there underlined the very big textile sales at the shops of the household co-operatives, though this was not wholly relevant since an important share of the sales of the household branches was made to the numerous Agrarian Reform staff working in Damira or in neighbouring regions. Nevertheless the general appearance of the beneficiaries and tenants there denoted a standard of living slightly higher than that of the average tenants in the neighbourhood. Their clothes were in better condition and more were wearing shoes. This fact was corroborated by various statements by people (school-teachers, &c.) connected

[11] Similar trends are reported in Mexico; see FAO, *Cooperatives and Land Use*, by M. Digby (1957), p. 21.

[12] A vivid illustration of this in the al-Khazan region may be found in an article in *al-Ahram*, 1 Dec. 1959, which gives as an example of the new prosperity the increase in the marriage rate. See also *al-Magallat al-Zira'iyat*, Aug. 1961, and al-Shenawani, *al-Ahram*, 20 Feb. 1960.

[13] First wife and 7 children, plus 1 brother and his family of 4, plus his mother and 2 other brothers.

with the estates. More tobacco, tea, coffee, and various drugs and narcotics (black molasses,[14] hashish, &c.) were consumed. In Damira all those interrogated acknowledged that this item, commonly called *al-mukayyafat* (pleasure providing), absorbed a very big part of the extra income of the smallholders. Nor was this peculiar to Damira, but was found in all the various *mantiqat* visited by the author, whether in Lower or in Upper Egypt.[15] There was a slight increase in purchases of household equipment, furniture, &c. Finally, smallholders made a greater effort to provide schooling for their children.

Notwithstanding the increase in consumption of the smallholders, the transfer of agricultural income from the large landowners to the smallholders was claimed not to have affected the prevailing balance between saving and consumption; this was probably true to a large extent since the surplus of Egyptian landlords[16] was in the majority of cases spent on unproductive items, or was invested in land purchase. Moreover, if one recollects the low standard of living of the rural population, the increased consumption of foodstuffs and clothing by the beneficiaries of the land distribution programme is quite natural and should not be too severely judged; on the other hand, patterns of consumption such as the increase of the marriage rate and of the consumption of drugs and narcotics might have been kept within more reasonable limits if a vigorous attempt had been made to provide social guidance.

Part of the extra income of smallholders was reinvested to expand their livestock production, which had increased by 15–20 per cent in prosperous regions. In a few rare cases, the increment of income was allocated to the building of houses, using red bricks and concrete roofing instead of the usual mud bricks and timber or reeds. As has been seen, cowsheds were built in the fields but this was not financed out of income since the building materials (mud, reeds), and the labour were plentifully available to the peasants. The provision of credit facilities, the reduction of indebtedness to money-lenders, and the greater affluence of the farm operators stimulated short-term investment, as they were

[14] Black molasses (*asal aswad*) is used to sweeten the taste when smoking hashish (marijuana) pipes.

[15] See above, p. vi. An investigation of conditions in the Egyptian village of Tahrus brought to light certain typical aspects of rural life: expenditure on food of 10 per cent of the villagers did not exceed £E20 p.a.; 58 per cent of the families were barefoot; 73 per cent of the inhabitants were illiterate; 40 per cent of the babies died before they were 2 months old, but 61 per cent of the families spent most of their income on *al-mukayyafat*. Studies undertaken in three villages in Giza province by research teams of the Sociology Department of Cairo University revealed similar facts (*al-Ta'awun*, 31 Jan. 1961).

[16] Issawi (*EMC*, p. 138) stated that larger proprietors tended to be 'capital consumers'.

now in a better position to increase outlay on seeds, fertilizers, and insecticides. But no investments on long-term projects such as fruit production were made.

The third objective of the land distribution programme, i.e. the raising of the productive capacities of the rural communities benefiting from its implementation, was by 1960 far from fulfilled. Indeed, little was done to stimulate long-term investment and to intensify and diversify production on the holdings of the smallholders, with the exception of a few regions where rice was introduced, thanks to the drilling of artesian wells which ensured a generous flow of irrigation water. Animal husbandry was making slow progress; underground tile drainage and vegetable, flower, and especially fruit crops were practically non-existent. Crop yields were improving, but this was true not only of Agrarian Reform areas but also of other large farms in Egypt and would not alone have been sufficient to ensure the permanence of the undoubtedly short-term success of the Agrarian Reform land distribution programme. Only high-value, high-labour-intensity forms of agricultural production could have coped adequately with the tremendous rate of population growth, of which the land distribution programme might well in the future become one of the first victims.

By 1960, nearly eight years since the enactment of the Agrarian Reform Law, the opportunity had not been taken to intensify to the maximum the productive capacities of the distributed holdings. But in the fertile lands of the Central Delta, at the co-operatives of Damira, Simbilawain, Shibin al-Kawm, and at Burgaya in Upper Egypt, innumerable successful smallholders could be found with a wide knowledge of agronomy and more drive than the agronomists who had been granted the exclusive privilege of receiving holdings planted in orchards.[17] Fruit and vegetable and livestock production could have given these peasants a real opportunity to make a big leap forward, bringing about a rapid and dramatic increase in their income which would have transformed their economic and social conditions as effectively as industrialization.[18]

[17] See above, p. 32.
[18] 'The hope of overcoming the Malthusian impasse in the countries of high population density and potential rests on achieving industrialization with such speed that the values of the low-birth-rate family would quickly spread and thus prevent each increase in productivity from being eaten up by the growing excess of births, as in India and Egypt, where, as generally in the underdeveloped areas, deaths have dropped so much more quickly than births that all efforts at per capita economic progress are repeatedly set back' (D. Riesman, introd. to D. Lerner, *The Passing of Traditional Society* (New York, 1959), p. 5). The procedure followed in the Italian Maremma region, for example, reveals the possibilities of transforming the economic and social status of smallholders by an intensification and a diversification of agriculture. Had the Italian authorities contented themselves with increases in yields of current crops, the situation in

Banana, mango, and citrus orchards or vineyards producing an annual gross and net income two or three times higher than that obtained per unit of land sown with the traditional crops could easily have been planted without disrupting the customary consolidated triennial crop rotation.

Two methods of approach could have been devised for this purpose. The lands of a redistributed estate could have been divided into four big consolidated blocks, instead of the customary three blocks. Beneficiaries would then have received holdings divided into four distinct plots, each located within one of the four blocks; three of these blocks would have been reserved for traditional crops while the fourth would have been used for planting fruit trees. Thus a beneficiary would have received one-quarter of his holding in the block reserved for fruit trees. The resulting consolidation of orchards would facilitate adequate technical supervision by Agrarian Reform specialists and the bulk sale of the fruit through co-operative channels, which would in turn ensure the settlement of debts.

The second alternative would be to link the planting of orchards to the rebuilding of the villages of Agrarian Reform smallholders. Hamlets of 50–100 houses could be built side by side in a straight line. Each house, facing north for the sea breeze, could be bordered on the east by a courtyard of about 100 sq. metres for cattle and poultry and to stock fodder; it could also provide space for a concrete manure pit and a silage pit. On the immediate south an orchard for bananas, mangoes, citrus, or grapes, equal to one-third or one-quarter of a holding, could be planted. All the orchards of the neighbouring smallholders would be next to each other, thus forming one big orchard of 25–50 feddans. This could be supervised by the technical staff of the co-operative. The fruit could easily be sold through co-operative channels. Each smallholder would, however, remain responsible for all the manual work on his own orchard, as usual in the system of land tenure set up in *mantiqat*. The remaining part of the holding (i.e. two-thirds or three-quarters of the area of a holding) could be distributed in three plots situated within the lands reserved for the crops of the

the Maremma would have been very different today; deep ploughing, irrigation, vegetable and fruit crops, and rationalized animal husbandry are some of the instruments which have transformed this region from an underdeveloped semi-pastoral economy into a diversified and flourishing one. The big changes observed in rural Lebanon since the expansion of citrus, banana, and apple production during the last two decades are also proof of the tremendous impact on a rural society of the rapid multiplication of gross and net returns per acre, and the fact that marketing problems have now to be faced in the Lebanon does not in our opinion invalidate the value of this example.

For further reference on the profitability of fruit production in Egypt see above, p. 5 n. 16. For Lebanon see J. Gauthier and E. Baz, *L'Aspect général de l'agriculture libanaise* (1960).

consolidated triennial crop rotation. It would even be possible to build several hamlets along the pattern described above to concentrate all the orchards in one zone, surrounded by the lands cropped according to the consolidated triennial rotation.

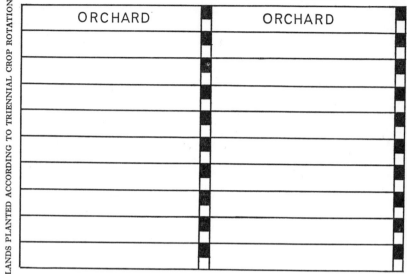

LANDS PLANTED ACCORDING TO TRIENNIAL CROP ROTATION

Fruit Production in Agrarian Reform Regions: Second Alternative Proposed

The increased income which smallholders would receive from this type of project would more than compensate for any administrative difficulties which might arise during its implementation. (In a successful co-operative such as that of Mit al-Mawz, Shibin al-Kawm *mantiqa*, the increment of income obtainable through fruit production in only a part (one-third) of a 2-feddan holding can be estimated at 65 per cent, compared with a holding entirely planted in the traditional crops).[19] Orchards require an investment

[19] Income from a 2-feddan holding planted in fruit crops and in the traditional crops:

Annual income from 0·66 feddans of bananas   £E100
Annual income from 1·33 feddans planted in the traditional crops on the basis of £E50 per feddan, including the value of livestock production, as estimated by the author in 1958/9   £E65
Total income £E165
Annual income of 2-feddan holding planted exclusively in the traditional crops   £E100

of £E50–450 per feddan according to the variety of fruit,[20] but part of this could come from the undistributed profits piling up in the prosperous *mantiqat*[21] which could be loaned to successful Agrarian Reform smallholders. More could be obtained by tapping the vast reserve of unemployed manpower available (a procedure all the more useful if it is recalled that labour represents an important share of the capital to be invested for the establishment of orchards). Finally, the planting of orchards could provide a unique opportunity to set in motion a campaign to promote savings and investment among the prosperous smallholders. The absence of any effort to stimulate saving by persuasion, or by a preferential fiscal treatment such as a remittance of payment of the basic land tax, remained, as late as 1960, a formidable obstacle to the take-off of a self-sustained process of growth in the prosperous *mantiqat*.

But the diversification of agricultural production, if attempted on a large scale, might demand a reduction of the area allotted to the cultivation of wheat, maize, and rice (except in the Northern Delta). Such a policy was frowned on by senior Agrarian Reform officials who in the summer of 1959 were already concerned at the rising cost of maize in rural areas and believed that it might be dangerous unless the Ministry of Supply undertook to make bread grains available in Agrarian Reform areas at the current official prices.[22] This in turn could not be envisaged, since it would have opened the door to big imports of grain, and thus conflicted with the autarky supposedly governing state policy.[23]

FINANCIAL RESOURCES OF THE CO-OPERATIVE ORGANIZATIONS

Fully to grasp the socio-economic and financial aspects of the land-distribution programme it is necessary to scrutinize at close range the operations of the various new co-operative organizations established under the auspices of the Agrarian Reform authorities, i.e. the 'local' co-operatives and the ACS as well as the central administration in Cairo.

The 'local' co-operatives, as has been seen, were destined to play a part of paramount importance in the land-distribution

---

[20] See also Said, *Iqtisadiat*, p. 183. According to Said, the annual income on invested capital was equivalent to 9 per cent p.a. in the case of fruit crops and only 5 per cent in the case of the traditional crops.

[21] See below, pp. 132–4 and App. V. [22] See above, p. 121.

[23] The economic union with the traditionally—with the exception of seasons of drought—grain-exporting 'northern province' of the UAR (Syria), which was then gradually taking place, might well have been the prelude to a policy of diversification; naturally the increase of grain yields in Egypt would have been an integral part of such a policy.

schemes. They thus had to be provided with adequate financial resources, but in practice these were mainly self-generated and were made up of:

1. Capital subscribed by members on the basis of one share at £E1 per feddan or part of a feddan. At the end of 1959 the subscribed capital in the various Damira co-operatives (to give an example) was £E18,056, the total supervised area then being 15,169 feddans.[24]

2. Commissions, profit margins, and interest on services or loans in cash and in kind.[25] The percentage varied according to the nature of the service and in most cases was the same or less than that charged by landlords for similar services to their tenants. As has been seen, interest on loans varied from 3 to 5 per cent per annum.

3. The *iradat al-gam'iya* made by landowning beneficiaries, before 1958/9 equivalent to 0·969 times the land tax and as from 1958/9 equivalent to the whole of the land tax.[26] Of this, 25 per cent was supposed to have been contributed to the GCS in Cairo to help meet its running expenses but the exact working of this arrangement was difficult to determine. Accountants in *mantiqat* stated that some 75 per cent of income from this source was paid to the GCS.

4. Rents by tenant members, originally seven times the land tax but from 1958/9 reduced to six times the land tax. In the case of Damira before 1958/9 rents were equivalent to seven times the land tax but annual instalments due as compensation to expropriated landlords (or, in the case of confiscated estates, to the state as legal successor) were only 3·921 times the land tax. This instalment was paid by the co-operatives to the state treasury. The rest of the rent (i.e. slightly over three times the value of the land tax) was divided into the following three further payments.[27] (1) The land tax and supplementary taxes, assessed at 0·110 of the land tax previously paid by a landowner. Responsibility for this payment was assumed by the Agrarian Reform authorities during the period between expropriation and redistribution in full ownership. Payment was in fact made by the co-operatives to the Agrarian Reform authorities out of the total amount received as rent, and the authorities remitted the sums due as tax to the state treasury. (2) A contribution to 'local' co-operative expenses equal to 0·969 of the land tax. (3) A contribution to meet administrative expenses of the Agrarian Reform authorities equivalent to the land tax. After the reduction in rents in 1958/9 the

---

[24] Net, including the new co-operatives of Urman Talkha and Manshiat al-Badri set up in 1960.
[25] See above, pp. 84–92 and below, App. II, p. 197.
[26] See above, pp. 43–44.   [27] See above, p. 46.

margin between the rents and the annual instalment was divided as before.

The vast majority of peasants were unaware of the intricacies of the accounting systems, and as far as they were concerned the only subject worthy of attention was whether they had to pay five, six, or seven times the basic land tax; the final breakdown of the amount they were charged and its redistribution among the various co-operative organizations was for them quite irrelevant.

5. Miscellaneous income. This consisted in the various fines imposed on members who disobeyed irrigation or drainage regulations or who refused to take part in pest control operations, &c.[28] The co-operatives also earned considerable income from the sale of timber obtained from trees previously planted as windbreaks.

Expenditure

In the Damira region, as a typical example, the following items were included:

1. The actual costs incurred for the various services and loans in kind to members.

2. The interest paid on funds provided by the Cairo authorities for loans in cash and in kind to members.

3. Depreciation on buildings, farm machinery, &c.

4. Administrative costs covering wages and other overhead expenses of the staff of the 'local' co-operatives, and the share paid by them in the wages and overhead expenses of the staff of the ACS (until 1957 the *mantiqa*).[29] The share of each 'local' co-operative in these expenses was made in proportion to the land under its supervision in relation to the total acreage of land under the supervision of the ACS.

Profits

Not all the profits (*arbah*) of the 'local' co-operatives were distributed. Their statutes prescribed several rules for their allocation: 25 per cent was set aside as legal reserve provisions (*kanuniye*), 20 per cent was placed in the Social Aid Fund, used for social activities,[30] and 55 per cent was distributed under *'a'id*, a refund paid after the deduction of the bonuses (*al-mukafa'at*) to the boards of directors, the *mushrifs*, &c. As soon as the statutory reserve of a co-operative amounted to double its capital, the board was entitled to make 80 per cent of net profits available for distribution, and the remaining 20 per cent was placed in the Social Aid Fund.

[28] See above, pp. 49–50.

[29] The wages of the *mushrif al-ta'awuni* (the ex-*mandub*) and all the other members of his staff were accounted for under this heading.

[30] See below, p. 134.

Co-operative profits from rent and lands not yet distributed in full ownership were entered in a separate account; members did not benefit from these profits. The profits distributed to members were a partial refund of money levied in excess of actual costs incurred for the various services the co-operative had provided during the agricultural year. A member was therefore entitled to claim a refund from profits in proportion to the value of the various services from which he had benefited. On a few services, such as irrigation and disposal of the cotton crop, the co-operative made a substantial profit. On others, where less profit was made, the refunds were paid in proportion to the profits. Hard-working peasants who often had to deal with co-operatives were entitled to substantial refunds from profits. These were paid at the same time as the payments made after delivery of the cotton crop, in the presence of the directors of a co-operative, so that complaints or accusations of embezzlement were rare. Promptness in paying these refunds, in the Damira region at least, strengthened confidence in the co-operatives, but this was in sharp contrast with most *mantiqat*, where considerable delay was reported.

Again in Damira, smallholders who were entitled to refunds were able to spend the money even if they were in debt to the co-operatives. In other Agrarian Reform regions before early 1960 this facility was only rarely granted. In Bahut, Nabaruh *mantiqa*, Agrarian Reform officials usually paid an indebted peasant his share of profits but immediately took it back, crediting it to the peasant's account in an effort to reduce outstanding liabilities. This procedure was motivated by the desire of the *mushrifs* to demonstrate a high percentage of collection of sums due to their co-operatives.

THE FINANCIAL OPERATIONS OF THE DAMIRA CO-OPERATIVES

The balance sheet in Appendix V gives a general idea of the financial management and the operations undertaken by Agrarian Reform co-operatives.

UTILIZATION OF FINANCIAL RESOURCES

The financial resources flowing into the coffers of the successful 'local' co-operatives were mopped up by the respective ACS, who then reallocated them to their legal reserve fund, Social Aid Funds, or as profits to be distributed. The Damira ACS provided a vivid illustration of the procedure adopted elsewhere. In this region such substantial profits had been accumulated by the 'local' co-operatives during 1954–8 that they were unanimously considered

TABLE 7

Profit & Loss Account of the Co-operative of Kafr Damira,
1957/8

(*feddans*)

Area under supervision	1,259	Paid-up capital £E1,564	
Area in full ownership	1,130	No. of members 397	
Area tenanted	129	(Landowners 345)	
		(Tenants 52)	

Profits and Losses (£E)

	Expenditure	Income	Profits	Losses
Lands operated by the co-operative on its own account	659·78*	247·686	181·708	
Upkeep of drainage network	110·754	146·486	35·732	
Ghufara'	1,166·160	1,288·546	122·386	
Pest control	403·015	443·318	40·303	
Measuring fields	43·650	36·355		7·295
Ploughing (& interest)	40·500	193·700	153·200	
Commission on disposal of cotton crop		2,037·437†	2,037·437	
Interest on fertilizers & price margins		407·843	407·843	
Interest on selected seeds & price margins		166·971	166·971	
Interest on jute sacks & price margins		6·807	6·807	
Interest on insecticides & price margins		56·578	56·578	
Upkeep of draught animals	103·152	74·042		29·110
Interest on loans provided for rice crop		23·340	23·340	
Interest on loans provided for picking cotton		21·460	21·460	
Miscellaneous income		254·903	254·903	
General overhead expenses incl. provision for amortization of machinery, farm buildings, & various other provisions	2,525·274			2,525·274
Income from *iradat al-gam'iya*		2,690·522‖	2,690·522	
Co-operative projects	398·100	427·555	9·455	
Rent due by tenants		4,322·252	4,322·252	
Ann. instalments & expenses of authorities in Cairo	2,536·384			2,536·384
Total	7,392·966	12,845·801	10,550·898	5,098·063
Net profits	5,452·835			

* Lands farmed directly under the supervision of the staff of the co-operatives not including the value of the instalments and land tax to be paid to the Agrarian Reform Central Fund (see above, p. 43).

† Commission of 5 per cent on the value (£E40,730) of the 1956/7 cotton crop sold through co-operative channels (see above, p. 117).
This item includes the 'voluntary' contribution of the landowning members of the co-operatives.

as the most prosperous of the Agrarian Reform co-operatives both in Daqahliya province and in the Northern Delta.[31] By 1959 profits totalled £E190,462.[32] Of this amount £E32,341 had been deducted for the Social Aid Funds, £E13,687 of which had been

[31] See Min. AR, *Agrarian Reform in Daqahliya Province* (1960).
[32] Not including the Damira co-operatives of Urman Talkha and Manshiat al-Badri, which had just been legally constituted and joined to the Damira ACS.

actually spent on social activities sponsored by these funds. Moreover, £E75,129 had been set aside as a reserve provision (depreciation of buildings, machinery, &c.), while £E40,000 had been distributed to farmers as refunds. It is thus clear that the proportion of annual profits of the co-operatives which finally found its way back into the pockets of affiliated members, either indirectly through the implementation of schemes sponsored by the Social Aid Funds or directly as refunds to members on their transactions, was less than one-third of total annual profits. The policy limiting the proportion of annual profits to be distributed to members was partly justifiable, since an important share of these profits came from rents of tenanted lands, and it would indeed have been contrary to the spirit of co-operation if the rents paid by the tenants (the less fortunate members of the co-operatives) had swelled the profits accruing to their landowning colleagues. However, the large share of profits put into reserve funds was said to have been only temporary, and after most of the Damira co-operatives had accumulated reserves more than twice the value of their capital, it was hoped that the setting aside of reserve funds would be discontinued as from 1960 and that refunds distributed to the smallholders would thereafter be equal to 80 per cent of net profits, the remaining 20 per cent being allocated to the Social Aid Funds. A less stringent financial policy would certainly have been more popular with the members of the Damira or other prosperous co-operatives, who were inclined to believe that surplus funds[33] were being diverted to bolster up other less successful *mantiqat*. This belief was not unfounded, though part of the surplus funds was in fact invested locally to swell the working capital of the prosperous co-operatives in order to expand their activities and to increase the variety of services they provided. It would have been advantageous if the other part could also have been invested locally on projects of prime importance, such as planting orchards or vegetable crops, the full mechanization of farm operations requiring draught power, a better balanced livestock production programme, a dynamic housing scheme, and, above all, vocational training programmes.

THE SOCIAL AID FUNDS

The role of the 'local' co-operatives was not confined to the economic field, and some of them were made to play an active part in the day-to-day life of the Agrarian Reform village communities

---

[33] i.e. those set aside for reserve provisions as well as those constituted by the profits on tenanted lands or those resulting from the accumulation in the Social Aid Funds of sums not yet earmarked for specific projects.

with the aim of fostering social equilibrium and cultural development.[34] As has been seen, each of the 'local' co-operatives was obliged by statute to place 20 per cent of its annual profits in a Social Aid Fund, administered by its Board of Directors, to finance various welfare projects. These included building schools and mosques and their upkeep and repair, improving street lighting in the villages, setting up dispensaries, nurseries, and clubs, and, above all, providing necessary financial help for members when in need and for the relief of destitute families. In practice, despite the size of the Social Aid Funds of many co-operatives, not more than half the money available was spent on or allotted to specific projects. Until 1960 most of the money was spent on needy members or the destitute inhabitants of the Agrarian Reform villages, who also received grants in kind on feast days. In about a third of the *mantiqat* visited, the co-operatives had set up household branches for their members which sold goods for consumption, such as textiles, leather goods, furniture, drugstore goods, and transistor radios. By 1960 the various household branches had been working for two or three years and were in a sound financial position, but their impact on the village economies was limited because they were not allowed to sell on credit. This deprived them of many potential customers who were too poor to make cash payments, and who preferred to buy at higher prices on credit from local merchants or grocers.

Schools, mosques, sports clubs, libraries, dispensaries, and nurseries financed by the Social Aid Funds were only occasionally set up in *mantiqat*. Sanitary conditions were not much better than in 1952, and were worse in some areas, such as Damira and Za'faran.[35] The growing demand for dispensaries to provide free medical care to all co-operative members led to an announcement by the authorities in March 1959 that a working arrangement was about to be made with the Ministry of Health to establish free dispensaries in all the Agrarian Reform villages. The capital outlay on this scheme was partly to be contributed from the Social Aid Funds, and their boards would thus have a hand in controlling their operations.[36]

---

[34] See App. VII, p. 203.

[35] In Damira a fully equipped hospital donated by the evicted landlords and supervised by the Ministry of Hygiene was only partially operated through a shortage of doctors. Members of the Damira co-operatives had to go as far as Naburah, 10 km. away, for medical treatment. In al Za'faran, another star co-operative, nearly 1,500 peasant families were deprived of medicinal care after 1957, when the existing dispensary was closed down. A Rural Combined Centre was being set up, but there was no doctor, so that its medical section was paralysed. Both these cases, witnessed by the author in July 1959, were also reported in the Agrarian Reform publication *al-Ta'awun*, Sept. 1959, p. 14.

[36] For further details see ibid. 8 Mar. 1960; also Warriner, Report to UN.

There is much to criticize in the nature and the limited scope of the social aid programme of the co-operatives seven years after Agrarian Reform. But it did introduce a ray of hope and a new outlook into Egyptian rural life. The idea of an interdependence between the social and economic status of the different inhabitants of an Egyptian village community was new and slowly made an impression on the peasant's mind. Its beneficial psychological impact might have been far greater, especially as far as the peasant's appreciation of the co-operatives was concerned, had it not been for the delays in obtaining the sanction of the central administration in Cairo prior to any payment from the Social Aid Funds.[37]

THE FINANCING OF THE LAND-DISTRIBUTION PROGRAMME

The keystone to the successful development of any agrarian reform is doubtless the provision of ample sources of finance for the central administration entrusted with its implementation. The Egyptian case was no exception to this rule, and major financial problems had to be solved to enable the Agrarian Reform Central Administration to begin operations. The authorities had started in October 1952 with empty coffers, and it was not until two months later that full state financial backing was obtained in the form of a state-guaranteed credit of £E1 million from the Agricultural Credit Bank.[38] A provisional budget for January 1952–June 1963 was submitted and approved, expenditure being estimated at £E820,000 and income at £E2,513,000.

In fact, however, the land-distribution programme was largely financed by rent from provisional smallholders,[39] who thus carried a large share of the administrative costs of the distribution programme.[40] This is particularly important when it is borne in mind that a very large area (about 100,000 feddans) was still tenanted as late as 1959.

Additional income came from the regular *iradat al-gam'iya*, from savings certificates issued to prosperous smallholders, and from the 10–15 per cent commission[41] on the price of holdings which was added to the instalments collected from landowning

[37] See above, pp. 67–68.
[38] Above, p. 82.
[39] Two-sevenths of the rentals paid by the latter had been (as previously explained) earmarked as a contribution to the expenses of the 'local' co-operatives and to cover administrative costs incurred by the Agrarian Reform authorities.
[40] See Garzouzi, p. 99. Also balance-sheet of the co-operatives of Kafr Damira, p. 133, and App. II, Accounts of the co-operatives of Za'faran and Rub' Shandid (p. 197).
[41] Above, p. 43.

beneficiaries. This last item amounted to some £E7–11 million (according to the rate due for settlement) during the redemption period of the holdings.

As a result of this large income, the financial plight of the Agrarian Reform authorities was short-lived, and by 1956 the money initially borrowed from the state through the Agricultural Credit Bank had been fully repaid.[42] In July 1959 accounts for mid-1957 to mid-1958 showed that the authorities had considerable assets, provisions, reserves, and surplus funds at their disposal. Moreover, the total capital of the 276 local co-operatives had soared to £E269,833[43] and their statutory reserves to £E117,546, while annual profits totalled £E1,161,796.

<h3 style="text-align:center">INVESTMENT PLANS AND LACK OF VOCATIONAL TRAINING PROGRAMME</h3>

In spite of the apparently big liquid assets, the financial situation of the authorities was not over-prosperous: certain regions were heavily in debt[44] because the co-operatives were not fully consolidated, so that part of the unused money in the prosperous regions was diverted to them, to buttress their efforts. The fact that much of the money supposed to be available in the Social Aid Funds remained idle rather than being allocated to specific projects bears out this statement. But the diversion of the surplus funds of prosperous regions to less fortunate ones may have diminished in 1960 and in 1961 as a result of a reduction in their indebtedness during these two years, thanks to improved crop yields on the one hand and to the lowering of instalments and rents decreed in 1958. On the other hand part of the funds supposed to be used to improve the lot of the smallholders had also been utilized to buy 13,000 feddans seized from English and French landowners in 1956, and which were ultimately to be distributed. A large part of the remaining funds was tied up in various dubious schemes such as the purchase of large quantities of farm machinery, or ambitious cattle-breeding projects directly and exclusively supervised by the Agrarian Reform administration.[45]

Even if all the liquid assets had been set aside and invested for the economic and social development of the smallholders, they would not have been enough to cope with the magnitude of the

[42] See *Agrarian Reform in Five Years* and Garzouzi, pp. 96–99.
[43] Nearly £E400,000 by 1961, when the number of co-operatives registered or awaiting registration had risen to 400.
[44] See above, pp. 99–100.
[45] For details on the schemes for livestock production in the *mantiqat* of Idfina, Abis, Itay al-Barud, Marg, &c., all of which were carried out exclusively by the Agrarian Reform authorities, see App. VIII, p. 206.

task in an area of about 450,000 feddans which was being assigned to some 700,000 human beings afflicted with all the problems typical of Egyptian rural life. The fact that beneficiaries of the Agrarian Reform measures, and not only the evicted landowners, were made to bear the brunt of expropriation and redistribution costs as well as the cost of running the co-operative organizations did not make things easier[46] and was doubtless partly responsible for the accumulation of big debts. The Egyptian land-distribution programme was different from a Western type of reform such as the Italian one, where considerable capital, lavishly supplied by the state (itself backed by a vigorous foreign aid programme) had been invested for land distribution and to alleviate the social and economic plight of these benefiting from it.[47] Bearing in mind the extremely low standard of rural life, the application of a similar procedure in Egypt would have required a tremendous financial and administrative effort which could only have been carried out at the beginning of the revolution with the greatest difficulty unless there had been considerable surplus human and material resources. As it was, the tight financial situation of the government and the dearth of trained technicians could only have been overcome with extensive foreign aid, at least during the initial stages of the land-distribution programme. No doubt the considerable investment in capital (£E25–30 million) and in trained personnel that has since been devoted to the ambitious Liberation province land-reclamation project, and which has yielded disappointing results,[48] could have been more profitably used for a thorough socio-economic transformation of the Agrarian Reform regions, which might have become foci of development. Part of this investment could also have been earmarked for the financing of a determined effort to raise the productivity of the human factor so profusely available in the redistributed estates, for the total absence as late as 1960 of an agricultural vocational training programme[49] remained one of the unexplained mysteries and one of the weakest points in the land-distribution programme.[50] Vocational training in agriculture and agricultural co-operation would have fostered entrepreneurship among smallholders and

[46] It has already been pointed out in Ch. III and in this chapter (p. 136) that the occupants of the distributed estates had been over-burdened.

[47] In the Maremma or Salerno regions, for example.

[48] See Ch. XI.

[49] The training centres to teach peasant women and young girls sewing and knitting or the manufacture of carpets which were to be found in a few ACS could hardly be considered adequate for this purpose.

[50] Crop failures of smallholders who had been agricultural labourers prior to becoming landowning beneficiaries, and who lacked the necessary farming experience, could well be traced back to this deficiency in planning, itself a reflection of an underestimation of the importance of the human factor in a process of economic and social development.

female members of their families and would also have provided
them with basic technical knowledge. It would, moreover, have
been the logical corollary to a 'liberal' approach to agrarian problems, which allows for the emergence of individual initiative
within a co-operative framework. But it would have been incompatible with the so-called 'co-operative socialist' ideology of
the present rulers of Egypt, itself springing from a deep-rooted
belief in the advantages and the effectiveness of direct state intervention in every aspect of social and economic activity.[51] One can
only wonder if state-directed initiatives alone (i.e. without the
prop of entrepreneurship, or that of an extremely active political
party) will be capable of coping with the formidable problems of
rural Egypt. The successes claimed by Chinese agrarian policy,
for example, before the communes experiment, appear to have
been mainly a result of state intervention supported by the tireless
efforts of the Communist Party, who had contrived to take in hand
every aspect of rural life with ruthlessness, inflexible thoroughness,
and terrifying efficiency. Whether in Egypt the state, assisted by
the government-sponsored party *al-Ittihad al-Qawmi*, can in
future succeed in whipping up and enforcing as much devotion,
enthusiasm, incorruptibility, and constructive effort is debatable.

The big investment plans of the Agrarian Reform authorities,
which totalled £E13 million[52] for the period 1960–4, and which were
to be implemented under their exclusive control and management,
may thus have yielded meagre results as far as the smallholders
were concerned unless very active political leadership was ensured.
Part of these investments would probably have contributed more
effectively to increase the productive potential of the smallholders, if
they had been channelled directly into their own hands, combined
with the establishment of vocational training centres in every

---

[51] A different appraisal of the prevailing official Egyptian ideology has been
put forward; it lists the following as one of the characteristics of the newly
emerging society of Egypt—'A rational distribution of the economic activities
between public and private sectors of the economy' (see Y. A. Sayigh, *Bread
with Dignity* (1961)). Professor Sayigh's appraisal does not seem to have been
substantiated by policy trends since 1961.

[52] Breakdown of total Agrarian Reform investment during the period 1960–4
in £E'ooo (for further reference see *al-Magallat al-Zira'iyat*, Mar. 1961).

	£E'ooo		£E'ooo
Housing	1,800	Fattening of calves	522
Orchards	150	Poultry	1,570
Livestock production	368	Animal feed factory	817
Distribution of calves	401	Mechanization	2,100*
Studs for breeding milk		Improvement of 40,000	
buffaloes	501	feddans of poor lands dis-	
Distribution of 4,165		persed in various estates	3,300
female buffalo heifers	125		

* Of which £E1,370,000 was for the purchase of artesian and canal irrigation
sets (*bahari*) and £E770,000 for repairs and the purchase of new stock.

mantiqa and with the improvement of the extension services and full mobilization of all human resources.[53]

In conclusion, the land-distribution programme could best be described in 1961 as a major delaying action, to win time by re-distributing wealth, to be repeated again and again if need arose. It had fulfilled most of its initial targets: the allocation of the large expropriated estates to smallholders had been successfully carried out without any grave disruption of agricultural production, and the political power of the feudal landowners had been broken. The state itself, though directly interfering in the reorganization of agrarian structures, had avoided the costs by passing on the bill to the interested parties, i.e. the evicted landowners and the new beneficiaries.[54] But it had also placed formidable obstacles in the way of a self-sustained process of economic, social, and cultural growth through its reluctance to envisage the emergence of any spontaneous constructive initiative in the redistributed estates, and through its insistence on itself implementing development projects designed to benefit the smallholders. It had thus impressed on the whole land-distribution programme static characteristics gravely endangering its successful long-term evolution.

[53] For further reference on the importance of the human element in processes of economic development see J. Chérel, 'La Mise en valeur agricole; problème d'ensembles humains', *Cahiers de Tunisie*, nos. 29–30 (1960).

[54] 'A capital problem when it comes to land redistribution is to fix the basis and the conditions relative to compensation payments to the ex-landowners, as well as those related to payments demanded from the new landowners. The solutions adopted, in addition to considerations of fairness, which they may raise, bear important results on the overall economy of the country and in particular on the State Budget' (UN, *Progress in Land Reform* (New York, 1963), p. 75, para. 55).

PART 2

OTHER AGRARIAN REFORM MEASURES

IX

CHANGES IN TENANCY AND SHARE-CROPPING AND IN THE STATUS OF AGRICULTURAL LABOUR

The improvement in income and legal status for a very large section of the farm population is by far the most valuable achievement of the reform, greatly exceeding in importance the benefits of redistribution.

D. WARRINER, *Land Reform and Development in the Middle East* (1957), p. 39.

SEVERAL measures included in the Agrarian Reform Law of September 1952 were designed to improve the conditions of tenure of tenants and sharecroppers other than those on the distributed estates. Only written contracts were to be permitted by law, while the minimum period of lease for agricultural land was fixed at three years. Rents were reduced to more reasonable levels by fixing them at a maximum of seven times the land tax, the ensuing reduction averaging approximately 33 per cent. In the case of sharecropping the share due to the landlord was reduced to a maximum of 50 per cent of the crops produced; all expenses were to be shared equally.

The Agrarian Reform authorities have claimed that about 6 million rural inhabitants benefited from the rent reductions, and that their income rose by about £E35 million per annum;[1] some experts have also expressed the belief that in 1953 alone the income of tenants and sharecroppers increased by 23 per cent.[2] In Upper Egypt, where rents had reached astronomical heights before 1952, there was undoubtedly a considerable reduction. In many cases where the big landlords had cheated the state by obtaining low valuations from the land tax committees, rents fell very sharply. At Girga lands previously let by large landowners at £E70 a feddan have since 1952 been rented at £E22 a feddan.

The new regulations for tenancy affected a very important percentage of the cultivated area (at least 50 per cent and probably 70 per cent if seasonal leases are included), and about 40 per cent of all farms. These regulations were hailed as an important step

---

[1] Marei, *Agrarian Reform*; also Warriner, *Land Reform*, p. 39.
[2] Thweatt, in *M.E. Papers, 1956*.

towards the reform of tenancy. In the years before the Agrarian Reform the conditions of tenants and sharecroppers had become unbearable owing to population pressure and the lack of legal protection. This situation was also detrimental to the sound development of the agricultural sector, whose short-term prospects depended in no small manner on the implementation of a rational programme involving a high rate of capital investment to intensify, diversify, and mechanize production, to improve agricultural techniques and research, to provide sufficient credit, and to expand marketing and processing facilities.

The fixing of a minimum period of three years for farm leases and the prohibition of the eviction of tenants and sharecroppers by landlords during the first years after Agrarian Reform provided a minimum of protection and security. It encouraged them to invest and to make better use of the land they cultivated, and freed them from the rapacious greed of big and small absentee landlords.[3]

The Land Reform Law seemed truly revolutionary to the Egyptian rural community, stifled as it was by an outmoded legal straitjacket and following a centuries-old routine. Probably because of this and because of the law's intention to define new methods of approach in the light of experience, the authorities abstained from enacting sweeping measures which would have still further raised the status of tenancy and sharecropping.

Since 1952 expired farm leases have been automatically renewed by special legislation enacted at various times. Renewal of leases ending that year was granted just after the enactment of the 1952 law, to be effective for one year. It was followed by three successive laws in 1953, 1954, and 1955, granting renewal for a further three years. (But at this stage, landowners were given the right to evict tenants and sharecroppers from half the lands whose leases had expired.) The procedure (*tagnib*) aimed at granting a respite to all tenants and sharecroppers threatened with eviction during which they could find new means of livelihood. Tenants or sharecroppers whose contracts expired were thus given the right to continue occupation of half the area of the lands they previously operated for another term of lease.

In 1956 a new law was enacted, renewing contracts expiring in the current years for three years ending in the agricultural year 1958/9 but this only covered half the area leased by a tenant or a sharecropper. Landowners were also compelled to accept payment, on a three-year instalment basis, of rents in arrears, which

---

[3] As previously mentioned, the tendency towards absenteeism was, and has remained, more prevalent among small landowners. It has even prevailed among smallholders in the areas supervised by the Min. AR (see above, p. 47, 75).

had grown considerably as tenant farmers believed all lands were about to be expropriated and redistributed and had, in numerous cases, ceased since 1952 to fulfil their contractual obligations. However, farmers not fulfilling their obligations were liable in the future to forfeit their rights automatically. Similar legislation[4] was enacted in the following years. In 1960 the government presented to the National Assembly a bill providing security of tenure for another three consecutive years, but this was rejected by the Assembly's agricultural committee under pressure from medium-size landowning groups.

By passing gradual and somewhat improvised tenancy legislation, the state had attempted to reconcile its desire for relative stability for reliable tenants and sharecroppers (i.e. those living up to their obligations) and the political expediency which prohibited a direct attack on the problem of stability. Long-term security and protection of tenants and sharecroppers, so beneficial to a rural community, were therefore still lacking in 1960–1. Considerable abuse of the law arose from the exemptions from the tenancy and sharecropping regulations of the 1952 legislation which had been granted to landowners leasing orchards or land for seasonal crops such as maize or vegetables, and from the liberty given to landowners to retrieve half their leased holdings. Judicial courts set up in 1952 for the settlement of disputes between landowners and tenants[5] generally sided with the landowners, nor did the Agrarian Reform authorities and the state propaganda apparatus pay much attention to this.

Throughout 1959 and 1960 most tenants and sharecroppers renting land from big or medium-sized landowners (50–200 feddans) paid rent at legal rates principally because landowners feared exposure and much-publicized penal sanctions. On the other hand the vast majority of tenants and sharecroppers who rented land from the very numerous small absentee landlords were made to pay rents far higher than legal rates,[6] as they feared the

---

[4] See Laws no. 406 of 1953, no. 474 of 1954, no. 411 of 1955, no. 315 of 1956, no. 24 of 1958, no. 183 of 1959.

[5] By Law no. 476 of 1953, modified by Law no. 23 of 1958.

[6] In the region of Simbilawain, Aga district, for example, rents exacted in 1957/8 and 1958/9 by small and medium-sized landowners (in areas not subject to Agrarian Reform supervision) reached £E50 per feddan. This, of course, was very much more than rent calculated according to Agrarian Reform tenancy regulations (£E25–30 per feddan). The great majority of breaches of the Agrarian Reform legislation were made by the above-mentioned category of landowners.

Disputes arising from breaches of tenancy regulations were submitted to a special committee (*Lagnat al-fasl fi'l-munaza'at al-khassa bi imtadad 'uqud igar al-aradi al-zira'iya*) under the chairmanship of the local public prosecutor; representatives of the Ministries of Agriculture and Agrarian Reform, the landowners, and the tenants sat on this committee. In practice, in Aga (and in all the other regions of Egypt) the public prosecutor played the decisive role in the

landowners because of family ties, local prestige, &c. By 1960 rents had been pushed far beyond their legal level, a fact admitted privately by senior Agrarian Reform officials who, early in 1960, estimated the instances at 80 per cent. Late in 1959 articles began to appear in the press on the subject,[7] a sure sign that some new measure was in the offing. It was therefore hard to believe then that the reform of the conditions of tenure initiated in 1952 would not be further pursued in order to achieve the comprehensive stabilization of tenure necessary for the setting in motion of a process of rationalization involving considerable capital outlay.

STATUS OF AGRICULTURAL LABOUR AFTER 1952

Nothing had been done as late as July 1961 to ensure the payment of a minimum wage to agricultural labourers or to encourage the formation of labour unions, despite very specific provisions in the 1952 law.[8] A decree issued immediately after the 1952 law fixed a minimum daily wage of 18 piastres for men and 10 piastres for women, but even in the *mantiqat* it was never applied to hired labour. The 3 million rural inhabitants in the agricultural labour force were thus condemned to oblivion, whereas reduced employment opportunities since 1952 and the tremendous rise in the price of maize, their staple diet, should have entitled them to more considerate treatment on the part of the state.

Some agricultural labourers joined the seasonal labour gangs (*tarahil*) hired by special labour contractors (*mokawil anfarr*) to farm operators, where they endured appalling conditions of work. Drawn from the overpopulated districts of Upper Egypt and the Delta (Kuwaisna, Mit Ghamr, &c.) and jolted from region to region in goods trucks, beaten by the contractors and fed on onions and bread, these labourers were among the most wretched people of rural Egypt[9] or for that matter of the African continent. One of the most astonishing phenomena of the social, economic, and political development of revolutionary Egypt was that nothing

handling of cases of breach of the Agrarian Reform Law. According to officials of the Aga co-operative, most of the fifteen or so complaints reaching the committee weekly were settled in favour of the landowners. A typical technique of extortion resorted to by landowners was to compel a tenant about to be evicted to subscribe to a new contract, with rent calculated at the legal rate, while obliging him to sign separate bills of exchange for the amount above the legal rate.

[7] *al-Ta'awun, al-Ahram*, &c.
[8] Arts. 38 and 39 of ch. vi of the law.
[9] According to a survey of the labour force conducted on behalf of the Central Committee of Statistics (Cairo, 1959), 30 per cent of the labour force occupied in agriculture in Southern Egypt and 9 per cent in Northern Egypt were employed less than fifteen days a month. This concealed unemployment was, of course, a legacy of the past and could hardly be attributed to the economic policies pursued since 1952.

was done during 1952–61,[10] not so much to raise the wages as to improve the general conditions of their employment and halt the ugly exploitation by labour contractors. These contractors took a net 12 per cent commission on wages, and pressured the workers themselves into making additional payments.

The formation of agricultural labour unions appeared to have been postponed indefinitely for political and possibly economic reasons. While it was feared that these unions would be rapidly infiltrated and dominated by extremists, it was also claimed that they might bring about a quick rise in agricultural wages which would out-price Egyptian agricultural products on the world markets. The advance of education and a more pronounced feeling of social and political responsibility in the rural masses may well increase the chances of the establishment of agricultural labour unions in the not too distant future. But such a change in policy, when it comes, will be inadequate unless it is preceded by the enactment of laws regulating the employment of agricultural labour in agriculture, prohibiting the employment of children under fourteen,[11] and extending to men and women labourers social benefits similar to those enjoyed by industrial workers.

[10] The unhappy lot of the *tarahil* seems only to have attracted the attention of the public and the government in 1960; since then articles have regularly appeared in the press on this subject.

[11] This would result in the loss of at least 3 m. labour units from the available force. And it could be applied in the densely populated areas of Upper and Central Egypt, wherever there are enough schools to cope with the enormous influx of pupils.

X

CO-OPERATIVE FARMING AND
SUPERVISED AGRICULTURAL CREDIT

*Agrarian science has the important task of finding compromise solu-
tions between family farming and kolkhozes.*

F. KUHNEN, *Agrarian Reform and Economic Development* (1961)

CONSOLIDATION OF FARM OPERATION

THE various laws regulating the pattern of agrarian tenure which
were enacted after September 1952 affected only one section of
the cultivated area. An important area in the hands of small landowners was hardly affected by the new legislation. In fact 1,573,917
feddans (27 per cent of the cultivated area) owned by 2,492,234
landowners in 1952 continued to suffer from excessive fragmentation, were poorly farmed, and remained plagued by low land and
human productivity; moreover, 45 per cent of the cultivated area
was owned by landowners whose holdings consisted of four or
more plots.[1] The moleculization and the fragmentation of holdings was bound to increase over the years if only as the result of
the application of the Egyptian inheritance laws. True, Articles
23 and 24 of the 1952 Agrarian Reform Law had clearly forbidden
the fragmentation of holdings of less than 5 feddans, but this legal
injunction was not given any practical application during the period
1952–60.

Rather than impose laws, the Agrarian Reform authorities
preferred to prevent the continuous disintegration of smallholdings and to reduce the excessive fragmentation of landownership and farm operation by devising methods common to Egyptian
agricultural traditions.[2]

The authorities accordingly started in 1955 an important
experiment in crop consolidation,[3] in the village of Nawag,
Gharbiya province, which was to serve as the basis for future
plans affecting an area of 3 million feddans.

---

[1] Statement of Min. AR. See also *Ann. stat. FI, 1956–7*, p. 236.
[2] See M. K. Hindy, *Reorganization of Land Use* (1962).
[3] See below, App. I, p. 190. For full details see Saab, 'Cooperation and
Agricultural Development in Poverty-Stricken Rural Zones in Italy and Egypt',
Commerce du Levant (Beirut), 17 & 20 Feb. 1960; also Warriner, Report to UN,
p. 69.

The system proposed to the landowners of Nawag was to persuade them to join voluntarily in a consolidation of crops which involved all the village lands. They were left entirely free to carry out their work on their individual plots. A triennial crop rotation was worked out for all the village lands and villagers were asked to comply with this rotation in so far as it involved planting the same crop as that chosen for the portion of the village lands within which their property lay. Whenever for some reason or other they did not wish to have all their property under the same crop, they were encouraged by the directors of the 'local' co-operative to enter into provisional exchange agreements with other small-holders. To foster this co-operative effort, the Agrarian Reform experts set up, in collaboration with the head of the 'local' co-operative, an extension service programme combined with super-vised agricultural credit.

The Nawag experiment succeeded beyond expectation. Crop yields and gross and net income increased considerably. Irrigation water was fully controlled and water requirements per unit of area diminished by 30 per cent. Plans were finally drafted in 1959 to extend the system gradually to 3 million feddans. Mansha'at Sultan[4] in Minufiya province and two villages in Upper Egypt were scheduled to start voluntary crop consolidation experiments in 1960. To provide the necessary inducements, the authorities promised that all villages undertaking crop consolidation and rotation would automatically receive top priority in the Nasir cattle-distribution programme.[5] Furthermore, such villages were promised that they would be the first to benefit from the underground drainage network, planned to be ready between 1960 and 1970.[6] In the spring of 1960 official statements indicated that crop consolidation was to be attempted in over 100 villages in the provinces of Minufiya, Qalyubiya, Sharqiya, Gharbiya, Daqahliya, and Minya. The over-populated Minufiya province was itself to receive the lion's share of this big experiment where 65 out of 320 villages were supposed to subscribe to the new drive.

Agrarian Reform publications have revealed that from autumn 1960 crop consolidation was in full application in 103 villages in these provinces. They claimed that the experiment had met with tremendous success.[7] As an example, it was claimed that in the pilot villages of Minufiya 94 per cent of the area planted with cotton had been consolidated in blocks of over 10 feddans; and

[4] In December 1960 increases in crop yields of nearly 80 per cent were claimed; they were said to have been due to the crop consolidation adopted in this village.
[5] See above, p. 116.   [6] See below, p. 170.
[7] See S. Marei, 'Crop Consolidation', *al-Magallat al-Zira'iyat*, May 1961, p. 9.

better still, that 70 per cent of this area planted in cotton had been consolidated in blocks of over 20 feddans. The full significance of this consolidation can be gauged where it is recalled that the average size of a farm unit in Minufiya was about 0·5 feddans.

By 1961–2 crop consolidation was due to be enforced in all the Minufiya villages. To give greater momentum to this drive, the Ministry of Public Works was instructed to be ready to fulfil the promise to install underground drainage networks in the villages which took part in the scheme.[8]

<h2 style="text-align:center">SUPERVISED AGRICULTURAL CREDIT</h2>

As in the organization of the expropriated estates, from 1952 co-operatives were made the channel for the distribution of agricultural credit, the Agricultural Credit Bank receiving instructions from the government to promote co-operative farming as much as possible and progressively to restrict its dealings with operators not participating in co-operatives. As a result of these directives, loans granted by the Bank to co-operatives rose to 41·7 per cent of its total transactions by 1957,[9] and it further expanded the scope of its short- and medium-term loans; by the same date short-term loans had risen by nearly £E3 million to £E18,292,242, and medium-term loans for the purchase of farm machinery and livestock, for land reclamation projects, &c., though still negligible in volume, had risen to £E144,297, a 60 per cent increase. To facilitate the implementation of the new credit policy, and to ensure the healthy development of the co-operative sector, an attempt at its reorganization was simultaneously made. The numerous village co-operatives supervised by the Ministry of Social Affairs[10] were grouped in regional federations (*ittihad ta'awuni*), financed by a 50 per cent share of the annual profits. All the regional federations were affiliated to a national co-operative federation. Changes in the membership of the Boards of Directors of the village co-operatives were planned to reduce the dominating position of the big farmers, and all operations were to be more strictly controlled by the Ministry of Social Affairs.

Another important change in agricultural credit policy was introduced in 1956, when the statutes of the Agricultural Credit Bank were amended to enable it to deal with all farmers, whether landowners, tenants, or sharecroppers, if they were members of

<hr/>

[8] 37,000 feddans in Minufiya province in the districts of al-Shohada, Tala, Minuf, and Shibin al-Kawm. See below, p. 170.
[9] As against 20 per cent in 1952 (see above, p. 8).
[10] The non-Agrarian Reform co-operatives were controlled by a Superior Advisory Council under the Minister of Social Affairs.

the co-operative. Credits in kind and in cash were placed at the disposal of the directors of the co-operatives for distribution to members according to their requirements (i.e. in proportion to the area they actually farmed), regardless of the mode of tenure. Board decisions were subject to the approval of a delegate of the Bank, who was entrusted with the control of all the financial operations, the allocation of loans within a limit of £E3,000, and the appointment of the co-operative accountant.

This system of supervised agricultural credit was successfully tried out in 3 districts (*markaz*) in 1957, and was later adopted in 15 more districts in 1958, and 35 more in 1959. By the end of 1959 2,046 village co-operatives under the supervision of the Ministry of Social Affairs and operating in these 53 districts were subjected to this new procedure. The co-operatives, with a total membership of 475,041, received £E7,698,184 in credits for distribution to 294,631 holders of an area of 745,741 feddans, but despite a big increase in the size of loans, the percentage of debts settled remained much the same as it had before.

The Bank encountered some obstacles in carrying out its new programme. The shortage of trained personnel[11] to carry out the duties of Bank agents or delegates (*mushrif* again) appears to have been a major bottleneck, rendered the more serious by the difficulties encountered in providing the agents with adequate living quarters and transportation. The dual control exercised by the Bank agents and by the staff of the regional federations also led to conflicts of jurisdiction between them. Though tenants and sharecroppers were supposed to present their contracts to benefit from the new credit facilities, it was thought necessary only to consider the opinion of the co-operative board as a sufficient proof of the status of tenure of a tenant applicant. In the case of sharecroppers, an additional guarantee from the landlord was required if the landlord was not himself a member of a co-operative. Tenants and sharecroppers were allowed to enjoy short-term loans in kind, under the same conditions as landowning clients, but loans in cash were restricted to half their current amount.

Though there were obstacles to the efficient administration of the supervised agricultural credit scheme, the situation of small-holders appeared to have slightly improved by 1959, and the grip of the village money-lenders and merchants was weakened in the pilot districts. In spite of the reluctance of the Bank to extend

---

[11] There were not enough Bank agents. Each was put in charge of several co-operatives in a given district. In practice, the accountants (*katib*) of the co-operatives and their board members were free to carry out the instructions of the Bank's agents.

the new system to new regions before a full assessment of the initial efforts, another thirty-three districts were brought under the scheme in 1960. There was thus a total of 3,101 co-operatives (some of which were especially set up in villages where none existed) with 672,437 members. The year 1961 was scheduled to see the completion of this programme to integrate the 4,000 villages of rural Egypt in an all-embracing co-operative structure, exclusively entrusted with the channelling of agricultural credit to all farm operators. Membership of a co-operative was made conditional on the purchase of at least one share of its capital, valued at £E0·5, which had to be paid 25 per cent cash down and 75 per cent in two annual instalments. The candidate members had to be actively farming, thus excluding all absentee landlords.

As a result of the sustained drive to expand the scope of agricultural co-operation, during recent years the Bank's operations have concentrated more and more on the provision of financial assistance to co-operatives. Its dealings with them amounted to 84 per cent of its annual transactions in 1960, and the target for 1961 was 100 per cent. Most of the beneficiaries of the Bank's loans were the small operators of less than 5 feddans (366,517 out of a total of 531,407, or 70 per cent of the Bank's clientele).[12]

The size of short-term loans by the Bank increased considerably to over £E35 million in 1960.[13] Medium-term loans for the purchase of farm machinery, cattle, &c., and for land reclamation also increased, totalling £E1·5 million in 1960. Nevertheless these amounts are still very far from coping with the credit requirements of agricultural production valued at more than £E500 million, especially since the increases in credit allocations have been partially offset by the rise in prices of certain imported inputs such as farm machinery, insecticides, fertilizers, and fuel.[14]

THE VILLAGE BANK PROJECT[15]

The Bank's attitude towards its rural clientele had not been very businesslike before 1952. Old habits are hard to change in rural

---

[12] The total number of farm operators of less than 5 feddans was about 1,025,000 in 1956, so that, despite the Bank's efforts, it was clear that a very high percentage of farm operators was still not benefiting from its services (see figures on distribution of farm operators according to the size of their holdings, p. 14).

[13] Volume of short-term loans extended by the Agricultural Credit and Co-operative Bank (in £E'000) during 1949–60:

1949	1950	1951	1952	1953	1954	1955
8,981	13,359	12,600	15,606	16,013	16,862	18,231
1956	1957	1958	1959	1960		
16,260	18,292	25,000	30,000	35,000		

[14] See above, p. 121.

[15] See *al-Ahram Economic Review* (Cairo, 1961), p. 32.

Egypt, so that despite seven years of revolutionary rule, by 1960 little had been achieved really to transform it into a bank clearly devoted to the service of the small peasant. No effort had been made to encourage or mobilize rural savings. Village branches were practically non-existent, and those established in important towns were not receiving deposits from private individuals. The dealings of the Bank with its customers were, moreover, characterized by the frustrating and tedious red tape and routine so typical of Egyptian governmental administration, thus considerably increasing the 'real' cost of the loans it granted.

A more effective approach to the problem of agricultural credit and co-operative farming was therefore devised early in 1960, when branches of the Bank were opened in eighteen villages to bolster the efforts of co-operatives operating under the supervised credit system. These village banks were managed by a delegate of the Agricultural Credit Bank, who was also appointed as *mushrif*. Warehouses were specially built close to the offices of the new branches to store the goods (fertilizers, insecticides, &c.), supplied on a cash or credit basis to the co-operatives and their members; they were also used to store the members' crops, thus facilitating their disposal by bulk sale under the auspices of the co-operatives.

The aim of the village banks was primarily to promote all forms of co-operative farming, such as crop consolidation, mechanization of farm operations with co-operative machines, pest control by co-operative units, co-operative marketing, and rural industries. They were also entitled to receive deposits from individual farmers. Official statements claimed at the end of 1960 that the initial experiment had been highly successful and that credits allocated had been repaid without having to resort to the customary procedure of legal seizure of a debtor's crops.[16] An additional 120 village banks were to be established in new area during 1961.

There is no doubt that a more active participation of the Bank at the village level helps to mobilize rural savings to finance agricultural expansion. According to S. Marei,[17] £E2·5 million in gold is purchased annually by rural couples when marrying. There is thus a considerable amount of rural savings now hoarded by villagers who keep their cash reserves in the form of gold bracelets and jewellery worn by the women. It is the duty of the village banks to tap this 'concealed' capital and to draw it back into the economy. But the trend of combining management and operation of the Agricultural Credit Bank (of which the village banks

---

[16] See above, p. 98.
[17] 'Sectors unemployed', *al-Magallat al-Zira'iyat*, Aug. 1959, p. 14.

are subsidiary branches) with those of other governmental agencies[18] is inconsistent with a skilful and intelligently planned attempt to gain the confidence of a rural clientele naturally shy of government initiative and state-sponsored institutions.

NEW POLICY DEVELOPMENTS

Criticism of the running of the co-operative societies, and especially of the agricultural co-operative societies, began to appear in various official publications in the late autumn of 1960. In December of that year it was officially announced that drastic changes in the whole co-operative organization and agricultural credit policy were impending, as the existing system was inconsistent with the overall agricultural economic policy of the second five-year plan. The nature and the scope of these changes were disclosed early in January 1961 and proved to be far more sweeping than expected; they seemed to pave the way for a thorough revision of agrarian patterns in the near future.

The area of jurisdiction of each local co-operative was to cover 1,500 feddans, and all the 4,000 village co-operatives integrated in the supervised credit system were to be subjected to very strict financial control. The Agricultural and Co-operative Credit Bank was to recover all debts still owed to the co-operatives by the legal means at its disposal,[19] and criminal charges were to be laid against board members who abused their prerogatives. Membership of the co-operatives was to be limited to persons effectively farming, thus eliminating absentee landlords. Boards of Directors were to be reshuffled and only people living within the boundaries of a village were to be eligible. An agronomist was to be appointed by the Ministry of Agriculture to direct and control all the agricultural activities of the lands of a given village. He was also to supervise the co-operative, to attend its sessions, and to co-ordinate its work with the short- and long-term plans for rural development. In short, he was to assume a role similar to that of the *mushrif ta'wuni* of the Agrarian Reform co-operatives. If he was successful in developing co-operative farming and marketing, crop consolidation, &c., he was to be rewarded by a bonus of more than three months' salary. This was to provide the necessary incentive and to encourage initiative. The village agronomist was, furthermore, to co-operate with the heads of the Rural Combined Centres in his neighbourhood.

---

[18] The Min. AR, and, above all, the Ministry of Supply, the Bank having in the last five years shouldered many of the latter's responsibilities.

[19] By 'legal means' was meant the legal seizure of all standing crops at the hands of officers (*sarraf*) of the state treasury.

All the local co-operatives in a *markaz* were to be grouped in a district ACS.[20] The secretaries of the boards of the different local co-operatives were to meet at the General Assembly of this organization, whose *mushrif* was to be the district agronomist. Helped by experts of the various departments of the Ministry of Agriculture, he was also to direct, co-ordinate, and control the work of the *mushrif* of the village co-operative.

At another level all the ACS of the various districts of a province were to be affiliated to a Central Co-operative Society presided over by the provincial governor (*Muhafiz*), who was to be assisted by a delegate of the General Co-operative Organization. The *mushrif* of this Central Co-operative Society was to be the provincial inspector of agriculture (*mudir al-mantiqat al-zira'i*), assisted by the provincial representatives of the principal departments of the Ministry of Agriculture. The presiding governor was to enjoy full powers not only over the administrative affairs of his province, but also over all matters relevant to its agricultural production (and to co-operation).

The twenty-one co-operatives thus set up in the twenty-one provinces were to replace the previous regional co-operative federations. They were all to be affiliated to the newly established General Co-operative Organization, which from its Cairo headquarters was to co-ordinate the co-operative movement. This organization was managed by a supreme Committee for Co-operation presided over by the Minister of Agrarian Reform and Agriculture. Its members included:

1. The directors of the Bank of Co-operative Organizations,[21] of the Agricultural Credit Bank,[22] and of the Co-operative Organization for Supplies.[23]

2. The secretaries of the Boards of the twenty-one Central Co-operative Societies.

[20] A district (*markaz*) in Egypt is an administrative sub-division of a province *muhafazat* (previously *mudiria*). It covers an area of approximately 50,000 feddans.
[21] A new establishment set up in 1961 to finance co-operative industrial undertakings. Its capital was to be paid up partly by the state and partly from the profits reaped by the fertilizer price stabilization fund, a state organization created in 1960.
[22] The former Agricultural Credit and Co-operative Bank, now transformed into a purely co-operative institution.
[23] Formerly the Royal Egyptian Agricultural Society. Under the name of the Egyptian Agricultural Organization, it had been joined to the Ministry of Agrarian Reform in 1956, but was now transformed into a co-operative society entrusted with the importation of all requirements (farm machinery, fertilizers, insecticides) of the various agricultural co-operative societies, and with the distribution of the selected seeds produced on the Ministry of Agriculture's experimental farms. The capital of this new society was to be subscribed by all the agricultural co-operative societies, including the Agrarian Reform co-operative societies.

3. Four experts in co-operative affairs, to be appointed by the head of state.

The supreme Committee for Co-operation was responsible for:

(*a*) all the different co-operative societies, including the local, associated, and central societies:

(*b*) the Agrarian Reform GCS, grouping all the Agrarian Reform co-operatives:

(*c*) the Agricultural and Co-operative Credit Bank;

(*d*) the Bank of Co-operative Organizations;

(*e*) the Fertilizer Price Stabilization Fund;

(*f*) all other co-operative institutions, including the Institute for Co-operative Studies of Ain Shams University,[24] and the various institutes training experts in the field of co-operation.

The Agricultural and Co-operative Credit Bank was to continue to finance agricultural production exclusively through co-operative channels, and was also to help in the financial control of the various co-operative organizations at all levels. A host of technicians was required for this complete reorganization. A crash programme to train some 4,000 *mushrifs*[25] for the village co-operatives was started in May 1961, and a thorough reorganization of the Ministry of Agriculture was planned. But the new co-operatives were first tried out in 100 villages of Minufiya province, where the crop-consolidation schemes were already in full swing. They were only later to be extended gradually to the provinces of Buhaira, Daqahliya, Qalyubiya, Minya, and Fayyum.

[24] Created in March 1961 in Cairo.
[25] In three centres established in Alexandria, Cairo, and Asyut.

XI

LAND RECLAMATION

It is often argued that, because people in a particular country are devoid of the initiative and drive of entrepreneurship necessary for economic growth, state action is required to make good this deficiency. It is not at all clear why governments or the public service should be able to muster the talents, which by hypothesis are lacking in the population.

P. T. BAUER & B. S. YAMEY, *The Economics of Underdeveloped Countries* (1957)

STATE–DIRECTED PROJECTS

A MORE rational distribution of manpower among the various sectors of the economy, and especially a lower concentration of manpower in the agricultural sector itself, were essential for greater human productivity in Egypt. The large population increase registered since 1947 and revealed by the 1960 population census (26 million inhabitants)[1] has made this redistribution of manpower more imperative, for with a density of 800 inhabitants per square km. in 1960, congestion in the Nile valley is becoming unbearable. Industrialization in rural areas and an intensification of agricultural production will relieve population pressure; the introduction of a new statute to regulate the employment of agricultural labour and to limit the employment of young children in rural areas could also help. But with a population growth of 2·6 per cent per annum, a no less urgent task is to expand the cultivated area by developing to the utmost water resources for irrigation and by implementing land reclamation projects rapidly, so as to prevent a greater imbalance between land and human resources. Indeed, assuming that cropping patterns remained unchanged and that cultivation techniques are not improved, it is necessary to double the arable land during the period 1952-77 in order to maintain the 1952 ratio of manpower annually available per cultivated feddan (i.e. approximately 170 man days and 130 woman days per cultivated feddan as against annual requirements of 55 man days and 60 woman days).

The plan to increase the cultivated area by 50 per cent envisaged after 1952 by the revolutionary government[2] implied, therefore, that by 1977 the already over-abundant manpower

---

[1] On the basis of this figure the population increase in 13 years is approximately 7 m. inhabitants.

[2] See Atef Sedki, 'L'Agriculture égyptienne', unpubl. thesis, Paris Univ., July 1958.

annually available per cultivated feddan would rise to 220 man days and 170 woman days. This serious situation would be further aggravated if the target was only partially fulfilled as a result of slackening of the pace of land reclamation. State intervention since 1952 in the field of land reclamation is to be understood in the light of these considerations. Land reclamation, which had made considerable progress at the beginning of the nineteenth century thanks to the efforts of private enterprise,[3] had, as has been seen, almost come to a standstill by 1952. The specialized large agricultural companies which were partly foreign owned[4] had lost confidence and only rarely embarked on new projects. Attempts by the Administration of State Domains to reclaim land had proved costly and were implemented with considerable delay.[5]

A new approach was deemed necessary to ensure that as soon as new water resources were developed, land reclamation would proceed at utmost speed. Thus changes in the pattern of tenure of waste lands were decreed, while new government agencies were established to work in the field side by side with the private sector. Foremost among these were the Liberation Province Autonomous Organization and the Egyptian–American Rural Improvement Society (EARIS).

The Liberation Province Autonomous Organization was entrusted with the reclamation of some 800,000 feddans of desert sandy soils lying to the north-west of the Delta. By 1959 25,000 feddans were under cultivation, including approximately 7,000 feddans of orchards. Some £E25–30 million were reported to have been expended on this not too successful venture, which had been undertaken on a scale unprecedented in Egyptian agricultural history.[6] High costs had been incurred due to faulty planning and

---

[3] In fifty years some 500,000 feddans were reclaimed by private companies one of which, the Buhaira Land Co., was alone responsible for bringing over 80,000 feddans under the plough.   [4] See Baer, p. 120.

[5] The Arabic for reclamation is *istislah*. But this leads to confusion when considering progress in land reclamation projects, for land reclamation in Egypt involves two distinct phases. The first, *istislah*, includes all agricultural engineering operations such as levelling, deep ploughing, and breaking up the hard pan, establishment of drainage, irrigation, and internal road networks as well as all other earth-moving operations. The second phase, *istizra'*, starts once all agricultural engineering operations are completed, and includes the periodic flooding of the land to accumulate Nile silt and to reduce salinity, as well as cultivation. The completion of both phases does not, however, mean that the land is anywhere near being fully productive, and it usually takes three or four years before the land yields sufficient returns to cover costs. It is therefore important to ascertain what is really meant when the word *istislah* is used in official statements, for it may well refer to lands which cannot be operated profitably before four or five years.

[6] In 1961 it was officially stated that the area reclaimed in the Liberation province totalled 50,000 feddans. This is plausible if area reclaimed is understood as including lands where agricultural engineering operations have been completed, but where preliminary cultivation operations are only starting.

mismanagement. An important industrial infrastructure inclusive of a large canning factory, a pasteurizing plant, &c., and a road network for an area of 100,000 feddans had been established. All this was far in excess of current needs, and until 1960 remained for all practical purposes completely idle. Large stocks of farm machinery had been accumulated, but by 1959 40 per cent of the implements were not working. The milk production of an imported herd of 500 Holstein cows was 3 tons daily, and it was trucked over 120 km. to a pasteurizing plant in Alexandria. Notwithstanding harsh criticisms voiced in the first National Assembly as early as 1957, and despite numerous setbacks and charges of corruption, some of which involved high ranking Agrarian Reform staff, appropriations of £E13·5 million were scheduled for the improvement of lands already cultivated and for livestock production in the Liberation province during 1960–5.[7]

The EARIS project was less ambitious. It aimed at reclaiming 33,000 feddans of barren land in the Buhaira and Fayyum provinces at a total cost of approximately £E10 million, part of which was contributed by the United States government. Though the project was very much more successful than the Liberation province project, its implementation was somewhat slow, and in the Buhaira province area, for example, only 5,000 feddans at Abis were in cultivation in 1960 (i.e. one-sixth of the targeted area eight years after the initiation of the scheme), though agricultural engineering operations had been completed in an additional 9,000 feddans.

By the end of 1959 the total area reclaimed in Egypt since the 1952 Revolution hardly amounted to 70,000 feddans (1·2 per cent of the cultivated area).[8] Appalled by this result, and in order to increase the rate of growth in the agricultural sector from a level of 2·8 per cent per annum,[9] President 'Abd al-Nasir decided in July 1959 to take things in hand personally. After consulting the various planning committees, he demanded that the rate of reclamation be increased to a minimum of 100,000[10] feddans per

---

[7] For further reference see Warriner, *Land Reform* and *Rep. to UN* (1961); Garzouzi; Saab, *Motorisation*; *al-Magallat al-Zira'iyat*, Mar. 1961 and NBE, *Econ. B.*, 15 Mar. 1962.

[8] 15,000 feddans by EARIS, 15,000 feddans by the Permanent Organization for Land Reclamation, 20,000 feddans by the Liberation Province Organization, and the remainder by the Administration of State Domains and private reclamation companies. In 1959–60 an additional 46,350 feddans were reported to have been reclaimed. (See *Agrarian Reform in Nine Years*; Miss Warriner, in her report to the UN gives the figure of 180,000 for the period 1952–9, but this is probably a printing error.)

[9] 'The rate of growth in all sectors was 4·65 per cent per annum during 1954–9, whereas it was less than 2·8 per cent in the agricultural sector' (official statement to the press, Cairo, July 1959).

[10] In 1962 official statements were issued implying that the target of 100,000

annum (a tenfold increase), so that the rate of growth in the agricultural sector should no longer lag behind that of overall economic growth. In fact, purely technical considerations were the main cause of the feeling of urgency which suddenly gripped the state planners. The precious Nile silt carried by the river during the flood season and utilized extensively when reclaiming sandy soils will tend to settle at the bottom of the artificial lake created by the High Dam, and will only be available in very limited quantities once the storing of flood water behind it begins. Yet frequent irrigation with the flood waters with a high silt content had proved to be the cheapest and most efficient method of increasing productivity in sandy soils, in particular in the Liberation province area; it was thus important to reclaim all sandy waste lands as fast as possible, so as to gain the maximum benefit from the silt deposits while they were still plentiful.

An ambitious programme was therefore drafted[11] involving an expenditure of approximately £E380 million. One million feddans were to be reclaimed and prepared for cultivation by 1970, on completion of the first phase of the High Dam, while 250,000 feddans of basin-irrigated land in Upper Egypt were to enjoy perennial irrigation.[12] Another 585,000 feddans were to be immediately reclaimed and prepared for cultivation by 1965. Irrigation water for this area was to be provided by slightly increasing the storage capacity of the old Aswan Dam, by economizing on current consumption of irrigation water on farms (i.e. by a rationalization of irrigation techniques, and the introduction of sprinkling), by occasionally diverting water pumped from drainage canals to irrigation canals, and by boring artesian wells wherever possible in the desert and in the Nile valley. This last alternative seemed to offer opportunities for land reclamation nearly as fruitful as those expected from the High Dam project, as studies of underground water resources indicated that artesian water was plentiful not only throughout the Nile valley up to 40–50 km. north of the town of Tanta (Gharbiya province) but also in the desert regions bordering on its north-western flank.[13]

feddans of land reclaimed was being fulfilled. But here again, to obtain a clear view of the progress it is important to differentiate between the completion of the phase of agricultural engineering operations and that of actual cultivation.

[11] See *al-Magallat al-Zira'iyat*, July 1959, pp. 11–19.

[12] In fact 750,000 feddans of basin-irrigated lands are to be perennially irrigated by the High Dam waters. But as 500,000 feddans of these lands are already receiving complementary summer irrigation by pumping from artesian wells, increased production due to double-cropping can only be expected from an area of 250,000 feddans, at present exclusively basin irrigated, during late autumn and left fallow in summer (see Marei, 'Sectors Unemployed', *al-Magallat al-Zira'iyat*, Aug. 1959).

[13] In May 1961 the first contract for boring 110 artesian wells (out of an expected total of 170) in various parts of the Delta was signed. An area of 80,000

The discovery in 1959 of important underground water reserves in the oasis regions of Kharga and Dakhla in the southern part of the Western Desert was the starting-point of another reclamation project—the New Valley project—whose execution was entrusted to a state agency—the General Desert Development Organization. The focal point of the activities of this agency, the New Valley project, aimed at reclaiming some 120,000 feddans of heavy clay and sandy soils during the period 1960–5, after an initial three-year trial in a pilot area of 20,000 feddans.[14]

To step up the pace of implementing all these projects, a shake-up of the various state agencies concerned with land reclamation was decided on; it was also recognized that state efforts alone would not be sufficient, and that the help of foreign and local companies specializing in large-scale land reclamation would be necessary. An Egyptian company for large-scale land reclamation was also to be set up, its capital being entirely provided by the state Economic Organization, which managed nationalized enterprises. Together with the speeding up of land reclamation, it was decreed that the whole of the area to be reclaimed was to be distributed exclusively to landless farmers in holdings of 5–10 feddans. The latter were to be allowed to occupy the holdings as soon as the agricultural engineering operations in a given area were completed; all preliminary cultivation operations were therefore from the start to be accomplished exclusively by the new beneficiaries and members of their family, who were to be grouped in co-operatives supervising the strict application of consolidated crop rotations according to customary Agrarian Reform procedure.

Following these principles, a contract was signed early in 1960 with an Italian firm, Italconsult, which undertook to reclaim 140,000 feddans in the Delta (Qusaibi, al-Hagar areas), in the Liberation province, and in Upper Egypt at a total cost of £E28 million. According to the terms of this agreement, the Italian firm was to provide mechanical equipment to carry out the agricultural engineering operations (entrusted to it) and to build 1 housing unit per 10 feddans; it was further specified that payment would be partly in local currency and partly in foreign exchange.

feddans was to be irrigated with the water pumped from these wells. The utilization of underground water resources in the Nile valley itself was in fact a long overdue measure. It aimed at economizing irrigation water from the Nile, so as to reserve as much as possible of it for saline areas under reclamation and for the cultivated regions of the Northern Delta where artesian water was brackish. Of course, farm operators irrigating with water pumped from artesian wells incur higher costs than those incurred in areas irrigated by gravity flow. But this additional expense may well turn out to be one of the most potent inducements to a rationalization of the present primitive irrigation techniques, which could save considerable quantities of water for additional land reclamation.

[14] See Gen. Organization for Desert Rehabilitation, *UAR Development and Land Reclamation* (1961).

The firm also undertook to hire local labour and set up schools to train tractor drivers and other workers handling mechanical equipment. The contract was further conditional on the establishment of experimental stations in the reclaimed area. On completion of the engineering operations, the firm was to transfer the area to the Ministry of Agrarian Reform, which was then to allot the holdings to smallholders for further reclamation and cultivation.

Work on this scheme began in the spring of 1960, and proceeded satisfactorily during the following year. Some delay in execution was already perceptible, mainly because of the administrative difficulties in obtaining rapid clearance through Egyptian customs of imported equipment, in spite of the fact that such equipment was exempted from tariffs under the terms of the agreement.

The agricultural economic aspects of this project were left to the supervising Agrarian Reform authorities. In principle, the consolidated crop rotation system was to be applied, a high proportion of the reclaimed lands being devoted during the initial stages to forage crops to improve soil productivity. The size of the holdings to be distributed had originally been fixed at 10 feddans, but in 1961 it was fixed at 5 feddans to satisfy a larger number of landless peasants. Changes in irrigation techniques were not envisaged, and the Italian firm was merely instructed to establish the main irrigation, drainage, and internal road networks as customary in similar Egyptian projects.

The traditional irrigation technique of flooding minute basins subdividing a plot of 1 feddan or less was therefore to remain standard practice, although it precluded all forms of mechanization of farm operations. While nothing was disclosed concerning the integration of the cropping system with industrial development in the area, a very determined effort was made to solve rural housing problems. The Italian firm was asked to erect the new houses in small villages dispersed among the fields but all situated within a radius of 2–3 km. of a big central village in which community centres (including a mosque, school, dispensary, Agrarian Reform offices, premises for a co-operative, and warehouses) were to be established. The concrete houses were not, however, to have running water facilities, and were not directly connected with the holdings of their owners.

A contract similar to that entered upon with Italconsult was signed in May 1961 with one of the firms owned by the state Economic Organization. This contract covers the reclamation of 40,000 feddans in the southern section of Liberation province, at a cost of £E240 per feddan, inclusive of housing, community services, &c.

PRIVATE ENTERPRISE AND RECLAMATION

Official statements issued at different times since September 1952 indicated that a substantial increase of the cultivable area could only be achieved rapidly and at reasonable costs by a full mobilization of all available energies in both the private and public sectors. But the rather general declaration of intentions of the public authorities[15] was never substantiated by any measures likely to induce private enterprise (private individuals or specialized companies) to shoulder its responsibilities and participate in the land reclamation drive. Indeed, the reluctance of private enterprise in the last two decades was further reinforced by the emergence since 1952 of new obstacles. Some of these were economic, such as the high prices demanded by the state for its waste lands, the fall in cotton prices, and reductions in land values resulting from the massive sales of landowners threatened by expropriation and from the sales of timid landowners expecting further legislative action. Some were technical, such as the high prices demanded for new earth-moving equipment[16] and the difficulty in obtaining spare parts. And some were institutional, such as the cloud of uncertainty which shrouded tenure conditions in wasteland areas since the promulgation of the Agrarian Reform Law.

Article 2 of the 1952 law listed certain exemptions to the provisions limiting ownership, some of which concerned waste land. Companies and societies could own more than 200 feddans of land under reclamation for purposes of sale; private individuals could own more than 200 feddans of fallow or desert land for improvement. These exemptions were only valid for twenty-five years from the day of acquisition, without prejudice to the disposal of the land before the termination of that period. Nevertheless private enterprise was unwilling to start or pursue land reclamation projects during 1952–7. This was partly the result of uncertainty about the application of the exemptions, as companies and societies were more or less left in the dark as to the criteria differentiating between land under reclamation and land under cultivation. Private individuals also hesitated to involve themselves in reclamation projects, as the twenty-five-year limit was considered insufficient. Their fears were born out by the fact that on numerous occasions land sold by the state for reclamation

[15] Some of these are included in the explanatory note of Law no. 84 of 1957, while others were made in official Agrarian Reform publications as late as 1959, and even in the press (see statement of S. Marei in *al-Ahram*, 22 May 1961).

[16] Prices of imported tractors rose considerably between 1946 and 1959. An international track tractor Model T.D. 18 valued at approx. £E2,500–3,000 in 1947 was selling at £E8,000 in 1959. The steepest rise in prices occurred between 1956 and 1959, e.g. a John Deere 55 h.p. priced at £E1,433 in 1955 was on sale at £E2,700 in 1959 (see Saab, *Motorisation*, pp. 277–82).

before 1952 had only been provided ten or fifteen years later with the necessary irrigation, drainage, and road networks. With similar shortcomings, the ten or fifteen years left to run could well be insufficient to cover reclamation costs. It might also be difficult to find prospective buyers if general economic conditions were unfavourable.

The very considerable capital (financial, human, and material) at the disposal of the large specialized reclamation companies thus remained, practically speaking, unemployed from 1952 to 1957.[17] Faced with this situation, the government set up in 1954[18] the Permanent Organization for Land Reclamation, a state agency empowered to survey and study the problems of waste land, to draft a general policy for reclamation and land settlement, and to undertake land reclamation, either itself or through the services of other organizations. The following new laws were passed early in 1957.[19]

1. Companies and societies were allowed to own more than 200 feddans of land under reclamation for purposes of sale subject to certain regulations. If the 'irrigation opening'[20] of such land was first made 25 or more years before, such land could be disposed of within 10 years from 1957. The land to be sold to a single individual could not exceed 200 feddans and the latter's total ownership thereafter should not exceed 200 feddans.

If the irrigation opening was first made less than 25 years previously, land above the 200-feddan ceiling could be sold within 10 years from 1957 or 25 years after the irrigation opening was made, whichever period was longest. Again the land to be disposed of to one individual might not exceed 200 feddans, and total ownership thereafter should not exceed 200 feddans. One-quarter of the area should be set aside for sale to small farmers (working in agriculture) owning not more than 10 feddans. The area of this land to be disposed of to a single individual was not to be under 2 or over 5 feddans. The Permanent Organization for Land Reclamation[21] was entrusted with the supervision of these sales, with fixing the sale price, the method of payment by instalments, the choice of beneficiaries according to standard Agrarian Reform practices, and the setting up of co-operatives similar to those already under Agrarian Reform auspices.

---

[17] The shares of these companies were in consequence depressed, with the exception of a rally in 1956, following an upward surge of cotton prices (see NBE, *Econ. B.*, x/2, 1957).

[18] Law no. 169 of 1954 amended by Law no. 33 of 1956.

[19] Law nos. 84 and 148 of 1957.

[20] 'Irrigation opening' is the official permission of the Min. of Public Works for farmers to draw water from irrigation canals or to bore artesian wells.

[21] A subsidiary department of the Min. AR since 1956.

2. (Industrial) agricultural companies processing the crops planted on their land were exempted from the 200-feddan limit, regardless of the date of their establishment.

3. Private individuals were allowed to own over 200 feddans of fallow or desert land for improvement for 25 years from the date of acquiring permission for their irrigation by Nile water or by artesian wells. At the end of this period the land, if not already sold, was to be requisitioned in compliance with the Agrarian Reform Law. However, in 1958 this exemption was withdrawn,[22] and private individuals were thereafter liable to the expropriation of waste land in excess of 200 feddans which they possessed in September 1952. Areas of waste land already disposed of by contracts with fixed dates were deductible from this amount.

The successive changes in the pattern of agrarian tenure in waste land hardly encouraged private enterprise, and by 1959 the time was ripe for some new initiative that would have added to the state-directed efforts the potential energy of private enterprise in an all-out drive to fulfil the annual target of 100,000 feddans of reclaimed land.

[22] Law no. 148 of 1958.

PART 3

AGRARIAN POLICIES AND THE SECOND AGRARIAN REFORM

XII

AGRICULTURAL AND AGRARIAN
POLICIES, 1952–61

*The return on industrial investment is not necessarily higher than
on agricultural investment.*
R. MOSSE, *Bull. de la Société française d'économie rurale*, Jan. 1957.
*Surplus workers cannot be absorbed in non-farm employment in the
early stages of industrialization.*
SAYED MAREI, *Principles and Scope of Agrarian Reform* (1965)

OBJECTIVES AND IMPLEMENTATION OF POLICY

THE new government at first attempted to rely as much as possible
on agricultural development to foster Egyptian economic growth
in the short run,[1] for it recognized that though industry was pro-
gressing rapidly it could not alone provide employment for the
expanding population.[2] The agricultural policy which it adopted
aimed at securing as fast as possible a horizontal expansion of
production through an enlargement of the cultivated area, and a
vertical expansion through an intensification of agricultural production. The first of these objectives was at first pursued at a
snail's pace and, as has been seen, it was not until 1959 that a
determined effort was really made. The second objective, though
less spectacular, was more energetically sought for. To counter
the stagnation and decline in crop yields registered since 1939, the
strict enforcement of the traditional triennial crop rotation (in
place of the biennial rotation which had become popular with
rising cotton prices during 1947–52),[3] was put into practice experimentally with varying degrees of success from 1952–3 onwards,
and a great effort was made to facilitate the utilization of the
selected seeds[4] and chemical fertilizers[5] indispensable to higher

[1] A. R. Sidqi, *Siyasat misr al-zira'iyat* (Cairo, Govt. Press, 1954).
[2] The very ambitious second five-year plan elaborated in 1959 targeted for an
increase in the gross value of industrial production from £E1,094 m. to £E1,814
m. in 1965. Despite this, only 300,000 new jobs for industrial workers were to be
created (see NBE, *Econ. B.*, xiii/2, 1960).
[3] See above, pp. 32-34.
[4] Quantities of selected seeds made available to farm operators in 1952 and in
1960 (in ardebs):

	Cotton	Wheat	Maize
1952	89,000	67,000	22
1960	900,000	288,000	23,340

[5] Over 800,000 tons of nitrogen fertilizer were consumed in 1960, of which
more than 600,000 tons were sold on credit or against cash payment by the

levels of production. By 1960 some 50 per cent of farmers were using selected strains of seeds for the three main crops, cotton, wheat, and rice. The planting of hybrid maize was successfully developed and the production of hybrid maize seeds was finally subsidized. At the same time the consumption of fertilizers, which was already widespread in 1952, increased by 33 per cent to well over a million tons in 1960, thus reducing the prevailing imbalance in essential soil nutrients.[6] The large-scale use of insecticides in cotton cultivation was, moreover, encouraged as from 1955; it yielded positive results and the bumper cotton crops harvested in 1959 and 1960 can probably be attributed to the growing efficiency of pest control, which unfortunately was not extended to other crops.[7] Poor drainage, a big obstacle to high yields in numerous regions, was also attended to, and a ten-year plan for the extension of an underground tile drainage system throughout Central and Northern Egypt was scheduled for execution from 1960 at an estimated cost of £E65 million.[8] A diversification of agricultural production was attempted and measures were taken to stimulate the cultivation and export of rice, vegetables, fruit, and flower crops; the area planted in vegetables thus rose to 400,000 feddans in 1960 (i.e. approx. 4 per cent of the cropped area, compared with 2·75 per cent in 1952), while the area planted in fruit rose to 130,000 feddans in 1960 (i.e. 1·3 per cent of the cropped area compared with 1 per cent in 1952).[9]

Agricultural Credit Bank (see Agric. Credit Bank, *Ann. Reports of Board of Directors* (Cairo, Imprimerie Misr, 1961)).

[6] It has been mentioned that Egyptian agriculture was suffering in 1952 from insufficient use of organic fertilizer. This problem, which can only be solved by an increase in the cattle population and by a more rational use of farm manure (part of which is presently consumed as fuel), will intensify during the next decade, not only in areas about to be reclaimed (see above, Ch. XI) but also in cultivated areas, because of the inevitable reduction in Nile silt deposits consequent on the High Dam. (See A. H. Mustafa, 'Fertilization and Agricultural Production in Egypt', *al-Magallat al-Zira'iyat*, no. 9, 1959; NBE, *Econ. B.*, xiv/4, 1961, p. 388.)

[7] See A. Bishara, 'Recent Developments in the Control of the Principal Parasites of Egyptian Cotton', *Egyptian Cotton Gazette*, 15–23 Sept. 1957, p. 32. Heavy attacks of cotton-leaf worm partially destroyed the 1960/1 cotton crop, the loss being equivalent to 33 per cent of the volume of the 1959 crop. These attacks have been attributed to a newly acquired immunity to pesticides commonly used, to faulty use of the pesticides, to the poor quality of some of these, and also to the unfortunate timing of the promulgation of new expropriation laws in July 1961 (see below, Ch. XIII).

[8] The effects of this scheme on crop yields may be short-lived, without higher standards of maintenance and upkeep of the main government-owned drains, to which underground drains will be connected. Experiments on underground drainage in the Tala' district, Minufiya province, conducted during the last fifteen years would have been very much more successful but for the lack of maintenance of the main drainage channels to which the underground drainage networks were connected (see Saab, *Motorisation*, pp. 233–4 and NBE, *Econ. B.*, 1959–61).

[9] The relative unimportance of fruit and vegetable production in Egypt's

Livestock and poultry production also engaged the attention of the agricultural policy makers, and a drive to extend free veterinary care throughout Egypt was initiated simultaneously with the distribution of pedigree stock and poultry. By 1961 approximately 100 veterinary centres were in operation in the provinces of Kafr al-Shaikh, Minufiya, Qalyubiya, Minya, and Fayyum; each was planned to provide free veterinary care for some 20,000 animals, so that an appreciable percentage of Egypt's 6 million odd animals was to benefit from this scheme, which aimed at reducing the annual loss of £E35 million through inadequate prophylaxy.[10] The mechanization of specific agricultural operations on small farms[11] in order to improve tillage techniques so as to reduce production costs and to eliminate draught cattle was also encouraged by providing credit facilities to co-operative organizations for the purchase of farm machinery. Attempts to consolidate voluntarily smallholdings were also carried out, and an agricultural credit policy designed to satisfy the short- and medium-term capital requirements of farmers, to help them to overcome marketing difficulties and to promote the industrial processing of crops, was put in motion.

The two main objectives of agricultural policy, the horizontal and the vertical expansion of Egyptian agriculture, were pursued throughout the seven years 1952–9 within a general framework of agrarian tenure spelled out in detail in 1952 and amended at regular intervals, as has been described. This framework had aimed at satisfying ideals of equity and social justice and at inducing higher rates of capital formation and investment both in agriculture and in other sectors. But when a general appraisal of the economy was made in 1959, the fruits of the agricultural and agrarian policies followed proved to be disappointing.

In seven years, the general index of agricultural production, which had stood at 110 in 1952, had hardly risen to 136.[12] In 1959 average crop yields were mediocre when compared with those obtained on well-managed Egyptian farms; for some crops they were even lower than those of an extensive type of agriculture, such as that of the United States.

rural economy as late as 1960 stands out in vivid contrast with the situation in the relatively prosperous Lebanese rural economy. In the latter, more than 14 per cent of the cultivated area (approx. 47,000 ha. out of a total of 324,000 ha.) was devoted to four main fruit crops (apples, bananas, vine, figs). (See Gauthier & Baz; Saab, *Motorisation*, pp. 233–4; and NBE, *Econ. B.*, xii–xiv/1–4, 1959–61.)

[10] Nearly 50 per cent of the gross annual income from livestock production (inclusive of the value of draught power). (See Saab, *Motorisation*, p. 362.)
[11] Mechanization has to be understood here in its restricted sense, i.e. as the replacement of animal draught power with tractors and irrigation pumps.
[12] See Issawi, *Egypt in Revolution*, p. 113.

TABLE 8

Crop Yields: Egypt compared with World and U.S.A. (kg.)

Crop	World Av. yields per ha.	Egypt Av. yields per ha.	% of av. world yields	U.S.A. Av. yields per ha.	% of av. world yields
Wheat	1,280	2,260	184	1,840	144
Rice	2,170	4,960	182·5	3,510	161·7
Maize	2,060	2,140	104	3,250	158
Potatoes	12,200	16,300	134	20,300	166
Onions	11,800	8,000	68	25,000	212
Tomatoes	16,900	14,400	85	20,600	122
Cotton (ginned)	300	560	187	520	140

Source: Marei, *al-Magallat al-Zira'iyat*, Dec. 1960, p. 14. See also M. A. Kilani, ibid. Apr. 1959, p. 8.

Though substantial increases in yields were recorded for cotton, wheat, and rice,[13] the yields of other crops, such as clover, maize,[14] vegetables,[15] and fruit were far from satisfactory. In addition, the ideals of social justice and equity were only partially fulfilled; a large number of landless peasants, still as destitute as ever, roamed the countryside despite the implementation of the land-distribution programme, while the exactions and rack-renting of landowners continued. Savings in the agricultural sector had hardly increased and investment—other than by the state—whether in the form of improved buildings, additional farm machinery, or the planting of new orchards, had not accelerated. Capital released by the Agrarian Reform and in the hands of the ex-landowners, and that released through sales of panicky landowners, had only slowly trickled into industry or the services sector; most of it had either been hoarded or had remained idle in the banks in the form of short-notice deposits,[16] or it had been invested abroad or diverted to the construction of luxury buildings in the two urban centres of Cairo and Alexandria, in spite of legislation specifically limiting this type of real estate investment.[17]

No wonder, therefore, that growth of gross and net agricultural income was small during 1952–9; official statements in 1959 dis-

[13] The percentage increases of these crops relative to 1935–9 was 10, 18, and 40 per cent respectively; nearly all these increases were recorded since 1952.

[14] Av. yield in 1935–9, 7·45 ardebs; in 1958–9, 5·76 ardebs. In 1959 large quantities (107,000 tons) of maize had to be imported to make up for the deficiency in local supply; this was equivalent to 7 per cent of local production.

[15] Av. annual yields of tomato fields (1,200 feddans = approx. production 10,000 tons) delivered to the Kaha canning factory, Qalyubiya province (and at that time the most successful of Egypt) fluctuated throughout 1952–9 around 8–9 tons per feddan. But in 1959 in the extremely well-managed 500-feddan farm of Taftish al-Lawandi, Aga dist., Daqahliya, the average yields of an 80-feddan late summer (*nili*) crop of tomatoes, delivered to the Kaha factory (and ascertained by the author), was over 17 tons per feddan.

[16] A 70 per cent increase in deposits between 1954 and 1961 was recorded, according to Issawi, *Egypt in Revolution*, p. 251.

[17] Law no. 344 issued in 1956.

closing that the rate of growth in the agricultural sector during that period had only been 2·8 per cent per annum (compared with 4·65 per cent in all sectors during the same period) expressed disappointment. But who was to blame? Was agricultural policy wrong, or were those supposed to implement this policy both in the public and in the private sectors to blame? Or was the framework of agrarian tenure unsatisfactory? And what was to be the next step?

AGRICULTURAL AND AGRARIAN POLICY AT THE CROSS-ROADS

The second five-year plan was drawn up in 1959, and it allocated £E392 million for agricultural development (including irrigation, drainage, and the first stage of the High Dam). It was supposed to raise gross agricultural income from its 1959 level

TABLE 9

Gross and Net Agricultural Income

(£E million)

Farm products	1951/2	1952/3	1953/4	1954/5	1955/6	1956/7	1957/8	1958/9
Field crops	325·0	296·0	286·1	311·0	303·0	360·6	363·3	345·5
Vegetables	11·0	14·0	13·4	14·1	15·8	17·8	23·7	28·5
Fruit	11·0	11·0	11·7	13·8	16·0	17·4	24·4	26·1
Aromatic seeds	—	—	0·4	0·6	0·7	0·7	0·6	—
Total	247·0	321·0	311·5	339·5	335·5	396·5	412·0	400·1
Livestock								
Carcases	37·0	30·0	30·7	36·8	44·8	43·7	43·4	46·4
Dairy products	—	—	27·9	31·2	33·5	33·5	33·2	33·1
Raw wool	—	—	0·3	0·3	0·5	0·5	0·4	0·4
Total	62·0	56·0	58·9	68·3	78·8	77·7	77·0	80·1
Poultry &c.								
Poultry	—	—	10·9	12·1	13·8	14·8	16·6	16·8
Honey & Wax	—	—	0·3	0·3	0·3	0·3	0·4	0·4
Total	12·0	10·0	11·2	12·4	14·1	15·1	17·0	17·2
Gross Income	421·0	387·0	381·7	420·2	428·3	489·3	506·0	497·4
Production costs*	115·6	117·4	119·6	119·4	116·5	114·4	125·4	133·0
Net Income	306·0	270·0	262·1	300·8	311·8	374·9	380·6	364·4

* Depreciation cost of agricultural machinery and buildings not included except for 1958/9 (£E4·7 m.).

Sources: 1951/2 & 1952/3: *Monthly B. Agric. Statist.* (Cairo), Jan. 1956; 1953/9: NBE, *Econ. B.*, xiv/1 & xv/2.

of approximately £E500 million to £E755 million in 1964–5; net agricultural income, which was estimated at £E364 million in 1959, was scheduled to rise to £E512 million.[18] Assuming an

[18] 'The overall target is to raise national income from £E1,282 million in 1959/60 to £E1,795 million in 1964/5, an increase of £E513 million or 40 per cent, of

egalitarian distribution of income from agriculture, and bearing in mind the expected population increase, the net annual income from this source would therefore not be higher than £E30 per rural inhabitant in 1965, despite a big increase in net national income from agriculture.

The second five-year plan did not carry any implications of a major shift in agricultural and agrarian policy. Official publications explained that all efforts in the future were to be concentrated on implementing the plan, and in particular on the expansion of the cultivated area and the intensification and diversification of agricultural production.[19] The disparity between land and human resources was to be bridged by the redistribution of large tracts of reclaimed land, and by industrialization and the growth in the services sector. As for suggestions that a different pattern of agrarian tenure might favour higher rates of growth while satisfying more largely the ideals of equity and social justice so loudly proclaimed, they were brushed aside. Reductions of the ceilings on landownership and farm operation, which had often been rumoured since 1952, were, moreover, considered unrealistic. It was argued that since 1952 all the large estates had been broken up, and that to limit ownership to less than 200 feddans would compel the Ministry of Agrarian Reform to expropriate relatively small scattered areas. This would prevent the establishment of a co-operative organization similar to that applied successfully in the expropriated large estates managed by the Agrarian Reform authorities and the introduction of a consolidated crop rotation. The fragmentation which would result from a new limit on land would harm land productivity and imperil the economic stability of the redistributed family holdings. Grave difficulties had already been encountered since 1952 whenever isolated smallholdings had been seized. It was officially recognized that the sale of these smallholdings to small independent farm operators, in 2- or 3-feddan lots (or less) which had taken place was very far from an ideal solution. It precluded the introduction of consolidated crop rotation and it made it extremely difficult for the Agrarian Reform co-operatives to extend to future beneficiaries the advantages derived from the supervision, large-scale operation, and credit facilities which their colleagues enjoyed in the large expropriated estates.

which £E112 from agriculture, £E267 from electricity and industry, and the rest from other sectors. The moderate contribution of the agricultural sector is attributed to the fact that the full results of the High Dam project and the conversion of basin lands into perennial irrigation will not be obtained during the second five year plan' (NBE, *Econ. B.*, xiii/2, 1960).

[19] Marei, in *al-Magallat al-Zira'iyat*, Aug. 1959; also *Agrarian Reform in Seven Years*.

THE WRITING ON THE WALL

The arguments expressed in official quarters in 1959 regarding eventual changes in the agrarian pattern, though plausible, were not convincing. The pressure of population on land had not diminished since 1952, and was, moreover, likely to persist even after the completion of the High Dam and the increase in the cultivated area. The union with Syria established in 1958 offered nothing but distant prospects for a massive emigration of Egyptian peasants that would have brought relief to the congested Nile valley. Attempts to intensify and diversify Egyptian agricultural production were only slowly yielding results. A new initiative in the agricultural sector was needed, and it was therefore hard to believe that it would not affect existing agrarian structures in some way or other. The chances that this initiative would involve a further limitation of landownership and farm operation were rapidly increasing, if only for political reasons. Indeed, early in 1961 the frantic efforts to extend government-controlled co-operatives to all villages, coupled with the attempt to spread throughout the countryside the crop-consolidation measures successfully experimented in Nawag, appeared to be omens of an impending and decisive change in agrarian policy.

For if the village co-operatives could be made to operate smoothly and efficiently under the guidance of state-appointed agriculturalists, as was the case in many Agrarian Reform regions, and if crop consolidation was adopted in every village, the expropriation of holdings as a result of new reductions in the ceilings on ownership and farm operation would be greatly facilitated, even if the expropriated holdings (ranging in size between the new and the old ceilings) were not large, and even if they were scattered. The operation of these holdings after their redistribution in 2–5-feddan units, as customary under Agrarian Reform procedures since 1952, would also be fairly simple, since the future beneficiaries would automatically be integrated in co-operatives already in existence at the village level and applying consolidated crop rotations. In short, all the arguments against a lowering of the ceilings on ownership and farm operation would fade out if the establishment of co-operatives and the adoption of crop consolidation was successful throughout rural Egypt.

The question arises whether further reductions in the ceiling on ownership and farm operation, which now seemed imminent, were inevitable. The answer to this question is definitely no, for as late as 1961 the gravity of Egyptian rural problems could have been alleviated by other less spectacular but no less effective measures. Until then the Egyptian rural economy offered numerous opportunities for constructive development within the framework of an agrarian tenure the broad lines of which had been defined in 1952 and during the following years. A genuine and comprehensive stabilization of land tenure for tenants and sharecroppers that would have extended agricultural leases from three to nine years, coupled with an automatic right for them to renew these leases at their expiration, would have greatly enhanced the value of tenancy titles, thus narrowing the gap between them and the peasants who had benefited from land-distribution measures in Agrarian Reform or land-reclamation areas. Landlords would have been allowed to retrieve their holdings, at the expiration of the nine-year leases, but only exceptionally if they decided to revert to owner-operation, and they would have been subject to penal and financial sanctions if they evicted their tenants under false pretence. The provision of the 1952 Agrarian Reform Law requiring written contracts between the parties involved should have been enforced, and these contracts registered at the regional or district headquarters of the Agrarian Reform Ministry. To facilitate this procedure, the co-operatives could have taken over the responsibility of dealing with the landlords for drafting agricultural leases as well as for fulfilling the obligations imposed in these leases. The co-operatives could also have been allowed to rent holdings from their owners (whether big or small) and then share them out to their members, while applying a consolidated crop rotation. In the event of the transfer of ownership by sale, the tenant or sharecropper could have been entitled to exercise a right of pre-emption as well as claiming compensation for any improvements he may have made, especially if these were carried out after consultation with district productivity committees specifically appointed for this purpose. The measures affording the necessary stability to tenants and sharecroppers could have been completed by other measures to peg effectively farm rentals at levels which would take into account the decrease in prices of the all-important cotton crop since the promulgation of the 1952 law. Indeed, even on the assumption that the law's provisions with regard to the level of rentals were respected by the parties concerned, rentals remained in 1959 extremely high compared with farm income, and in numerous cases they were equal to over half the gross receipts of farms. The percentage of gross agricultural income cashed in 1958 by absentee landlords throughout Egypt was therefore large; if calculated on the basis of the rates prescribed by the Agrarian Reform Law, it was still over 10 per cent (compared with 20·7 per cent in 1952); but if calculated on the basis of the rentals effectively paid by tenants, it was larger still. A 50 per cent reduction of agricultural rents below the level prescribed by the 1952 law would still have provided (in 1959) more than 3 per cent on capital invested in the purchase of agricultural land—a higher yield than that obtained by absentee landowners in many north European countries.

A stable system of tenure and cheap agricultural rents would in 1959 have left farm operators renting lands from large and small absentee landlords with substantial savings for investment in the working capital they were so short of. It would also have relieved them from the nefarious habit of tying down their savings in the acquisition of land. Landlords with available capital could, exceptionally, have been permitted to increase their rentals above legal rates if they would invest it to improve agricultural production or housing conditions on their tenanted land. This increase, which could have been equal to 7–8 per cent of the sums invested on a long-term basis (i.e. the normal rate of interest of the Crédit Foncier d'Égypte for long-term loans), could have become effective after being sanctioned by district agricultural productivity committees, to which reference has already been made, and whose responsibility, among other things, would have been to ensure that the investments envisaged fitted in with district development plans.

Obviously proposals in favour of drastic improvements of the status of tenancy and sharecropping would have involved the streamlining of the administrative machinery entrusted since 1952 with the settlement of the disputes arising between tenants and sharecroppers and their landlords, as well as the setting up of consultative committees for agricultural leases and land productivity committees. They would also have involved a considerable effort by the state propaganda departments[20] to make tenants, sharecroppers, and landlords fully aware of their rights and obligations, and a vocational training programme to provide farm operators with the necessary know-how for them usefully to channel the savings derived from rent reductions to investment rather than to the traditional forms of consumption. No doubt the impact of improvements in the status of tenancy and sharecropping might have been partially impeded by a number of obstacles such as the ignorance and weaker economic and social position of the sharecroppers and tenants, the cumbersome nature of the machinery set up for the settlement of disputes, and, above all, the constant population pressure, inevitably reflected in rentals and tenure conditions. But despite these shortcomings, until as late as 1961 the remodelling of land tenure on the above pattern seemed

[20] Most of the efforts of the highly efficient state propaganda departments had until 1961 been directed towards such distant and debatable causes as the Congo.

preferable. It offered one big advantage, that of bringing relief to the pitiful lot of the landless masses more rapidly, and to very much larger numbers than redistribution measures resulting from a reduction in the ceilings on ownership and farm operation. It also provided a solution to that other plague of the Egyptian rural world, the small absentee landlord so prone to rack-rent, which a lowering of the ceiling on ownership would not affect. Moreover, some of the difficulties that would be encountered in enforcing this new pattern of tenure successfully were in any case being encountered in the land distribution areas, where sub-letting by beneficiaries to landless peasants at high rentals was already taking place, and where a cumbersome administrative machinery was functioning often at great human and financial cost.

At the same time as the status of tenancy and sharecropping might have been set on a permanent and sound basis, thus restoring to those constructive landowners and farmers the confidence in the future without which no economic progress is possible, a few changes in agrarian tenure as applied to waste land could have been made.[21] Coupled with a liberal agricultural credit policy and preferential fiscal treatment, they might have whetted the appetite of private enterprise without necessarily playing havoc with the basic principles of the 1952 Agrarian Reform legislation. Reclamation areas could have been exempted from a strict application of tenancy and share-cropping regulations (such as those suggested by the author) for twenty-five years from the day irrigation rights were conceded. Also land-reclamation companies or individuals could have been allowed to retain land above the 200-feddan limit, equivalent to one-third or a quarter of the reclaimed area, forty years from the day irrigation rights were conceded. A generous and flexible policy of agricultural credit for reclamation areas could have been drafted by the Agricultural Credit and Co-operative Bank, whose loans under this heading had remained (as already mentioned) ridiculously small until 1960. Companies and individuals venturing into the field of land reclamation could have been exempted from the payment of the basic land tax ten years from the day irrigation rights were granted, If they were willing to process the crops grown on their land they could have been exempted from the payment of the tax on industrial and commercial profits for fifteen years. Such companies or individuals could have been given top priority at the time of allocation of long-term loans by the state Industrial Bank. Similar treatment could have been extended to actual industrial and

---

[21] These suggestions were first published by the author in 1959 in 'Rationalization of Agriculture and Land Tenure Problems in Egypt', *ME Econ. Papers*, *1960*.

commercial concerns which settled in the reclamation areas. In compensation for these advantages and fiscal inducements, the state could have demanded from companies and individuals a minimum of social and political responsibility. Housing and health conditions in the reclamation areas could have been made subject to strict state control. Under no circumstances should the state have allowed the new settlers of the reclaimed areas to sink into the misery and degradation still characteristic of Egyptian villages as late as 1960. The luxury in which the top officials of the land-reclamation companies lived or even the comfort enjoyed by members of the Agrarian Reform staff in land-distribution areas were indeed shocking in places where thousands of peasants lived in mud and filth.

The expansion of the co-operative sector and a decided and well-planned effort to provide members of the newly created co-operatives with the necessary vocational training and leadership, side by side with a gradual lifting of administrative control and an extension of the crop-consolidation experiments, would also have yielded very positive and rapid results. The active partici-pation of the private sector in agricultural development plans could also have been obtained, at little cost, by granting fiscal advan-tages to certain activities of prime importance such as livestock and fruit production, the operation of farm machinery by con-tractors, repair workshops for agricultural equipment, &c. This active participation would have greatly increased the chances of success of a rapid diversification of agricultural production, which would have taken full advantage of the temperate climate during the fair winter months,[22] while establishing Egypt as one of the principal exporters of vegetables, fruit, flower, and livestock products in the Mediterranean. Friendly commercial relations and technical co-operation with the developed nations would have ensued an outlet for production and helped diversification, whilst the lifting of the stranglehold of administrative routine on exports of fresh products would also have been useful.[23]

Of course, a slowing down of the rate of population growth would have also been imperative. The prohibition of child labour in agriculture could have been one of the most effective ways of achieving this without running the risk of a direct attack on religious taboos by birth-control measures. It would have

[22] Egypt's climatic advantages have become the more valuable with the cumulative rise in the demands for vegetable, fruit, flower, and livestock products in Western Europe, the Arabian Peninsula, and the Persian Gulf Shaikhdoms. These last are being supplied by Europe, the Lebanon, and even Kenya (see further J. Besançon, *L'Homme et le Nil* (Paris, 1957), p. 307).

[23] Incredible as it may seem, no less than twenty different formalities were required in 1960 to export a consignment of fresh tomatoes.

prevented fathers from considering their offspring as an economic asset obtainable at no extra cost and providing them with cheap labour for the cultivation of their holdings. Gradually enforced in rural areas where adequate school facilities had been established, it would have reduced the total manpower available for farm work by several million child units who are at present depressing agricultural wages and increasing the intensity of chronic rural unemployment.

Finally, a concentration of all human resources of the various state agencies on the immense tasks of education, agricultural extension, vocational training, crop consolidation, co-operative organization, agricultural credit, improvement of rural housing, &c., rather than their involvement in new land-distribution schemes, would have provided the necessary administrative support for all these changes. But a liberal approach to rural Egypt's ailments which gave due consideration to technical necessities and which respected the framework of agrarian tenure broadly defined in 1952 was unlikely to appeal to Egypt's rulers, naturally inclined to spectacular political initiatives. Their apparent hesitation and reluctance to face agrarian issues squarely, in particular with regard to the status of tenancy and sharecropping, the constant population pressure, the increasing attraction inside Egypt of socialist agrarian policies such as the Chinese[24] had all combined during the last nine years to narrow considerably their margin of choice. By the late spring of 1961 their decision was finally made, and the plunge taken with the course firmly set towards complete state socialism in all sectors of the economy.

[24] The force of attraction of Chinese agrarian policies was observed by the author in numerous conversations held during 1959–60 with young Agrarian Reform experts and with persons connected with Egyptian university circles. The possilility of Egypt eventually being led to follow the Chinese way, or what has rightly been termed 'the economics of neo-barbarism', has been alluded to by one of the leading experts on Middle East affairs, Prof. C. Issawi of Columbia University (see 'Egypt since 1800: a Study in Lopsided Development', *J. Econ. Hist.* (New York), 1961, p. 23).

XIII

THE SECOND AGRARIAN REFORM

*The point is that in all the above proposals, ceilings are visualized
as a prelude to joint farming. Now if the ultimate aim is merely
to place the agricultural labourers back into large scale farming
under a managerial bureaucracy, the slogan 'land to the tiller'
appears to be a deception. For their giving land to the tiller in the
immediate future is meant only as a means, so to speak, of later giving
the land as well as the tiller over to a manager. What is intended
for him is just a change from landlessness under a large owner cultivator, to landlessness under a manager.*

R. KRISHNA, in *Economic Development and Cultural Change,*
April 1959

DRAMATIC changes in economic and fiscal policy were announced
on 21 July 1961, the ninth anniversary of the Revolution. Approximately 300 industrial and commercial establishments, i.e. the
bulk of Egypt's industry and commerce, were nationalized. All
foreign trade was declared a state monopoly. Heavier taxes on
real estate were imposed, and a new assessment of buildings was
promised. Higher rates of income tax were levied to limit annual income to a maximum of £E6,000 per person. Workers in
the nationalized sector were granted a 25 per cent share of annual
profits distributed as well as a participation in the management
of the nationalized firms. Working hours in factories were shor-
tened to seven hours a day, but to keep production constant more
shifts were scheduled and operated with additional workers
specially recruited for this purpose; the ensuing increase in the
labour force was in turn destined to reduce unemployment in all
sectors, and in particular in the agricultural sector.[1]

REDUCTION OF CEILINGS ON LANDOWNERSHIP AND FARM OPERATION

A few days later, on 26 July, new measures affecting land tenure
policy were announced. These measures (Law no. 127 of 1961)
were more limited in scope than the sweeping changes in the industrial and commercial sectors. Landownership was limited to
an area of 100 feddans per person, this being applicable to fertile

[1] See Y. Sayigh, 'The Social Philosophy of the Revolution', *Middle East
Forum*, Mar. 1962; also Issawi, *Egypt in Revolution.*

or waste land. All land owned above the prescribed ceiling was to be expropriated within a period of one year. The 1959 ceiling, allowing for a total landownership of 300 feddans per family, was not changed. A father, his children under age, and his wife were thus entitled to own 300 feddans, as long as not more than 100 feddans were registered under one name. All lands above the legal limit, which were still registered in their owner's name but which had been disposed of by a contract with a certified date, were exempted from expropriation procedure. Those persons to whom land accrued in excess of the legal limit, either as a gift or as an inheritance, were thereafter required to dispose of the excess to small farmers within a period of one year, according to conditions to be laid down by the Ministry of Agrarian Reform.

The ceiling on farm operation was reduced even more drastically. Whereas the 1959 law had limited the area that could be rented by one person to the equivalent which he was legally entitled to possess (i.e. 200 feddans if he was a bachelor, or 300 feddans including members of his family), the 1961 legislation specified that a maximum of 50 feddans could be rented by one person and his family. Moreover, anyone already possessing 50 feddans or more could not rent land, but if he owned less than 50 feddans, he was entitled to rent land on condition that the total area operated did not exceed 50 feddans. Land in excess of the new ceilings on farm operation was to be taken over by the Ministry of Agrarian Reform and leased by the latter to small farmers.[2]

Though the law was put into force on 26 July 1961, excess land was to be expropriated gradually as from 1 November 1961. Expropriation formalities were to be completed, according to official statements, by November 1962. The total area to be subjected to expropriation was originally estimated at 500,000 feddans, affecting 5,200 landowners, 1,800 of whom owned 200 feddans and the remaining 3,400 from 100 to 200 feddans. There were no figures for the total area affected by the ceiling on farm operation.[3] Subsequent statements on the impact of the second Agrarian Reform Law established that the area to be expropriated from 3,205 landowners was approximately 250,000 feddans,[4] a more conservative estimate. By 1963 some 214,132 feddans had been taken over by the Agrarian Reform authorities in accordance with the 1961 law.[5]

It is interesting to note that the new law did not specify any

---

[2] This was in compliance with the amendment to Art. 37, sect. 3, Law no. 173 of 1952; this amendment was enacted in Sept. 1959 (see above, p. 23).

[3] 34·9 per cent of the cultivated area in 1956 was operated by 1 per cent of farm operators occupying holdings of more than 50 feddans. See above p. 14.

[4] See *al-Magallat al-Zira'iyat*, Sept. 1961, p. 1.

[5] *Agrarian Reform in Eleven Years* (1964), p. 29, table showing Agrarian Reform lands according to the various sources of acquisition.

exemptions for lands planted in orchards, or highly productive farms. It has already been pointed out[6] that this was one of the notable deficiencies of the first Agrarian Reform Law. This failure may well deprive Egypt of some of its most progressive farmers. Moreover, medium-sized farm operators of 10–50 feddans, some of whom are highly efficient, may well fear that their turn also will be coming and that they will soon fall prey to new land-redistribution measures.

TABLE 10

Landownership in 1952 and 1961

Holdings (feddans)	1952*		1961†		After reform of 1961	
	No. of owners	*Area owned ('000 feddans)*	*No. of owners ('000)*	*Area owned ('000 feddans)*	*No. of owners ('000)*	*Area owned ('000 feddans)*
Under 5	2,642	2,122	2,870	2,660	2,920	3,040
5–10	79	526	79	530	79	530
10–50	69	1,291	69	1,300	69	1,300
50–100	6	429	11‡	630	11†	630
100–200	3	437	3	450	5‖	500‖
Over 200	2	1,117	2	430	—	—
Total	2,801	5,982	3,034	6,000	3,084	6,000

* Actual census.   † Estimates.
‡ The increase in this category in both the number of owners and the area owned is estimated to result mainly from the provisions of the 1952 Agrarian Reform Law, as it authorized owners of over 200 feddans to concede 50 feddans to each child, with a maximum ceiling of 100 feddans for all the children of each landlord.
‖ There seems to be some mistake in this table since with the application of the new 100-feddan ceiling, this category of landowners should disappear. Issawi (*Egypt in Revolution*, p. 156) expresses the belief that these figures apply to estates of exactly 100 feddans.

Source: NBE, *Econ. B.*, no. 3, 1961.

Pending expropriation, owners of areas larger than those allowed by the new law were allowed to continue cultivation and to enjoy the right of disposing of their crops. On the other hand, they were absolutely forbidden to dispose of their lands, by any means, until they were taken over by the Agrarian Reform authorities. The sale of excess lands to small peasants during the interim period preceding expropriation, which had been authorized by Article 4 of the 1952 law, was therefore prohibited this time. But landlords who, pending expropriation, had been subjected to an additional tax, equivalent to five times the basic land tax (in accordance with the 1952 law), were now relieved of this burden. Landlords liable

[6] Above, p. 32.

to expropriation were, moreover, forbidden to move tenants or sharecroppers from one section of their lands to another until the Agrarian Reform authorities took them over. This measure was enacted to prevent fraud on the part of landlords or of tenants, as had often been the case after 1952.

Land to be expropriated was on the whole fertile, as much of it included the residual holdings belonging to people affected by expropriation during 1952–6, who had then kept the most fertile parts of their estates. The situation was therefore different from that after the 1952 law, when a high proportion of the estates taken over in 1952–6 had been waste land (20 per cent), or low-productivity lands (5 per cent).[7]

COMPENSATION

The 1961 legislation introduced some changes in the treatment of expropriated landowners. The basis for the calculation of compensation was the same as that specified in the 1952 legislation, i.e. 70 times the land tax plus the value of fixed and mobile installations and equipment. But whereas the landlords expropriated under the 1952 legislation received non-transferable bonds redeemable in 40 instalments bearing an annual interest rate of 1·5 per cent, the new batch of expropriated landowners were compensated under more favourable conditions. The bonds were nominative but were transferable by sale on the stock exchange. They had an annual interest rate of 4 per cent and were redeemable in 15 instalments.[8] The preferential treatment granted to those affected by the second Agrarian Reform Law may well have been to prevent antagonizing too strongly the bourgeoisie and medium-sized farmers, from whose ranks much of the Egyptian officer class were drawn. Whatever the case, the actual payment of compensation for lands expropriated in accordance with the first and second Agrarian Reform Laws proceeded slowly. By 1964 state bonds to the value of £E50,084,252 had been issued to the expropriated owners of 257,258 feddans.[9]

REDISTRIBUTION OF EXPROPRIATED LAND

The new legislation did not change the general rules governing redistribution as specified in Law no. 179 of 1952. The lands

---

[7] This was land not fertile enough for redistribution to landowning beneficiaries, but was occupied by tenants under a provisional status, paying a rental often adjusted to productive capacity. It has already been pointed out that some of these so-called weak lands had suffered from losses in productivity since 1952 (above, p. 42).

[8] UN, *Progress in Land Reform* (1965), Ch. 3, p. 28.

[9] *Agrarian Reform in Eleven Years*, p. 30.

expropriated were redistributed in holdings of 2–5 feddans; beneficiaries were the tenants or sharecroppers actually occupying
and farming the lands and in their absence neighbouring destitute
families, large families being granted preferential treatment. The
investigations preceding the allocation of holdings to candidates
were carried out by joint teams of Agrarian Reform technicians
and representatives of the provincial governor, the government-
sponsored National Union party,[10] and village councils.

All the beneficiaries of the second land-reform distribution
programme were grouped in co-operative organizations similar
to those already set up in Agrarian Reform areas. Wherever the
expropriated holdings were small or dispersed, the beneficiaries
were integrated either in the nearest Agrarian Reform co-operative,
or in the village co-operative within whose boundaries the expropriated lands lay. The co-operative structures set up since the
autumn of 1960 were thus utilized to overcome the obstacles to
a successful operation of small dispersed holdings; as previously
foreseen by the author.

The new legislation took into account the fact that with low
cotton prices some of the inexperienced beneficiaries might find
it difficult to meet their financial obligations. The redistributed
holdings were therefore sold to beneficiaries at a price equivalent
to half the value of the lands as assessed for compensation; the
price was to be redeemed in 40 annual instalments, with interest of
1·5 per cent per annum. But the state carried the burden of fully
compensating the expropriated landlords.

This important innovation was also extended to all the Agrarian
Reform smallholders who had benefited from redistribution
measures during the period 1952–61. But so far as the latter were
concerned, the reduction was applicable only to that part of
the purchase price of their holdings which was still outstanding.
This facility, granted to all Agrarian Reform smallholders who
had benefited from the 1952 legislation, and to the beneficiaries
of the 1961 legislation, cost the Treasury over £E50 million.
It substantially reduced the annual payments to be made by
Agrarian Reform beneficiaries (old and new). The latter
would have paid the equivalent of four times the basic land
tax if the 1952 legislation (as amended in 1958) had remained
in force, plus the voluntary contribution to co-operative expenses
equivalent to the land tax, i.e. a total of five times the land tax.
After 1961, they were made to pay (according to our calculations)
the equivalent of 2·5 times the basic land tax, plus a voluntary
contribution equivalent to the tax, i.e. a total of 3·5 times the basic
land tax.

[10] *Ittihad Qawmi.*

Another concession granted to those beneficiaries who had accumulated debts on their holdings was that their debts were collected over a period of five to ten years on an instalment basis. In addition, occupants of lands seized from the ex-royal family, who had accumulated outstanding debts to the latter before the seizure of royal family property in 1954, were granted total remission of these debts whenever their holdings were less than 5 feddans; larger operators were allowed to settle these debts on an instalment basis.

On 24 March 1964 a new concession was granted to all Agrarian Reform beneficiaries by Law no. 138 of 1964. This law stipulated that the redistributed holdings were in future to be sold to Agrarian Reform beneficiaries at a price equivalent to one-quarter of the value of the lands as assessed for compensation payable to expropriated owners. The reduced purchase price was redeemable in forty annual instalments, free of any interest charge. All beneficiaries having received land in conformity with the 1952 and subsequent Agrarian Reform Laws were immediately allowed to benefit from the new concession; instalments and interest previously collected from these beneficiaries were taken into account when calculating the balances due by them on the purchase price of their lands.

As a result of this important change, the annual payments made by landowning beneficiaries were not to exceed, according to the author's calculations, 2·5 times the basic land tax, and that inclusive of a voluntary contribution to co-operative expenses. The down-scaling of the instalment payments of beneficiaries from the initial 1953 level of six times the land tax was a generous concession, showing that the state had now chosen to take over, with the expropriated landowners, the burden of Agrarian Reform, rather than leave it to the expropriated landowners and the beneficiaries as had been the case during 1952–61.

TENANCY, SHARECROPPING, AND STATUS OF AGRICULTURAL LABOUR

Though no legislation on sharecropping and tenancy was issued in July 1961, the Ministry of Agrarian Reform announced that new laws were in preparation to enforce stricter observance of existing tenancy and sharecropping laws. In October 1962 a law was issued further extending leases expiring in 1961–2 until 1964–5, as well as all leases ending during this period. This law, aiming at ensuring security of tenure, was soon followed in February 1963 by another law regulating tenancy and sharecropping more strictly: landlords and tenants were thereafter required to register their contracts at the local village co-operative.[11]

Contravention of the tenancy laws was now made liable to heavier penalties. In addition, to prevent evasion of the law fixing a ceiling on farm operations and to put a curb on sub-letting, the operation of holdings of more than 50 feddans by proxy was strictly forbidden.[12]

New laws regulating agricultural employment and extending social insurance benefits to agricultural labour were contemplated. The extension of social insurance to agricultural labour was to be partly financed by the employers (i.e. the farmers hiring labour) and partly from the Social Aid Funds of the village co-operatives. However, the social insurance legislation had not yet been issued by the end of 1964; in their own limited field the Agrarian Reform authorities had devised procedures for insuring beneficiaries against death or disability, benefits being payable in instalments.[13]

AGRICULTURAL CREDIT

One of the most important measures decreed at the same time as the Second Agrarian Reform Law was the decision to grant all loans to farmers supplied by the Agricultural Credit Bank free of charge.[14] This was destined to give new impetus to the agricultural sector.

FUTURE TRENDS

It is difficult to assess how radical Egyptian agrarian policy may become in the future. In view of the major changes in general economic policy since July 1961, and with the elimination of the possibility of mass emigration to Syria or other neighbouring Arab countries, it is hard to believe that the agrarian structure will not be drastically reshaped. This may happen within a few years, as soon as the co-operative organizations are firmly established throughout the countryside and once the distribution of lands expropriated as a result of the Second Agrarian Reform and subsequent legislation is successfully completed. In fact expropriation and distribution proceeded fairly rapidly after 1961. By the end of 1963 an area of 214,132 feddans had been taken over in compliance with the Second Agrarian Reform Law, as well as

---

[11] See Laws no. 139 of 1962 and no. 17 of 1963.
[12] A measure which seems to have been prompted by the recommendations of the second conference on agriculture and irrigation held in Cairo in June 1961 (see *al-Magallat al-Zira'iyat*, July 1961, p. 17).
[13] UN, *Planning for Balanced Social and Economic Development in the UAR* (Mar. 1965, mimeo), p. 34.
[14] Law no. 1250 of 1961.

all the *waqf* lands (some 148,750 feddans)[15] and some 61,910 feddans owned by foreigners, who are now strictly prohibited from owning land.[16] The area directly controlled by the Agrarian Reform authorities had thus increased to 970,435 feddans by 1964 as against 628,684 feddans in late 1960. To this figure of 970,435 feddans must be added the 135,000 feddans which in 1959 had been scheduled to be transferred from the State Domains Administration to the Ministry of Agrarian Reform. Bearing in mind the 145,000 feddans sold to small farmers by about-to-be expropriated landowners in compliance with Article 4 of the 1952 law, it becomes apparent that the area transferred or about to be transferred to smallholders was approximately 1,250,000 feddans in 1964, i.e. over 20 per cent of the cultivated area in 1952. Official publications disclosed that 646,775 feddans had been distributed by 1965 to 263,862 smallholders, whose families numbered 1,300,000 persons. In addition to this area distributed through Agrarian Reform channels, an area of 192,903 feddans, part of which was recently reclaimed and part of which was state lands, was also distributed to small farmers by various government agencies. The total amount distributed thus reached 839,678 feddans.[17] Another 297,678 feddans expropriated had not been distributed by the Agrarian Reform authorities as this land included poor and unproductive lands, orchards, and lands subject to judicial disputes.

Further reductions of the ceilings on landownership and farm operation are probable, and the chances are that soon the limit on ownership will be fixed at 5 feddans or less. An egalitarian redistribution of the 6,200,000 feddans which were fully productive in 1961 could provide roughly 2·5 million farm operators with holdings averaging 2·5 feddans, since on average a rural family numbered 5·5 persons in 1960; such a redistribution could satisfy the land hunger of some 14–15 million rural inhabitants. Only 1 million rural inhabitants, less than 200,000 families, would then be landless. But they would stand to benefit rapidly from the distribution measures implemented within the scope of the vast land-reclamation programme if this is carried out as announced,[18] at a projected rate of 723,000 feddans during 1960–5 and another 150,000 feddans annually during the next five years.

A highly efficient co-operative framework, under strict state supervision, will doubtless be necessary if such an egalitarian redistribution is to succeed. Judging by present patterns, this

[15] *Agrarian Reform in Eleven Years*, p. 29.
[16] By Law no. 15 of 1963.
[17] UAR, *Statistical Handbook, 1952–64* (1965).
[18] UAR, *The Year Book 1965*, pp. 142 ff.

might result in stifling bureaucracy. Birth-control measures instituted on a national scale, a remodelling of the status of tenancy and sharecropping, legal controls on the purchase and sale of lands, industrialization of agriculture and rapid land reclamation, all combined in a co-ordinated programme, might provide an alternative to a drastic redistribution of landownership. But time is flying by, and with the increasing intensity of Egyptian social and economic problems, the premium may well be once more on political as against less spectacular technical solutions.

APPENDIX I

The Nawag Experiment

ANY survey of Egyptian agrarian reform would be incomplete without a note on the important and interesting experiment of Nawag, a small village 10 km. north-east of the big town of Tanta (Gharbiya province). The method of approach and technique evolved in the experiment in crop consolidation and co-operative farming initiated here in 1955 served as a model for dealing with the problems inherent in small-scale farming elsewhere in the Delta.

At Nawag the village lands comprised 1,735 feddans, of which 192 feddans were *waqf* land rented to tenants and the remaining 1,543 feddans were owned by 1,585 landowners, i.e. an average of 1 feddan per owner. There were 1,181 farm units and 3,500 plots, each differently drained and irrigated. It was thus a classic case of very small-scale farming. There was a semi-dormant co-operative run by the Ministry of Social Affairs, no more than 10 of its 321 members regularly dealing with it. The total value of fertilizers bought and sold under its supervision did not exceed £E465 per annum (a situation common to many of the 2,000 odd co-operatives supervised by that Ministry).

It was decided to introduce the triennial crop rotation system, with all its advantages that have already been described in irrigation control, use of fertilizers and insecticides, the promotion of agricultural credit, &c., and the first step taken was to infuse new life into the co-operative and give the farm operators some inducement to join it and overcome their natural reluctance to participate in a government-sponsored programme. To achieve this, late in 1955 senior officials of the Ministry of Agrarian Reform visited Nawag and offered to supply the co-operative with selected cotton seed and fertilizers at official prices—a highly tempting proposal at a time when both were obtainable only on the flourishing black market at a premium of 30 to 40 per cent. All the Nawag smallholders, whether landowners or tenants, were given the opportunity of drawing seed and fertilizers on credit on the usual condition of purchasing one share (valued at £E1) in the co-operative, on an instalment basis. To guard against surreptitious disposal of crops before settling debts, in some cases members were made the legal custodians of their crops and seizure writs (*mahdar hagz*) were drawn up by the *sarraf*. This attempt to win the confidence of the peasants succeeded; they flocked to join the co-operative and to apply for the loans. To encourage them further the authorities supplied 150 tons of cotton-seed cake to the co-operative, which was sold at official prices against-cash payments (black market prices being 30 to 40 per cent higher). At the end of the cotton season all outstanding liabilities were settled without difficulty, a clear proof of the soundness of the methods adopted and that a constructive approach could yield positive results.

To encourage the smallholders to accept the introduction of consolidated crop rotation during the 1956/7 season, the authorities enlarged on the advantages of using a powerful new insecticide, toxaphene, in large consolidated fields of cotton. They underlined the dangers to children and cattle if spraying was done in small intermingled holdings, and the peasants were also told that if they agreed to apply consolidated rotation, they would be granted ample credits in cash and in kind. In early autumn they would be granted cash loans equivalent to 80 per cent of the value of the cotton crop to enable them to hold out for maximum prices. Nevertheless it seems to have required much persuasion and moral pressure from the Agrarian Reform and other provincial authorities to obtain agreement to carry out the experiment. Since most of the Nawag farmers operated holdings split into several plots dispersed throughout the village, many of them were afraid that all their holdings would fall exclusively in an area to be devoted to cotton or to winter crops, but this was overcome by encouraging farmers to resort to the customary practice known as 'suiting'. This meant that a peasant whose total holding fell in a block growing only cotton could exchange part of his crop with one whose total holding fell in a block growing winter crops, a practice which enabled each peasant to have four crops annually, i.e. cotton, clover, wheat, and maize. It was, however, very difficult to carry out since every farmer believed his land was better than any other. In the end it was found that the only way to reach agreement was to let the farmers conclude such exchanges on their own initiative without outside interference.

The crop rotation was finally worked out by the Agrarian Reform regional inspector and the neighbouring Sabarabay *mandub*. To prevent the surreptitious disposal of seed and fertilizer issued as loans, farmers were informed that pest-control spraying costs would be charged to them on the basis of the area they declared when submitting demands for seeds and fertilizers. Farm operators were charged £E4 for insecticides sprayed under supervision, a reasonable price for four sprayings. Peasants were satisfied with this arrangement though they seemed afraid that the authorities might involve them in unnecessary expenditure.

By 1959/60 the experiment had the full support of the leaders of the co-operative and of the peasants. Membership of the co-operative rose to approximately 600, 400 of whom were actively dealing with it. Loans in kind regularly provided included, besides cotton seed and insecticide, fertilizers and wheat seed. Superphosphates, available only for the clover crop, and cotton-seed cake were also sold on a cash basis. Farmers received a cash loan of £E12 per kantar of cotton as soon as the crop was picked and stored in approved warehouses, but tenant farmers complained that in 1959 they had not received this loan and had been compelled to sell their crop cheap (at £E15 per kantar instead of the £E17–19 obtained by other Nawag operators) to meet their obligations to the co-operative and to their landlords.

The success of the experiment was demonstrated by a 58 per cent increase in cotton production in 1956/7 compared with 1955/6 over the same area planted. All crop yields were at least 20 per cent higher than in smallholdings bordering Nawag. After 1957, despite delay in planting because peasants dragged on with a snatch clover or beans crop, cotton yields rose spectacularly, as the following figures show:

Cotton Yields

kantars

1955–6	4·3
1956–7	6·8
1957–8	6·0
1958–9	7·5

Wheat Yields

ardebs

1956–7	7
1957–8	8

Cotton prices also rose, although as late as 1960 it had not been possible to attempt the bulk sale of the crop through co-operative channels because of the lack of adequate storage buildings. The crop was thus sifted and sorted under the supervision of Agrarian Reform officials and then sold individually to local merchants. Prices were as follows:

1955–6, £E15 per kantar; 1956–7, £E18 per cantar. (The *mantiqa* of Sabarbay obtained £E22 per kantar for its crop.)

1957–8, average £E14 per kantar (Sabarbay managed to dispose of its crop at £E17 per kantar).

Though the Nawag farmers had not been included in any schemes for livestock evolved by the Agrarian Reform authorities for Sabarbay *mantiqa*, they were entitled to benefit from the services of the government veterinary centre which operated in the vicinity, and buffalo and Holstein Friesian bulls were available for breeding purposes at the neighbouring agricultural extension service unit (*widha zira‘iya*). While there were no plans for developing poultry production, it was interesting to note that the Nawag farmers were already breeding Rhode Island poultry, which they had purchased from smallholders in Sabarbay and other neighbouring estates. This was proof of the impact of the poultry programme in Agrarian Reform regions. The marketing of livestock and poultry products was undertaken individually by the farmers themselves, though some form of co-operative organization for marketing could have been established, if only to operate a milk collecting centre, dormant since 1957, in a nearby Rural Combined Centre.

The rise in gross income of the Nawag smallholders was impressive: in three years it amounted to approximately £E150,000 from increases in yields of the cotton crop alone. Rough estimates valued the increase of annual net income at nearly 50 per cent. The net annual income per feddan, including the value of livestock production but excluding labour costs, was estimated in 1958/9 at approximately £E50, i.e. an income nearly as high as that in the most successful co-operative of Mit al-Mawz, which occupied the leading place in the outstanding Shibin al-Kawm. The outward signs of this increase in income were apparent in Nawag, but unfortunately, as elsewhere, most of it seemed to have been spent on consumption or on the purchase of lands whose price had soared. The lands of Nawag were valued at £E1,000 per feddan by their owners, a colossal sum for not particularly productive land; the neighbouring estate of Sabarbay had been expropriated and distributed by the Agrarian Reform authorities at approximately £E250 per feddan.

The administrative costs, amounting to about £E1,000 per annum, involved in the experiment were nearly all assumed by the Agrarian Reform authorities: they paid the salaries of the staff entrusted with daily supervision and control. The co-operative paid the salaries and wages, £E114 per annum, of the *ghafir* entrusted with preventing the surreptitious removal of the cotton crop. The Agrarian Reform officials responsible for the day-to-day development of the experiment were not entitled to any bonus as a reward for their efforts. This might have been understandable during the first two years but something was needed if the necessary effort and psychological incentive were to be kept up.

In 1959–60 a very loose system of triennial crop rotation was in use, with cotton occupying a slightly higher percentage of land than normal (40–50 per cent instead of 33 per cent). Crop consolidation was complete for cotton, but wheat and clover were intermingled. Rice had not been introduced through lack of water and adequate drainage, though Board members of the co-operative mentioned that they were negotiating a loan with the Agrarian Reform authorities for the boring of artesian wells. The land was irrigated by gravity flow with the help of *saqias*. None of the main irrigation canals had been kept up and all urgently needed to have silt deposits removed. There was no internal drainage network and the main drainage ditch bordering the lands was not deep enough. Internal roads were hardly developed, though there were narrow paths that could have been used by light tractors if they had been slightly enlarged. Most of the holdings were owner-operated, less than 2 per cent of the area being leased. The average land tax was approximately £E3·5, so that annual rent per feddan should have been £E24·5 according to the provisions of the 1952 law on tenancy, but in some cases were as high as £E40–50, regardless of regulations (as also occurred in neighbouring areas).

The main criticisms of the scheme were, first, that although several development projects had been elaborated, by 1960 none of them had been implemented, although they entailed only a limited expenditure that could have been recovered in a very short time, while they would have ensured the full utilization of the untapped resources of the village. Investment in the building of a big warehouse to store fertilizers, seeds, and the cotton crop, &c., would have solved many of the co-operative's problems. It would also have resulted in higher cotton prices, and would have enabled the co-operative to deduct a commission on sales and thus dispose of capital for investments. Another undertaking that would have been of the utmost benefit would have been the establishment of an underground tile drainage network. It was not possible to

establish an effective open-air drainage system because tertiary drainage
ditches would have reduced the size of the already minute holdings,
while the main drainage ditches would have cut across many holdings.
Effective drainage would have gone a long way to ease the problems
of mechanizing tillage operations and, combined with the digging of
artesian wells, would have made it possible to cultivate rice. It was
also regrettable that the promoters of the Nawag experiment should
not have encouraged the elimination of draught cattle and the mechanization of tillage, transport, waterlifting, and threshing operations in
particular by awakening interest in the Nawag scheme among farm
machinery dealers. All farm operations except pest control were
carried out individually and manually: nearly all tillage was done with
draught cattle, tractors being rented for use in approximately 15 per
cent of the cultivated area.[1] Farmers were reluctant to make cash payments to contractors of farm machinery and preferred to use their own
cattle even if it meant reducing milk production, especially since there
was no outlet for dairy products.[2] Mechanization of tillage operations
would have improved cotton yields; it would have enabled farmers to
plough and to plant their cotton crop on time, notwithstanding the delay incurred through late harvesting in March of snatch clover and
bean crops, which occupied the fields to be planted in cotton. The use
of small tractors for irrigation, threshing, and for transport could also
have worked miracles; in fact the village was nearly 2 km. away from the
furthest of the Nawag lands and precious effort was being wasted as
farmers, leading donkeys loaded with farm manure, moved to and fro
from their houses to their fields at the rate of one trip an hour.

The second main criticism was the one that has already been made
in discussing the Agrarian Reform estates elsewhere, i.e. the neglect of
the potentialities for vegetable and fruit production.[3] With its high
population density and very small holdings, Nawag was well suited to
market gardening, and vegetable crops planted in consolidated blocks
within the framework of a loose rotation would have provided employment for the under-employed village labourers, at the same time ensuring
high net and gross returns. The cultivation of grain crops whose yields
were merely average (7–8 ardebs of wheat or maize) was nonsensical in
this village where the main problem was to induce the small farm
operators rapidly to intensify production to the very limit of potential
capacity. The only obstacle to an expansion of market gardening was
the lack of channels for bulk disposal of the crops in internal and export
markets. But some sort of arrangement could have been worked out
with canning factories and private exporters, rather than with state
agencies, to overcome marketing difficulties. Past efforts in Sabarbay,

---

[1] Miss Warriner, in her report to the UN (p. 74), states that in the winter of
1961 a tractor bought by the Nawag co-operative was being rented to its members. As its horsepower was not indicated, it is difficult to judge whether it was
sufficient to mechanize cotton tillage operations.

[2] This may change once the big UNICEF milk processing plant in Sakha,
Kafr al-Shaikh province (only 40 km. north of Nawag) and the 20-ton-daily
pasteurising plant scheduled for Mansura begin functioning.

[3] See above, pp. 126–9.

where marketing arrangements had been made with the state Organization for the Promotion of Exports, had not been encouraging.

Fruit production, which had not been considered, would have been the short cut to a really decisive increase in the income of the peasants. While the establishment of orchards would have encountered difficulties because of the minute size of the holdings, these difficulties could have been solved along similar lines to those followed in implementing the cotton crop consolidation scheme. An area equal to 20 per cent of the cultivated lands, i.e. approximately 360 feddans, dispersed in different parts of the village lands to constitute 6 to 12 units of 30 to 60 feddans, could have been reserved for fruit production. All farm operators could have been allotted orchard plots equivalent to 20 per cent of the area of their total holding, in exchange for forgoing, for a period of three to four years, an equivalent area of their original holding, this to be reserved to compensate and reconstitute the holdings of farmers who had received an orchard plot but had lost 80 per cent of their holding for the establishment of an orchard unit. Inducements to abandon grain cultivation might have been provided by allocating grain for home consumption and animal and poultry feed on credit at stable prices; the share in the orchard would have provided more than adequate collateral. Young fruit trees could have been distributed free of charge and the orchards established on a three-year basis and planted in bananas. This fruit is well suited to the conditions of Nawag, with its big labour force and abundant stocks of farm manure. It also comes into production rapidly and yields high gross (£E200 per feddan) and net returns (£E150 per feddan), while requiring investment mainly in the form of labour and farm manure. The technical supervision of the orchards could be entrusted to an agricultural engineer hired by the Nawag co-operative and not connected with the Agrarian Reform administration. But all manual operations other than pest control could be left to individual operators who would carry them out in the plots allocated to them in the orchard. Ample agricultural credit could be supplied with the fruit crop as collateral, and the bulk disposal of the crop could be left to the co-operative, who would thus easily recover loans to farmers At the end of three years the planting of long-term fruit crops (citrus, mangoes, vines, &c.) could be considered. Farmers would in the meantime have benefited from a tremendous increase in income without being involved in revolutionary changes in their cropping programme. The increase in income per feddan would be at least 35 per cent if not more. Net income in a three-feddan holding could be estimated at:

From 2·4 feddans planted according to the
prevailing crop pattern £E50 per feddan = £E120
From 0·6 feddans planted as orchard land £E150 per feddan = £E90
Total £E210, i.e. £E70 per feddan instead of £E50 as estimated for 1958–9.

The implementation of such a scheme would require some capital outlay on the part of the farm operators. This could be forthcoming from the increase in income due to the consolidation of the cotton crop, and the necessary inducement could be provided by preferential fiscal treatment, such as the provisional suspension of a basic land tax.

Contributions from the co-operative could only be hoped for from income from commissions on cotton marketed through co-operative channels, since no other large source of income was available, but this in turn would depend on the availability of storage. This again underlined the necessity for the erection of warehouses, which could have been erected on a co-operative basis by inducing farm operators to supply the labour and providing a long-term loan for the purchase of building materials. Co-operative efforts of this type have been promoted with considerable success in Italy during an experiment in voluntary co-operation sponsored since 1955 by Shell Italiana in the Tuscan village of Borgo à Mozzano, where agricultural lands extended over 6,700 hectares. A network of mountain roads built in less than three years solely with the help of co-operative labour gangs working free of charge was one of the most spectacular achievements there. A similar use might have been made of unemployed labour to improve housing conditions, which were as bad in Nawag as in other Egyptian villages.[4] This might also have succeeded in usefully channelling the increases in income.

Notwithstanding these criticisms, the Nawag experiment stood out as an outstanding success, above all because of the dedication and faith among the responsible technicians, illustrating the paramount importance of human factors in economic and social development. But it remains to be seen whether the initial impulse would be sufficient to sustain co-operative efforts, given the absence of a long-term plan and of an all-embracing self-sufficient scheme. In contrast to Nawag, the tremendous impact of the Borgo à Mozzano experiment was due to the advanced research and planning carried out by the Institute of Agrarian Economics in Florence, as well as to the implementation of a succession of co-ordinated projects in various fields such as agricultural credit, road building, irrigation, mechanization, crop rotation, seed selection, pest control, bulk disposal of crops, livestock and poultry production, home economics, and extension training. The scope of action and the impact of the Borgo à Mozzano experiment was increased a hundredfold by the establishment of a centre for agrarian studies in the village itself, to which students were flocking from all over the world to learn how to tackle the problem of an underdeveloped rural community.

[4] Clean drinking water had been provided since 1957 by the Ministry of Public Works.

APPENDIX II

Accounts of the Agrarian Reform Co-operatives of Za'faran and Qism Awwal Rub' Shandid, 1957–8

(a) ZA'FARAN

Area under supervision of the co-operative, 4,891 feddans: paid-up
   capital £E5,337.
Area in full ownership, 3,672 feddans: area tenanted 1,219 feddans.
Members; landowners, 743; landowners and tenants, 219; tenants,
   389; total (1957/8), 1,462.

Balance sheet drawn up on 24 November 1958

	Expenditure (£E)	Income (£E)
Irrigation[1]	7,541[2]	14,264[3]
Ploughing[1]	4,800[4]	6,014[4]
Threshing[1]	231[5]	241[5]
Pest control (actual costs)	4,969	5,265[3]
Upkeep of drainage network	6,726	7,011[3]
Ghufara'	2,386	2,541[3]
Draught animals	1,006[6]	265[3]
Cars used by staff	2,412	—
Field measuring	502	979[3]
Commission on fertilizers, seed, &c. provided to members	—	3,981
Commission on members' crops disposed of	—	7,525
Lands operated by the co-op. on its own account	154	464
Administrative costs contributed by landowning operators only	—	6,797[7]
Overdue instalments	11,383[8]	—
Rents due by tenants	—	17,837[9]
Rentals readjusted	7	—
Miscellaneous	22,733[10]	4,263[11]
Total profits	12,510	—
Total	77,353	77,353

[1] Running costs, not including amortization.
[2] Irrigation was carried out by means of 7 fixed and 3 mobile pumps.
[3] Price paid by co-op. members for this service.
[4] The co-op. owned 8 track tractors, 2 old and 6 caterpillar-type international
   harvesters (TD9 45 h.p.) bought in 1955.
[5] The co-op. owned a 4·5 ft Ruston grain thresher. The very low figure against
   this item shows that mechanization of threshing operations was no further
   advanced in Za'faran than in Damira (see above, pp. 103–7).
[6] The upkeep of draught animals for emergencies seems to have been costly.
[7] Includes 'voluntary contributions' of the landowning members.
[8] Covers the instalments due to the Agrarian Reform Central Fund for the lands
   that had not yet been distributed (these were handed over to the state
   Treasury); also includes the local expenses of the Agrarian Reform authorities
   in Cairo.
[9] Includes rents due for the lands which had not been redistributed in full
   ownership and occupied by tenants. It is clear that rents constituted one of the
   main sources of profit.
[10] Covers (1) amortization quotas on buildings; (2) salaries and travelling
   expenses of Agrarian Reform staff; (3) rents for buildings and lighting costs;
   (4) purchase of office furniture; (5) telephone calls and telegrams; (6) station-
   ery; (7) miscellaneous purchases; (8) transport costs and equipment.
[11] Includes proceeds from sale of felled trees and fines imposed on members.
   Note: Discrepancies in totals due to rounding of figures.

(b) QISM AWWAL RUBᶜ SHANDID, ITAY AL-BARUD MANTIQA

Mantiqa area: approx. 10,000 feddans; 3,363 smallholders.
Area supervised by the co-operative, 2,100 feddans.

	Expenditure (£E)	Income (£E)
Irrigation	2,433	2,671
Ploughing	1,130	1,243
Threshing	53	5
Pest control (728 f. of cotton)	5,287	5,816
Upkeep of drainage network	1,040	1,200
Ghufara'	1,396	1,535
Draught animals	1,511	106
Field measuring	117	369
Cars used by staff	864	—
General expenses	5,179	1,544
Commission on goods provided	—	655
,, ,, crops disposed of	—	430
Lands operated by the co-op. on its own account	1,124	2,524
Orchards not redistributed	1,059	1,886
Instalments due	6,714	—
Income due for administrative costs	—	4,555
Rents due by tenants	2,544	9,237
Total	30,451	33,776

Net profit: £E3,325

APPENDIX III

Income and Expenditure Account of GCS and Co-operatives for the year ended 30 June 1958

Income	£E000	£E000	Expenditure	£E000
Services			Agric. & admin. expenses (salaries, wages, fuel, upkeep, fertilizers, seeds)	2,937
(a) Operational (irrigation, pest control, upkeep of drains & canals, agric. services, admin., &c.)	2,236		Amortization	376
(b) Supply & disposal of goods (fertilizers, seeds, cotton, wheat)	443			3,313
		2,679		
Operation of land (orchards & lands rented, owner-operated, or sharecropped) after deduction of ann. instalments, rent reductions, and provision for unpaid rent)		1,355		
Miscellaneous income		441		
		4,475		
Surplus on account carried over		1,162		

Source: al-Magallat al-Zira'iyat, July 1959.

APPENDIX IV

Balance Sheet of GCS and Co-operative Societies Registered and about to be Registered on 30 June 1958

Assets

	£E000	£E000
Value of lands distributed and to be repaid in 30 ann. instalments		73,266
Value of land bought from trustees of sequest. agric. land, at 70 times basic land tax, redeemable in 10 ann. instalments		1,571
Buildings, machinery, &c. expropr. at prices determined by expropriation commissions or at cost	3,855	
Less amortization quotas	1,533	2,322
Co-op. profit-yielding projects (some in process of being undertaken)		1,726
Stocks		
Farm crops	316	
Spare parts, fuel, seeds, fertilizers, &c.	1,753	2,069
From landowning beneficiaries, incl. instalments, land taxes, suppl. taxes (£E1,019,500) due for period 1 July–31 Oct. 1958		6,509
From tenant beneficiaries, incl. rentals & services (£E1,168,460) for period 1 July–31 Oct. 1958	4,550	
Less reserve provision for debts	1,298	3,252
Due by debtors for lands expropriated for state projects		637
Debtors & other debit balances (Ministries, companies, clients, &c.)		4,910
Investments		687
Letters of guarantee	107	
		96,950

Liabilities

	£E000	£E000
Gen. Org. of AR & beneficiaries' lands		73,266
Gen. Org.: buildings, machinery, equipment requisitioned, value redeemable in 30 instalments	2,319	
Less amount that has already come up for redemption	429	1,891
Amount that has already come up for redemption		429
Gen. Org.: payments due to Agr. Ref. Fund up to 30 June 1958	7,051	
Less amounts paid	6,053	998
To trustee of sequestr. agric. property: value of land bought at 70 times the basic land tax	1,571	
Buildings, machines, equipment	105	
Less payments made	100	1,576
Capital of AR co-op. societies		270
To AR beneficiaries		11
To AR tenants		63
Income & accounts for period ending 31 Oct. 1958		
Purchase instalments, land taxes, suppl. taxes	1,019	
Rentals & services	1,168	2,187
Indemnities for lands expropr. for state projects		637
National Bank of Egypt: Balance of accounts opened with Treasury		503
Creditors & other credit balances (Ministries, companies, clients, &c.)		7,246
Provisions		4,290
Reserves		117
Surplus funds to be invested for increasing AR smallholders' output		2,303
Income & expenditure accounts of AR co-ops.; surplus of income for 1 July 1957–30 June 1958		1,162
To bearers of letters of guarantee	107	107
		96,950

Source: al-Magallat al-Zira'iyat, July 1959.

APPENDIX V

The Financial Situation of the Damira Co-operatives, 1954–8 (£E)

(Area supervised by the Damira ACS in 1958: 15,169 feddans)

	1953/4	1954/5	1955/6	1956/7	1957/8	Total 1954-8
Capital	902	6,784	14,629	14,934	18,164	
Expenses	23,979	47,900	112,160	73,138	100,996	358,173
Income	20,307	80,345	145,993	96,199	161,720	504,564
Losses	3,672	—	—	—	—	
Profits (net of 1953–4 losses):	—	32,445	33,033	23,661	60,724	145,591
Share to be distributed	—	8,587	17,484	12,161	32,399	70,631
Share distributed	—	7,741	11,972	2,451	11,572	33,736
Share not distributed	—	846	5,512	9,710	20,827	36,895
Social Aid Fund:	—	3,441	6,606	4,594	12,144	26,785
Sums allocated	—	2,951	2,185	548	4,576	10,260
Remainder (at disposal)	—	490	4,421	4,046	7,568	16,525
Statutory & extraordinary reserve provisions	—	20,097	8,259	5,766	15,181	49,303
Bonuses to members of Boards of Directors, *mushrifs*, & their staff	400	320	684	540	1,000	2,944
Provisions for amortization of machinery	1,364	506	1,433	632	2,356	6,311
Ditto of buildings	3,681	5,217	4,835	3,284	3,211	20,228
Various provisions	64	65	311	200	297	937
Misc. income (*ksur al-millim**) expended on projects not included in annual budget	—	—	—	5,012	6,507	11,519

* i.e. fraction of a millième (£E.001). The accountants of the co-operatives were entitled to calculate in millièmes when dealing with members. Fractions of a millième were not paid, and thus considerable sums accumulated annually and were utilized to meet expenditure on items not included in the annual budget.

Source: Information supplied by the Agrarian Reform officials in Damira.

APPENDIX VI

Livestock Owned by the Landowning Beneficiaries of the Damira Co-operatives

Co-operative	Area (feddans)*	No. of beneficiaries	Cows	Buffaloes	Calves	Donkeys	Horses
Damira	2,787	893	178	714	350	895	90
Kafr Damira	1,271	370	74	253	125	350	35
Mit Zankir	1,205	325	64	289	140	300	35
al-Manyal	1,282	379	84	214	108	365	35
al-Manakhulla	1,279	388	88	313	162	378	12
Kitama	1,344	403	92	378	185	315	58
Busat	1,717	464	101	372	190	413	14
Kafr Busat	993	294	63	115	77	205	10
Kfur al-'Arab	2,327	844	42	703	320	798	81
Sursuq	1,049	309	86	278	144	215	12
	15,254	4,669	872	3,629	1,801	4,334	382

* This includes expropriated lands occupied by landowning beneficiaries and the tenants; the figures refer to June 1959.

Source and Note: figures supplied by the vet in charge of the veterinary unit, Damira estates, July 1959. These figures refer to the cattle owned or part-owned by landowning beneficiaries but do not include those owned or part-owned by tenants. Two pairs of bullocks owned and fed by the local co-operative were also kept on every block of 1,000–1,500 feddans for emergency cases of default in executing agricultural operations at the prescribed time.

APPENDIX VII

Social Activities of the Damira Co-operatives

THE co-operatives of Damira *mantiqa*, on the west bank of the Damietta branch of the Nile, within the boundaries of the districts of Talkha and Balqas and approximately 10 km. from the large urban centre of Mansura, were reputed to be the most successful of all the Agrarian Reform co-operatives. In 1957 the total population of the Damira villages amounted to 30,000, of whom 5,060 were members of the 12 co-operatives.

The Social Aid Fund

By the end of 1958 (i.e. within four years) £E26,795 had been devoted to the Damira co-operatives' Social Aid Fund, of which £E10,260 had been allocated to carry out various projects for the village communities, the relief of destitute families, and for national defence.[1] By January 1960 the total amount paid into the Fund from co-operative profits had increased to £E32,341, of which £E13,687 had been spent.

(a) Projects of interest to the village communities

Schools. Three primary schools had been built by the local co-operatives of Kafr Damira al-Jadid, Kafr Damira al-Kadim, and Kitama, but the need for more schools was still acute, and in 1960 approximately 60 per cent of children of school age were still not attending school.[2] Though no schools for agricultural (vocational) training had been set up, two other training centres had been created, the first to teach peasant women and girls sewing and knitting and the second to train boys and girls to manufacture carpets (the latter employing 46 persons).

Upkeep and repair of mosques. Regular sums totalling over £E1,500 had been allocated for this. Decisions on the upkeep of the mosque of al-Manakhulla village were taken at a meeting of the Board of Directors of the local co-operative in the presence of the author (June 1959); this was also the case at Kafr Damira. One mosque had been built and 18 others repaired in the previous four years.

Provision of street lighting. The local co-operatives spent part of the funds available through the Social Aid Fund for the purchase of kerosene lamps for the village streets.

Relief of distressed villages. The entire village of Kfur al-'Arab was destroyed by fire twice in one year. All the local co-operatives drew on

---

[1] In 1955 the sums fixed by statute for the Social Aid Fund were contributed by the co-operatives to the national defence effort and remitted to the War Ministry.
[2] Schools available in the area for approximately 6,500 children of school age consisted of primary schools in the 12 villages supervised by the Damira co-operatives, 1 preparatory school opened in 1958 for boys, and secondary schools in the neighbouring towns of Talkha, Nabaruh, Shibin, and Balqas.

their Social Aid Funds to contribute to rebuilding. The total sum provided was £E3,000, of which £E1,200 was provided by the Kfur al-'Arab co-operative's Fund.

Purchase of mobile cinema unit. In June 1959 nine of the Damira co-operatives decided to buy a mobile cinema unit for £E3,500. The directors of the Kafr Damira co-operative, despite the exhortations of the regional co-operative adviser, flatly turned down the proposal and refused to contribute their share, but a few months later they relented.

Purchase of ambulance. This was given by the Damira co-operative to the Talkha First Aid Centre.

(b) Relief of destitute families and help for educational purposes

A monthly allocation, not exceeding £E3, was extended from the Fund to all needy widows living in the Damira villages, and £E5 was contributed to cover burial costs of any individual of Damira, whether a member of the co-operative or not. Financial help was also given for medical purposes; this often amounted to more than £E50 if surgical treatment was required or if admission to hospital was imperative. At a meeting of the Board of Directors of the Kafr Damira al-Jadid local co-operative, at which the author was present, various sums ranging between £E5 and £E50, were granted for this purpose (June 1959); this was also the case at a similar meeting at al-Manakhulla local co-operative. Considerable sums were also allocated every year at the time of the feasts of 'Aid al-Saghir and 'Aid al-Kabir to buy clothes and food for the destitute members of the village communities. This usually amounted to less than £E500–1,000 throughout Damira.

Grants were given to the boys and girls of the destitute inhabitants of Damira to help them complete their studies, whether in school or at university. Over 100 such grants had been made by 1959. One of them was given to the son of an Agrarian Reform beneficiary to enable him to continue his studies in a professional training centre in Germany.

2. Committees for Cleanliness and for the Settlement of Claims

Each of the Damira local co-operatives had a Committee for Cleanliness (*Lagnat al-Nazafat*): their members had been chosen among the members of the Boards of Directors. As far as street lighting was concerned, a great and useful effort had been made, but the degree of cleanliness and tidiness of the villages (streets and houses) was no more than that of the neighbouring villages. Each co-operative likewise had a Committee for the Settlement of Claims and Disputes (*Lagnat al-Musalaha*) to ensure smooth and peaceful relations between members and to prevent the outbreak of violence whenever differences arose between them. Their main responsibility was to settle the numerous claims and disputes arising between the peasant farmers: in many cases they were dealing with differences that had sprung up between members of the families of the Agrarian Reform beneficiaries.[3]

[3] A survey by the sociology section of Ain Shams University conducted in Mit Khalaf, Shibin al-Kawm *mantiqa*, revealed the paramount importance of the

3. *Other Activities*

A system of fire insurance was introduced and supervised by the co-operative organization. Each household paid a yearly premium of £Eo·5 for full cover, and this was automatically debited to the account of the beneficiaries.

There was no programme for the provision of welfare workers to advise the peasant families of Damira, but at the Mit Khalaf co-operative, Shibin al-Kawm *mantiqa*, a female assistant was appointed to advise the peasants. This was the first and only experiment of its kind attempted by the Agrarian Reform authorities.

The collection and redistribution of the tithe (*zakat*), due according to Islamic law by all well-to-do Muslims as a yearly contribution to their poorer brethren, was arranged by collecting 5 millièmes (PTo·5) from each farmer for every feddan of land he occupied, the proceeds being distributed to the poor and needy in the Damira villages.

The Boards of Directors of the local co-operatives provided the Damira village communities with a form of political and social leadership to replace the feudal relationship prevailing before 1952. As the elected spokesmen of the members of the various co-operatives, the directors seemed aware of most of the day-to-day agricultural problems of their respective communities, and were conscious of their responsibilities, but the political trends they reflected were those of the authorities. Whether this was the result of personal conviction or outside pressure was debatable.

local *'umda*, to whom families appealed to settle most of their disputes. Only 1·4 per cent of the families consulted the co-operative supervisor for advice on their family problems; 2·1 per cent resorted to him to arbitrate in disputes with their neighbours; and 76·8 per cent to discuss their agricultural problems.

APPENDIX VIII

Notes on Livestock, Poultry, and Land Reclamation Schemes

I. ITAY AL-BARUD

IN Itay al-Barud, Gabaris *mantiqa*, Buhaira province, 100 km. south of Alexandria (20,446 feddans; approximately 5,000 smallholders), schemes for the improvement of livestock and poultry were begun after 1952, for the smallholders owned a considerable number of cattle (many of which were kept for draught purposes). The total was 5,745 animals, excluding donkeys. But a conspicuous sign of poverty in this region was the high percentage of cows, prosperous Egyptian peasants always preferring the relatively high milk yield of the buffalo to the low yield of the cow.

The animals were fed in winter on clover and in summer on wheat straw, cotton-seed cake, and leaves from maize stalks. The peasants were not prosperous enough[1] to over-feed their cattle with cotton-seed cake in summer, since it was only available at the co-operative warehouses against cash payments (and this only during 1958),[2] and their cattle contrasted sharply with those in the wealthier regions of Damira or Shibin al-Kawm.

The projects implemented in this region to improve livestock and poultry production included:

The Fattening of Calves. Year-old calves were bought in local markets by the Agrarian Reform authorities and were distributed among the various co-operatives, who were debited with all the expenses involved and who supplied the technical staff entrusted with the supervision and operation of the project.

The calves were fed in winter on clover and in summer on concentrates, but the attempt proved a complete failure and was discontinued after diarrhoea wiped out a large part of the herd.

The Improvement of Livestock. Three pedigree buffalo bulls and three pedigree Holstein Friesian bulls were placed at the disposal of the members of the co-operatives for breeding. Smallholders whose animals were covered by the insurance policies issued by the veterinary unit could use these bulls at reduced rates.

Distribution of Cattle on Credit. About 300 buffalo heifers, covered by insurance policies issued by the veterinary unit, were distributed to peasants without cattle. Fifty per cent of the purchase price of the animals was paid in cash and the remainder in five annual instalments.

---

[1] See above, p. 100.
[2] Peasants buying cotton-seed cake at official prices promptly turned it over to the black market and cashed a premium. This could easily have been countered by distributing a balanced concentrate mixture as no black market ever existed for the latter.

The Veterinary Unit. This unit supervised the whole of the Itay al-Barud–Gabaris region; it was similar to that set up in Damira and functioned along the same lines, but was nowhere near as successful. It supervised about 600 animals in 1959, mainly buffalo cows, a low figure compared with the total number of cattle owned in the region (over 5,000). Poultry production was also encouraged by the distribution of nearly 150,000 chicks in exchange for a promise to deliver 4 eggs per chick. The main obstacle to the smooth running of the veterinary unit was the lack of mobility of its staff, as transport was not easily available, but transport costs for the Itay al-Barud co-operatives (i.e. an area of 10,000 feddans) totalled nearly £E3,300 in 1957/8 alone. Thus transport facilities clearly existed.

The Milk-Collecting Centre. This project was begun in January 1957, and started functioning in March that year. It seems to have been the most valuable of all the attempts to expand the livestock production of the Agrarian Reform smallholders of the Northern Delta.[3] The centre was set up in the town of Itay al-Barud, within the precincts of the *mantiqa* offices. Three subsidiary collecting centres were distributed throughout the Itay–Gabaris region, all within a maximum radius of 9 km. from the principal centre. Three vans equipped with weighing machines left Itay every morning to collect and weigh the milk delivered by the smallholders to the subsidiary centres. The milk was tested and cooled at the Itay centre while the churns were washed, sterilized, and returned the following morning to the subsidiary centres. The cooled milk was then loaded in churns on a truck belonging to the Alexandria Siclam pasteurizing factory,[4] which undertook to buy all the milk collected for PT3·4 kilo (6–6·5 per cent butter fat). The truck taking the milk to Alexandria also collected milk produced by private farms in the Damanhur region half-way between Alexandria and Itay; on the way from Alexandria to Itay, it carried ice used for cooling in Itay.

The project was in 1959 in the charge of the Co-operation Administration in Cairo, where a special control officer was appointed. The Itay *mandub* had no authority over it, though losses incurred were debited to the account of the Itay *mantiqa.* Four Agrarian Reform employees, helped by three drivers and a few labourers, were entrusted with the actual operation of the centre.[5]

The price received by farmers for their milk was originally PT3·2 per kilo,[6] the difference being kept by the centre to cover handling costs. In January 1959, as a result of losses sustained throughout 1957 and 1958 (£E2,000 per annum), the price was lowered to PT2·7 to meet the protests of the *mandub*, who was anxious to increase the profits of the co-operatives of his region. The smallholders were paid weekly in cash.

In 1957, over a 10-month period starting in March, 122,000 kilos of milk were delivered by the smallholders, and during the 12 months of 1958, 133,000 kilos. Throughout 1959 the quantities delivered remained

---

[3] For details see the 1958 edition of *Agrarian Reform in Egypt.*
[4] Set up in 1950. For further details see Saab, *Motorisation*, pp. 334–87.
[5] It was reported that, before the appointment of the control officer, this staff had been much larger.
[6] 1 kilo = nearly 2·25 rotls.

the same, mainly as a result of the cut in prices, and average daily deliveries did not exceed 400 kilos. Naturally fluctuations in the quantities of milk delivered monthly were large: during the winter clover crop season deliveries rose to 25,000 kilos but fell in summer to 4,500 kilos because of inadequate feed.

Evaluation of the Itay Project. The project could have raised the low level of livestock production in the Itay–Gabaris region and also provided a striking example of the great possibilities of improving economic and social conditions in the not too fertile zones of the Northern Delta. Its success was limited for the following main reasons:

1. Insufficient psychological preparation of the smallholders and members of the Agrarian Reform regional staff. The very poor peasants of this region only partly owned their cattle, according to the *shirq* system—their partners, who had contributed the necessary capital for the purchase price, were afraid of losing them, so they spread rumours that cattle were about to be nationalized, that the value of the milk delivered would be deducted from the outstanding liabilities, &c. These rumours reinforced the natural tendency of Egyptian peasants to look on sales of milk as a sure sign of the laziness of the womenfolk and an admission of poverty: the transformation of milk into melted butter (ghee), cheese, &c., for subsequent sale, after allowing for family consumption, was customary. But thorough preparation could have overcome this. In the meanwhile only 500 peasants delivered milk to the collecting centre, most of whom were co-operative members who had received their cattle on a credit basis and who had been 'coaxed' into participating in the scheme.

2. The employees of the collecting centre were looked upon as the black sheep of the Agrarian Reform regional staff, mainly because of the losses incurred in operating the scheme, but losses were inevitable at the start of such a venture.

3. Inadequate planning and execution of the livestock development programme. The rate of mechanization was slow, and farmers preferred to use cattle for draught operations even if it meant reducing milk production. The staff of the veterinary unit rarely answered calls for help. True the staff of the agricultural extension unit included a vet, and the Rural Combined Centre was supposed to be operating in the region, but their level of activity was low.

4. The breeding, veterinary, and nutrition programmes were inadequate and there was no plan to develop fodder production. The winter clover crop was poor mainly because of the failure to use superphosphates (which were only supplied against cash payments), there was no green maize forage crop in summer, nor were there plans for the conservation of forage by silage; moreover, methods of hay harvesting were poor.[7] Credit for the purchase of livestock or animal feed was scarce. There was no vocational training programme for livestock production (elementary training of cowhands, shepherds, &c.) and no attempt to inculcate a spirit of competition in breeding; it was not until late in 1959 that prizes were given for the best cattle. Methods of handling

[7] On nutrition problems in Egypt see further Saab, *Motorisation*, pp. 334–85.

and cooling the milk collected were primitive, although a complete plant fully equipped to cool 5 tons of milk daily had been installed 1 km. from the centre and had been idle since 1957, apparently because no competent mechanic could be found to run it (the total outlay on the buildings, machinery, &c. of this plant was well over £E12,000).

5. The whole project was inadequately managed and there was no co-ordination between the staff directly attached to it and that of the *mantiqa*. Those in charge of the project did not have sufficient authority or the full backing of the central authorities, even though this was said to have been one of the pet projects of the central Ministry of Agrarian Reform. Nor was there adequate financial backing. The project could have become self-sufficient financially if the milk collected averaged 2 tons a day in summer and winter. Given the cattle population in the region, such a figure could have been attained within three years if a completely integrated scheme had been devised and put into effect. Losses incurred during the first phase would probably have been recovered before long.

6. The prices paid for the milk were not high enough, especially after the January 1959 price cut. Buffalo milk collected within a 40-km. radius of Alexandria was bought for PT3·5 a kilo in winter and PT4 in summer, but additional costs of transport to Itay were no more than PT0·25. The relatively low price offered (PT3·2 a kilo during the first two years and PT2·7 from January 1959) to buffalo owners by the centre was insufficient to encourage farmers to make cash payments for agricultural operations done with hired machinery, in order to reserve their cows for milk production. This was all the more true in the case of the numerous owners of cows whose milk fetched a lower price because of its low butter-fat content. In consequence, despite the high percentage of cows in the region, nearly all the milk delivered to the collecting centre was buffalo milk. Higher prices should have been paid for buffalo and cow milk, even if this meant subsidizing livestock production by as much as £E2,000–3,000 per annum. Compared with the outlay on some other highly dubious cattle-breeding projects undertaken by the Agrarian Reform authorities, this does not appear excessive,[8] especially since livestock production was one of the most labour-absorbing outlets open to smallholders in the Delta, and the main short cut to big increases in soil fertility.

2. *Simmental Cattle-Breeding Project*

At the end of 1956, to check the rise in meat prices resulting from illicit manipulation by butchers and cattle merchants in the big towns, a contract was concluded with Hungary to supply 2,000 2-year-old Simmental bull calves, to be fattened in Egypt and then slaughtered. Plans were then changed and it was decided to import non-pedigree 2-year-old heifers in calf, to upgrade them and later distribute the calves to Agrarian Reform beneficiaries in areas being reclaimed. As the Agrarian Reform authorities were unwilling to increase the price offered (£E60–70 per calf c.i.f. Alexandria), the heifers were bought

[8] See above, p. 116.

haphazardly in Hungarian village markets. Some were in calf, others old enough to be mated. Some brown Swiss cattle were included in the lot, as well as a number of pedigree Simmental bulls imported from Germany.

The cattle arrived in Egypt in January 1958 after a very rough voyage. They were immediately divided into two groups of approximately 1,000 head each, one being dispatched to the Idqu Agrarian Reform land reclamation estate 25 km. east of Alexandria, and the other to the large EARIS reclamation project in Abis, 4 km. south of Alexandria. On both these estates farm buildings, cowsheds, &c. were practically non-existent, and fodder, whether green or otherwise, had not been provided. Some of the heifers started calving as soon as they reached their destination. Open-air sheds were immediately set up, and the cattle fed with concentrates and straw.

In Idqu especially the animals suffered severely from the damp, chilly sea wind blowing over the neighbouring swamps; in summer they were insufficiently protected from the heat and glare. Stabling was badly planned and the heifers were kept in their pens the whole year round, never being given any exercise; inadequate quantities of rice straw were spread on the cement floor. As a result, many cattle died, particularly in Idqu. Over 40 per cent of the new-born calves were wiped out, while various diseases attacked the fully grown cattle; in Idqu alone over 100 heifers were lost during the first 10 months. In February 1959 it was decided to move these cattle, some to the big Idfina estate 15 km. east, and some to the estates of al-Marg, al-Wadi, and al-Muʿtamadiya.[9]

Idfina. Idfina (approx. 15,595 feddans) was a large estate previously operated by the royal *waqfs*. In 1952 it had been taken over by the Ministry of Waqfs, which was compelled to hand it to the Ministry of Agrarian Reform in November 1958. In July 1959 nearly 16,500 feddans were nominally under the control of that Ministry; 1,300 feddans expropriated in 1956 had also been added to the estate, which comprised nine *ziraʿat* of 1,500–2,200 feddans each, each supervised by *nazir ziraʿat*. The land was mainly poor, either under reclamation or reclaimed since 1930. Until 1952 part had been owner-operated by the royal *waqfs* (only the lands under reclamation), part tenanted by share-croppers who turned over half of their crops to the landowner. Owner-operated lands were planted with clover, barley, and Sudan grass, grazed by a big flock of sheep (approx. 10,000) and a herd of nearly 500 milch cattle (buffalo and foreign breeds). There were many well-planned farm buildings (administrative buildings, peasant houses, cowsheds, garages, &c.); 1,500 brick houses had been built for the share-croppers and their families, and 2 hospitals and 3 schools (elementary preparatory, secondary) had been erected by the administration of the royal *waqfs*. All these had been provided to entice peasants from over-crowded regions to settle in underpopulated Idfina. After 1952 upkeep slackened considerably, the only notable innovation being the installation of fountains of clean drinking water.

⁹ The former near Cairo, the two latter near Tal al-Kabir, Sharqiya province.

When the Ministry of Waqfs took over in 1952 the cattle were removed and only 2,000 sheep were left. Most of the lands were leased to the sharecroppers, who were allowed to occupy the holdings against payment of a rent (in compliance with the new Agrarian Reform tenancy regulations). As in the past (due to fraudulent manipulation by the royal *waqfs*) tax had been assessed at the low rate of £E1 per feddan, the rent now paid was low, and peasants grew prosperous. However, in 1956, after carrying out some drainage improvements, the Ministry of Waqfs obtained a writ enabling it to readjust the tax. As a result, rents were increased, and in 1959 the tenants were paying on the average £E13 per feddan (the maximum was £E18, the minimum £E3·90). There were about 1,600 tenants in July 1959, farming some 11,000 feddans, and operating holdings generally of 10 feddans, though 10 per cent averaged over 25 feddans; 2,000 feddans were owner-operated by the Agrarian Reform authorities, and nearly 4,000 feddans were waste or were being reclaimed.

After 1952 compulsory crop rotation had been abandoned and each farmer chose the crop rotation that suited his holding best. The main crops planted were cotton (2,000 feddans), rice, clover, beans, barley, maize, vegetables (tomatoes, cucumbers, &c.). Cotton was a very recent innovation; its cultivation had only become possible since 1956 with the availability of potent new insecticides. But yields were not high (2·5–3 kantars) compared with other seaside regions such as Mandara, where they reached nearly 6 kantars in 1959. Rice yields averaged 1·5 daribas,[10] wheat 3 ardebs, barley 5 ardebs. Clover was not well tended since it only yielded three cuts of about five tons each, compared with five cuts in the Mandara region; upkeep of the drainage and irrigation networks was also poor. Average net annual income was estimated at £E15 per feddan, including the value of livestock production.

The Idfina estates were on the point of being redistributed in full ownership to their actual occupants in mid-July 1959. A social survey had been carried out and a complete replanning of operational methods had been devised to fit in with the consolidated triennial crop-rotation system. Some of the peasant families operating big holdings felt insecure as they feared they would lose part of the area they were farming, since regulations limited redistributed holdings to 5 feddans. The general feeling was that the seven years of administration and management by the Ministry of Waqfs, though it had improved the condition of the smallholders, had led to stagnation, if not a falling off in crop yields. The estate, previously a striking example of sound agricultural management, had by 1959 sunk to the level of the other large *waqf* estates supervised by the Ministry. Agrarian Reform officials, who could point with pride to their achievements in a number of other estates which had not been as well provided as Idfina with farm buildings, machinery, and organization, were on the whole rather bitter about the heritage left them by their colleagues in the Ministry of Waqfs.

Nearly 500 full-grown cows had been transferred from Idqu in February 1959 and had been put in large cowsheds still in fairly good

[10] 1 dariba of rice (husk) = 945 kg.

order, built before 1952 in al-Busairi. As at Idqu, the cows were kept in the sheds all the year round and never allowed any exercise. Despite a litter of rice straw they had contracted foot-rot through continuous contact with the damp cement floor. The animals themselves were fairly clean, but appeared to be suffering from heat and from unbalanced feeding, while numerous cases of abortion occurred. They were fed on wheat straw and 6 kilos of concentrates a day; late in July 1959 no green maize stalks had yet been supplied, though 600 feddans of owner-operated land were supposed to have been planted for fodder. There were 343 cows, with an average total yield of 1,500 kilos of milk daily, with a butter-fat content of 3·5 per cent, but this quantity did not cover the considerable upkeep expenses. The milk was sold at 3·2 an oke[11] to the Siclam factory, which took it to Alexandria. This relatively low price aggravated the losses incurred and it was reported that the cows had already cost nearly £E130, i.e. double their purchase price.

Malnutrition played havoc with the calves, and many were born blind. They were kept in cowsheds close to the main administrative buildings of the *mantiqa*, and they suffered from diarrhoea, lack of calcium, &c.: over 100 had been lost since February 1959. Young 3–6-month-old calves were fed with concentrates and wheat straw. Sick animals and cows about to calve were also kept in the sheds. A vet was in charge, but despite this the overall condition was far worse than those of the cattle at al-Busairi. After weaning, calves were dispersed among the various *zira'at* of the estate. But though the cowsheds there and at the administrative seat of the *mantiqa* were lavish (by Egyptian standards), they were not well adapted for foreign breeds.

The EARIS Project at Abis. EARIS, the Egyptian–American Rural Improvement Society, is a joint operation. The Egyptian government allotted £E5,450,000 and the U.S. government $10 million for the project. The broad objectives are to improve social and economic conditions by carrying out a demonstration programme for land reclamation, development, and community service in the provinces of Buhaira and Fayyum. This includes the following operations:

1. The reclamation of about 33,000 feddans of barren land in the two provinces of Buhaira (Abis, 24,000 feddans) and Fayyum (Kuta, Kom Ushim, 9,500 feddans). This operation includes one year of reclamation and 2–3 years of cropping.

2. The construction of about 6,000 improved houses in 11 villages.

3. The resettlement of approximately 6,000 landless families on the land after reclamation.

4. Demonstration of improved methods of reclamation, water application, soil and crop management practices, and the extension of irrigation and drainage to new lands.

5. The establishment of schools of various levels, and agricultural youth-training centres.

6. Provision of agricultural extension services, financial and other assistance to co-operatives, improvement and development of roads

---

[11] 1 oke = 1·248 kg.

and public health through improved sanitation, clinical service, training, and health education.[12]

The Abis *mantiqa* had been under Egyptian–American supervision since March 1953, but after the Suez crisis, both the Abis and the Kuta projects were put under the exclusive authority of the Ministry of Agrarian Reform. American financial participation, which had been suddenly interrupted, was resumed early in 1958; in 1959/60 only three U.S. experts were participating in the implementation of the scheme in Abis, on a purely advisory basis.

The Abis project extended over an area of approximately 31,000 feddans of salty marshy land, most of which (24,000 feddans) was 3·5 metres below sea-level, the rest being part of the Mariut lake, designed to be drained and leached.[13] In July 1959 the area under full cultivation was approximately 10,000 feddans. It included 460 feddans of fairly fertile land distributed in 1955, 3,500 feddans of supposedly productive land, and approximately 6,000 feddans which were productive but not sufficiently to be distributed. With the exception of the 460 feddans occupied by smallholders, the whole area was owner-operated by the Abis *mantiqa*, which employed a considerable number of agricultural workers especially hired for this purpose. It was planted according to the following cropping pattern: cotton 865 feddans, rice 5,800 feddans, maize 2,200 feddans, jute 500 feddans, sweet sorghum 400 feddans. The area still being reclaimed was also owner-operated by the *mantiqa* and it consisted of (1) 4,000 feddans in a preliminary stage of cultivation involving an annual expenditure far above its subsequent income; (2) 9,000 feddans in which earth-moving operations had been completed; this area was being flooded and washed regularly with irrigation water to desalinate it; (3) 7,000 feddans of swamp land, reclaimed from lake Mariut, in which earth-moving operations were scheduled to start fairly rapidly.

The 460 feddans distributed in 1955 were allotted to 88 smallholders, some of whom had been agricultural labourers participating in reclamation operations, while others were fishermen from the Lake Mariut area or war veterans. Each was given a pleasant modern house or flat in the first of the two model villages recently erected under EARIS auspices. The distributed holdings were all of 5 feddans and lay in a block of lands already reclaimed by the Administration of State Domains. These lands were therefore quite fertile and had been under the plough for more than ten years, though the general appearance of the holdings was very untidy. Upkeep of the internal irrigation, drainage, and road networks was not good, but the Casuarina trees planted by EARIS had been allowed to grow. The triennial crop rotation was strictly applied but crop yields per feddan were not high: cotton 2–3 kantars,[14] wheat 3–4 ardebs, barley 5–6 ardebs, rice 1·5 daribas, although vegetable production was developing rapidly.

---

[12] See R. M. Anwar, *The Land Settlement Programme of EARIS*. Centre of land problems in the Near East, FAO Country Project No. 6.
[13] See Anwar, Garzouzi; and Warriner, report to UN.
[14] Cf. yields at al-Mandara, below, p. 218.

Despite the abundance of machinery at the Abis *mantiqa*,[15] most agricultural operations were done with draught cattle. This was because the first batch of 88 settlers had been provided with various services (fertilizers, selected seeds, &c.) for which they had never paid: these rebellious-minded operators had even refused to settle the instalments on their holdings and continually lodged protests on every possible subject. Big debts had thus accumulated and the authorities were reluctant to increase them further by providing tractors for ploughing on a credit basis.

No co-operative had been set up, and the disposal of crops was left to the initiative of the settlers. In 1959 cotton was sold by the *mantiqa* at £E16·5 per kantar apparently for the first time. One big item of income was the sale of green clover taken into Alexandria by horse-drawn carts, but this was equivalent to exporting humus from an area which needed every scrap of it. Another important item was fresh milk sales, which were said to have averaged 7–10 kilos daily per family. Total annual gross income (including the value of livestock production) was estimated to average £E155 per holding, and net annual income approximately £E100, before the settlement of the instalments due for the purchase of the land and house.[16] Minus these it totalled approximately £E90 during the first four years of occupation.

Abis was suffering from acute water shortage in the summer of 1959. This, according to the *mantiqa* authorities, was the fault of the Ministry of Public Works, who installed pumps on the main Idqu drain to satisfy the water requirements of the Abis area,[17] as the flow from the Mahmudiya canal was insufficient. But although the outlay on the pumping station was contributed from the budget of the Abis project, the water thus made available was being diverted to other areas. As a result, progress in land reclamation was slow and the yields on the lands about to be distributed were very poor (cotton 1·2 kantars, rice less than 1 dariba, &c.). The rice fields instead of being flooded with water were nearly dry, particularly in the area south of the first model village. While low yields were due to lack of water, negligence by hired agricultural labourers must also have played a part. Conditions in the area in the first stage of cultivation were no better.

[15] Ten big tractors of over 80 h.p.; 111 of over 45 h.p.; 116 of between 20–45 h.p.; ten big threshing machines (3·5–4·5 feet); five self-propelled Massey-Harris combines.

[16] Average gross income on a 5-feddan holding came from the following sources:

Cotton (3 kantars)	£E45
Rice (3 daribas)	£E51
Grain (wheat, barley)	£E20
Clover	£E40
	£E156

[17] This area was irrigated from the Mahmudiya canal, but since the flow of water in this canal was not enough for the whole area, after careful studies concerning the mixing of drainage with irrigation water, a near-by main drain, Idqu drain, was selected. The average salt content of this drain permitted mixing it with the water of the canal, and thus a pumping station was installed at the end of Idqu drain for this purpose. In addition, five secondary canals were constructed to irrigate the whole area by gravity (see Anwar).

In mid-July 1959 430 families (approx. 2,500 people) were moved to Abis from the villages of Kuwaisna district, in the densely populated province of Minufiya. The head of each family was 50 or younger; he received a 5-feddan holding and a modern house in one of the two main villages. Each family also received on arrival 1 sack of flour (plus an additional 25 kilos for families of over four), 2·5 kilos each of sugar and tea, a kerosene lamp with fuel for a month, basic furniture for the house and 2 woollen blankets, a cash grant of £E5, repeated two months later, enough cotton-seed cake for animal feed, and travel expenses. All expenses were added to the purchase price of the holdings.

The peasants were allowed to occupy the holdings allotted to them immediately and were also given the right to half the crops, the other half being retained by the Abis authorities to cover expenses. This right amounted to over £E10 per holding (after deduction of the price of barley, wheat straw, and cotton seed previously distributed). Buffalo heifers and heifers in calf were distributed on a long-term credit basis, the purchase price being redeemable in 15 annual instalments. This was new, since the first batch of settlers were required to repay in five annual instalments. The price of the buffalo heifers was reasonable (approx. £E50–60 each). The heifers, bred on another Agrarian Reform estate,[18] were of the Baladi type, but had been mated with Friesian bulls. Five hundred animals were distributed, all in good condition. In January 1960 these, and about 200 animals brought by the Minufiya peasants, were about to be included in the insurance programme[19] of the veterinary centre recently set up, which had already distributed 5,000 2-day-old pedigree chicks to the peasants (each receiving 20) and was about to distribute another 10,000.

In January 1960 about 4,000 feddans were being farmed by 766 settlers, more than half of whom came from Kuwaisna. The distribution of another 4,000 feddans to new groups of eager Kuwaisna peasants which was being prepared was hampered by lack of housing in the two newly constructed EARIS villages.

Plans were being drafted for new housing projects. These were certainly revolutionary compared with all previous approaches to the problem of rural housing. Hamlets of 25–30 houses, dispersed among the agricultural land, were to be built instead of big villages of 300–400 houses. The main advantage was that this enabled the settlers to be closer to their holdings (each hamlet was surrounded by 125–150 feddans of land) and transport problems were thus considerably eased. It was certainly a big step forward, since the settlers in the two EARIS

[18] This estate, the Adda estate, 'Abadiya Hamul, Kafr al-Shaikh province, was part of the Za'faran *mantiqa*. It covered about 1,000 feddans and was used as a livestock-breeding centre under the control of the Livestock Breeding Dept. of the Ministry of Agrarian Reform, which, however, had no say whatever in the estate proper; all decisions on agricultural matters were in the hands of agronomists under the supervision of the Za'faran *mandub*. In consequence, there was no co-ordination between the livestock nutrition programme and the programme of fodder production executed by the agricultural section. Maize and sweet sorghum for fodder were therefore provided late in August instead of in June.
[19] See above, pp. 114–15 for similar procedure in Damira, &c.

villages were compelled to cover more than 1 km. to reach their holdings, and there was no mechanized transport.

In both the EARIS villages co-operatives were set up. The boards
of 15 members included delegates of the three main blocks into which
the lands were divided to fit in with crop rotation, the regional Agrarian
Reform delegate,[20] the *mufattish al-ta'awun*, the agricultural supervisor, the doctor in charge of the local hospital, and the headmaster of
the local school. Household branches were set up in both co-operatives; despite the limited capital of each branch (£E350), transactions
were running at a high level (daily average £E35) as the new settlers
found it convenient to purchase their requirements on the spot. The
whole of the new co-operative organization was under the guidance and
control of the *morakib*. A very capable man, Mr Hilmi 'Abd al-Barr
(former *mandub* in Sabarbay), was appointed to this office early in 1959
to straighten out affairs which had become disorganized since the
departure of the USOM experts in 1956.

It was too early in January 1960 to appraise the status of the new
settlers, though there were certain outstanding facts:

1. The area allotted to them had completely changed in appearance.
The Minufiya peasants, though they had received no preliminary
vocational training, were naturally gifted and immediately understood
that good crop yields depended on thorough drainage. They were
working all out to deepen the subsidiary drainage ditches bordering
their holdings, though unfortunately this was useless as it was the main
ditches that needed excavating.[21]

2. In many fields the clover crop had been heavily attacked by cotton-
leaf worm.

3. One of the methods devised to solve summer irrigation difficulties was the installation of *saqias* drawn by cattle. This seemed a rather
retrograde solution, and meant using cattle for draught purposes.

4. The new settlers seemed fully satisfied and very hopeful about the
future. They had emigrated from densely populated regions where
holdings, whether tenanted or owner-operated, were minute (often
less than half a feddan). Rents were extremely high[22] and wages for
agricultural labour very depressed.[23] Their net annual income in
Minufiya province, whether they were tenants or agricultural labourers,
was no more than £E40–45 per family and often less. In Abis during
the first years they were expecting a minimum annual gross income of
£E120 and hoped for a net £E60–70. At the same time they were
counting on obtaining some employment in the lands owner-operated
by the *mantiqa*, which was suffering from acute shortage of labour and
was paying relatively high wages.[24] A minimum increase of 33 per cent

[20] Known in Abis as *morakib*, i.e. controller, instead of the usual title of
mandub.
[21] The main drain had not been cleared for three years; yet five huge exca-
vators had been lying idle on the doorstep of the *mantiqa* for over three years.
[22] £E40–50 per feddan.
[23] Av. daily wage: £E0·10 for men; £E0·5 for children.
[24] £E0·15 daily for men; £E0·07 for children.

in the standard of living of the new settlers was thus expected during the first years.

5. The settlers were fairly satisfied with their houses, though certain details had not been adequately studied. The main complaints were dampness and leakage of water in winter and the lack of dividing walls between the houses.

6. There was no organization for the bulk disposal of livestock and poultry products.

7. Community life was working fairly well but there was no cemetery, communications by road[25] or telephone, and post office facilities were practically non-existent, and the hospital had not yet been provided with medicines.

According to the Agrarian Reform authorities each 5-feddan holding cost;

		£E
Bare land	(£E30 per feddan)	150
Reclamation costs	(£E80 per feddan)	400
House	(£E300)	300
		850
Administrative costs	(10 per cent of total)	85
Total cost (per feddan £E187)		935

This money was redeemable in 33 instalments, starting at the rate of £E2 per feddan. The settlers were also supposed to pay the customary land tax, estimated at about £E1·5 per feddan, so that after the eighth year they were to be debited with £E8 per feddan, i.e. £E40 per 5-feddan holding. In February 1960 the redemption term of the purchase price was lengthened to 40 years at 1 per cent interest rate.

The Simmental herd in Abis. In January 1960 about 500 Simmental cattle (250 mature cows) were bred in a livestock centre set up since 1958. The main defect of the cowsheds, built overnight, was that they were insufficiently protected from the damp sea winds. The animals were kept in their pens all the year round; a litter of rice straw covered the cement floor but it was used very sparingly. They were fed on clover, wheat straw, and concentrates; but throughout the summer of 1959 they had had no green fodder. The cowsheds were far from clean, and the general upkeep of the animals was worse than at the al-Busairi section of Idfina, though they looked healthier and were said to be suffering far less than in Idfina or Idqu. The vet in charge explained that this was because the waste lands of Abis (a dried-up lake) had not been contaminated by local cattle. The cowhands employed by the centre had received no advance training but they were supervised by a vet and his assistants.

This livestock breeding centre was completely independent from the Agrarian Reform regional authorities in Abis. This independence was limited, however, to the immediate precincts of the centre, and the staff in charge of it did not have any authority over the neighbouring agricultural lands. All the fodder, &c. produced on the Abis lands and used by the centre was debited to its account by the Abis Agrarian

[25] By 1960 the 27 km. of asphalted roads built by EARIS were barely usable.

Reform authorities, who considered it had been sold to the centre. This set-up was responsible for the lack of co-ordination between the nutrition programme drafted by the staff of the livestock centre and the schedule of forage crop production laid down by the Abis *mantiqa*. The limited success of the whole venture may well be attributable to this absence of a unifying authority.

Milk production was low, the daily average yield of 250 cows being about 900 kg. The milk was delivered to dairies in Alexandria at nearly the same price as that of al-Busairi. Plans were being drafted for the distribution of the Simmental cattle on a mid-term basis to new beneficiaries who did not possess livestock. It was uncertain, however, whether the latter would agree to raise a delicate single-purpose type of cattle, incapable of draught work, especially since its milk production was not high. At the same time vast new cowsheds were being erected in Abis to house large numbers of buffalo heifers. These were supposed to be distributed later to poor landless peasants on a credit basis, in compliance with the Nasir cattle distribution scheme.[26]

Mandara. In Mandara, which was part of the Alexandria *mantiqa*, a holding of about 220 feddans had been expropriated in 1959 by the Ministry of Agrarian Reform from the Ministry of Waqfs: the latter had bought it in October 1952 at a very low price. This holding, before the revolution, had belonged to the 800-feddan, owner-operated al-Mandara model farm,[27] which had specialized in milk production. The holding had well-planned farmbuildings and excellent cowsheds open on three sides; housing conditions for the agricultural workers were good and included two-storeyed concrete buildings which were well maintained. Clean drinking water had been made available by the Mandara farm. A loose triennial rotation was followed throughout; cotton, liable to be heavily attacked by pests, was not at first often included in the rotation. The main crops were clover, wheat, beans, rice, forage maize, and some vegetables; consolidation of crops was an established principle, and big blocks of 100-150 feddans were reserved for each of them. Since the discovery of potent insecticides in 1955, cotton had become a crop of major importance, yields rising in this seaside region to 6 kantars per feddan.

The holding taken over in 1952 by the Ministry of Waqfs was in a pitiful condition by 1959. It had been leased to small tenants, in holdings of about 2–5 feddans, against payment of a rent of £E18–21. Farm buildings were allowed to fall into disrepair, irrigation (previously by gravity flow or pumping) now depended on the use of *saqias* driven by cattle. Crop rotation and crop consolidation had been completely abandoned and peasants were free to plant their holdings as they desired. In consequence, the holding looked untidy and ill kept: its drainage, irrigation, and internal road networks were in a deplorable state, and crop yields, in particular cotton, were far below the level of the Mandara farm proper, and well below those of some independent farmers operating medium-sized (10–30 feddans) holdings in the immediate neighbourhood.

[26] Above, pp. 116–17.   [27] See Saab, *Motorisation*, p. 335.

About 100 Simmental cows and calves had just arrived from Abis in July 1959. The cattle were not in as good a condition as those in al-Busairi; in Mandara they were fed on wheat straw and 6 kilos of concentrates, as no plans for the production of green fodder had yet been made. There were many cases of abortion resulting from total lack of exercise. Milk production averaged 300 kilos a day. It was reported that the Agrarian Reform authorities had decided to replan the operational organization of the holding, one of the measures to be decreed being the elimination of a number of tenant holdings to make room for fodder production.

The al-Marg 1,500-feddan estate, in Qalyubiya province on the outskirts of Cairo, had a reputation as one of the best-managed owner-operated farms of Central Egypt. It had been expropriated at the end of 1953, as its owners were members of the ex-royal family, but part of it had already been sold by them to small operators in compliance with Article 4 of the Agrarian Reform Law. In December 1959 the condition of the smallholders on this estate was better than it had ever been in the days of the ex-landowners (the Mukhtar family), who had employed hired labour and rarely rented land other than on a seasonal basis. However, the irrigation, drainage, and internal road networks were in a very bad condition, particularly in the area sold by the ex-landowners. But even in the Agrarian Reform area the underground tile drainage installed by the ex-landlords had been allowed to fall into disrepair. The triennial crop rotation was observed strictly in the Agrarian Reform area but was completely ignored in the smallholdings that had been purchased. A very limited number of these smallholders lived in Cairo and had purchased smallholdings of 5 feddans and established fruit orchards.

The trees lining the roads and the open-air drainage and irrigation ditches were in poor condition; many trees had already been cut down. Crop yields were at best equal to their level before the Agrarian Reform; some of the orchards planted by the ex-landlords, and not distributed by the Agrarian Reform authorities (but supervised by them), were inefficiently managed and the trees attacked with various diseases or pests.[28] The numerous farm buildings erected by the ex-landlords were falling into disrepair.

Al-Marg had always been a centre of dairy production. The need for large quantities of manure for the light sandy soils had prompted the ex-landowners to raise a herd of over 100 buffaloes. This had been discontinued after Agrarian Reform, and it was not until spring 1959, when 100 Simmental cattle were sent from Idqu, that the big cowsheds were used to capacity. In December 1951 this herd, which had been deprived of green fodder throughout the hot summer period, was being fed with concentrates, some wheat straw, and clover. The animals were in better condition than in Idqu, though they did not seem to be bearing up well in the Cairo climate. Milk production was low: 140 kilos from 38 milch cows. One of the principal obstacles was the low fertility rate; only 18 cows were in calf on their arrival, and great difficulty had been

[28] Black rot, *Phenococus hersitus.*

encountered since. Cases of abortion and blindness among the mature cattle and their offspring were frequent.

Appraisal of the Livestock Development Projects

The overall conclusion drawn from the various Agrarian Reform livestock centres was that the authorities were not in a position themselves to enter the field of livestock production, without first-class personnel with the necessary authority. The difficulties of livestock production in Egypt were such that only highly efficient farms could successfully venture into this field, for which the top-heavy administration of the Ministry of Agrarian Reform was ill fitted. The promotion of a more indirect method of approach, such as that put into practice with some hesitation in Itay al-Barud, seemed to offer greater chances of success at far less cost, and was undoubtedly better adapted to the unwieldy organization of governmental agencies.

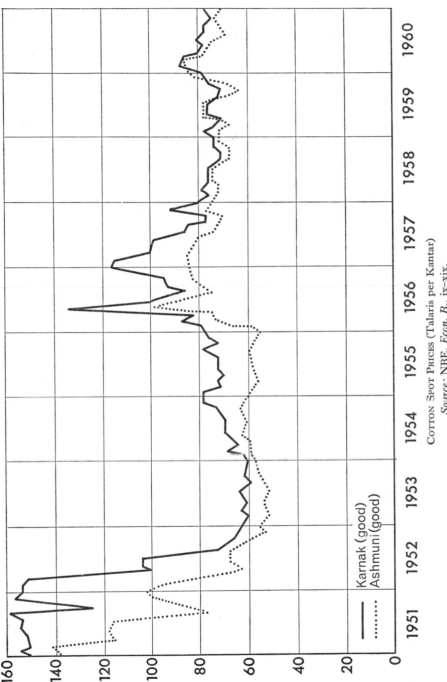

COTTON SPOT PRICES (Talaris per Kantar)
Source: NBE, *Econ. B.*, ix–xix.

Karnak (good)
Ashmuni (good)

GLOSSARY

Note: This glossary includes terms that are more or less frequently used in the text, but not those used only occasionally and which are explained in the text.

Ghafir (pl. *ghufara'*): field warden.
Idarat al-Ta'awun: Co-operative Department of the central administration in Cairo.
Iradat al-gam'iya: so-called 'voluntary contribution' to Agrarian Reform co-operative administrative expenses.
Lagnat al-Musalahat: Committee for the Settlement of Claims and Disputes.
Mandub: official delegate of the central Agrarian Reform authorities.
Mantiqa: regional administrative district; also used for the administrative centre of the district.
Mufattish al-ta'awun: co-operative expert.
Mushrif ta'awuni: co-operative supervisor (often simply called *mushrif*).
Mushrif ta'awuni al-'amm: general co-operative supervisor.
al-Musta'jirin al-mu'alliqin: tenants on probation.
Nawrag: threshing cart.
Nazir al-zira'a(t): agronomist.
Saqia: water wheel.
Sarraf: tax collector.
Shirq: form of partnership commonly practised in rural Egypt (see p. 87 n. 14).
'Umda: village headman.
Waqf: endowed property, its income being assigned by the founder.
Waqf ahli: 'family waqf', income of which is assigned to specified persons before going to a religious, cultural, or charitable institution.
Waqf khairi: 'charitable *waqf*', founded for religious, &c., purposes only, with none of the personal beneficiaries surviving.
Zira'a(t): operational unit of land.

SELECT BIBLIOGRAPHY

Austruy, J. *L'Égypte et le destin économique de l'Islam*. Paris, 1960.
Ayrout, H. C. *Fellahs d'Égypte*. Cairo, 1952.
Baer, G. *A History of Landownership in Modern Egypt, 1800–1950*. London, OUP for RIIA, 1962.
Berque, J. *Les Arabes d'hier à demain*. Paris, 1960.
Besançon, J. *L'Homme et le Nil*. Paris, 1957.
Dabbag, S. M. *La Réforme agraire en Égypte et en Syrie*. Beirut, 1961.
Darling, M. 'Land Reform in Italy and Egypt', *Year Book of Agricultural Co-operation 1956*, ed. by the Plunkett Foundation for Co-operative Studies. Oxford.
Ducruet, R. P. J. 'Problèmes démographiques en Égypte', *Travaux et Jours* (Beirut), no. 1, 1962.
FAO. *Interrelationship between Agrarian Reform and Agricultural Development*, by E. Jacoby. Rome, 1953.
—— *Cooperatives and Land Use*, by M. Digby. Rome, 1957.
—— *Improving Agricultural Tenancy*. Rome, 1957.
—— *The Owner Cultivator in a Progressive Agriculture*. Rome, 1958.
—— *FAO's Role in Rural Welfare*, by H. Santa Cruz. Rome, 1959.
—— *Methods for Evaluation of Effects of Agrarian Reform*. New Delhi, Aug. 1958.
Fromont, P. *L'Agriculture égyptienne et ses problèmes*. Lectures at the Faculty of Law and Economic Science. Paris, 1954.
Gadallah, S. M. *Land Reform in Relation to Social Development in Egypt*. Columbia, Mo., Univ. of Missouri Press, 1962.
Garzouzi, E. *Old Ills and New Remedies in Egypt*. Cairo, Daar el Maaref, 1958.
Gauthier, J., and E. Baz. *Aspect général de l'agriculture libanaise*. Paris, INSEE, 1960. 3 vols.
Ghunaimi, M. R. *al-Islah al-raifi fi misr* (Rural reform in Egypt). Cairo, Salafia Press, 1957.
—— *al-Takwin al-iqtisadi li'l-Kariya* (Economic structure of an Egyptian village). Cairo, Permanent Council of Public Services, 1954.
—— *Hiazat al-aradi fi misr* (Land tenure in Egypt). Cairo, Salafia Press, 1956.
—— 'Investment effects of Land Reform in Egypt', *L'Égypte contemporaine*, Dec. 1954.
—— *Mazahir al-banyan al-Iqtisadi al-zira'i fi'l-riaf al-misri* (An analysis of the basic features of the agricultural and economic structure in rural Egypt). Cairo, Sahifat al-Khadamat, 1956.
—— 'Resource Use and Income in Egyptian Agriculture before and after the Land Reform, with particular reference to economic development'. Raleigh, North Carolina State College, 1935; Ph.D. thesis.
Hartman, W. A. 'Review of Problems and Proposed Actions.' Cairo, USOM, March 1953; unpubl. report.
Hindy, M. K. *Reorganization of Land Use*. Cairo, FAO Regional Training Centre on Agricultural Development Planning, 1962, mimeo.
Issawi, C. *Egypt at Mid-Century*. London, OUP for RIIA, 1954.
—— *Egypt in Revolution*. London, OUP for RIIA, 1963.
Kayser, B. 'Réformes foncières dans le bassin Méditerranéen', *Tiers Monde* (Paris), July–Sept. 1960.

224   *Select Bibliography*

Kuhnen, F. *Agrarian Reform and Economic Development.* Berlin, Inst. für ausländische Landwirtschaft, 1961.
Lahita, P. *National Income.* Cairo, La Renaissance, 1951.
Lerner, D. *The Passing of Traditional Society.* Illinois, 1958.
Marei, S. *Agrarian Reform in Egypt.* Cairo, 1957.
—— *UAR Agriculture Enters a New Age.* Cairo, 1960.
—— *Principles and Scope of Agrarian Reform.* Papers presented to the Technical Advisory Group, International Labour Office, Geneva, Feb. 1965.
Money-Kyrle, A. *Agricultural Development and Research in Egypt.* American University of Beirut, 1957.
Pissot, P. 'La réforme agraire en Égypte', *Bulletin de la Société française d'économie rurale* (Paris), Oct. 1959.
'Pression démographique et stratification sociale dans les campagnes égyptiennes', *Tiers Monde* (Paris), July–Sept. 1960.
Saab, G. *Motorisation de l'agriculture et développement agricole au Proche-Orient.* Paris, SEDEIS, 1960.
——'Co-operation and Agricultural Development in Poverty-stricken Rural Zones in Italy and Egypt', *Commerce du Levant* (Beirut), 20 Feb. 1960.
——'Rationalization of Agriculture in Egypt and Land Tenure Problems', *Middle East Economic Papers* (Beirut), 1960.
Sa'id, G. al-Din. *Egyptian Agrarian Reform.* Alexandria, Dar al-Misrya li'l-Tiba, 1954.
Sayigh, Y. *Bread with Dignity.* Beirut, Dar al-Talia, 1961.
—— 'Economic Conditions and Development in the Middle East', *Colliers Encyclopedia* (1961).
Sedki, Atef. 'L'agriculture égyptienne'. Paris, 1958, unpubl. thesis.
Shell Italiana, Centro Studi Agricoli. *Shell Italiana*, Genoa, 1957–61.
Thweatt, William. 'The Egyptian Agrarian Reform', *Middle East Economic Papers*, 1956.
Tofani, M. *Borgo à Mozzano.* University of Florence, 1956.
UAR. *The Year Book 1964.*
United Nations. *Agrarian Reform.* New York, 1951.
—— *Progress in Land Reform.* New York, 1954 and 1965.
Warriner, D. *Land Reform and Development in the Middle East.* London, RIIA, 1957.
—— 'Land Reform and Community Development in the UAR', unpubl. report to UN, May 1961.

PUBLICATIONS OF THE MINISTRY OF
AGRARIAN REFORM*

Agrarian Reform in Buhaira Province. 1954.
Agrarian Reform in Daqahliya Province. 1960.
Agrarian Reform in Five [to Thirteen] Years. 1957–65.
Agrarian Reform in Sharqiya Province. 1954.
Agrarian Reform in Upper Egypt (Matay and Minya). 1954.
Damira Agrarian Reform Region. 1953 and 1956.
Land Distribution and Income Statistics. 1954.
Nawag; An Experiment in Crop Consolidation and Co-operative Farming. 1958.

* All published in Arabic in Cairo.

Shibin al-Kawm Agrarian Reform Region. 1959.
Simbilawain Agrarian Reform Region. 1961.
UAR, Desert Development and Land Reclamation Projects. 1961.
Za'faran Agrarian Reform Region. 1955.

PERIODICALS
al-Ta'awun, 1959-62.
al-Magallat al-Zira'iyat, 1959-62.

PERIODICALS

Agricultural and Co-operative Credit Bank, *Reports of Boards of Directors,* 1947-60 (Cairo).
Al-Ahram Economic Bulletin (Cairo).
American University of Beirut, *Middle East Economic Papers.*
Bulletin de la Société française d'économie rurale (Paris).
Bulletin of the Institute of Rural Economics (Beirut), series of lectures and discussions by Dr F. Kuhnen, C. Barberis, C. Vanzetti, L. Virone, S. A. K. Hrass, C. Issawi, H. Wilbrandt, &c. on 'Agrarian Tenure and Agricultural Co-operation in the Mediterranean Basin'.
Bureau de Documentation syriennes et arabes.
Le Commerce du Levant (Beirut).
L'Égypte contemporaine, 1952-61 (Cairo).
Federation of Industries in the United Arab Republic, *Year Book,* 1952-60. Cairo.
Journal of Economic History (New York).
Middle East Forum (Beirut).
Monthly Bulletin of Rural Economy, Statistics and Legislation (Cairo).
National Bank of Egypt, *Economic Bulletin* (Cairo).
Sélection de législation arabe (Damascus).
Tiers Monde (Paris).
UAR, Central Agency for Public Mobilisation and Statistics. *Statistical Handbook, 1952-64.* Cairo, 1965.
—— Dept of Statistics & Census. *Annuaire statistique, 1954-1958/9.* Cairo.
—— Information Dept. *The Year Book 1965.* Cairo, 1965.

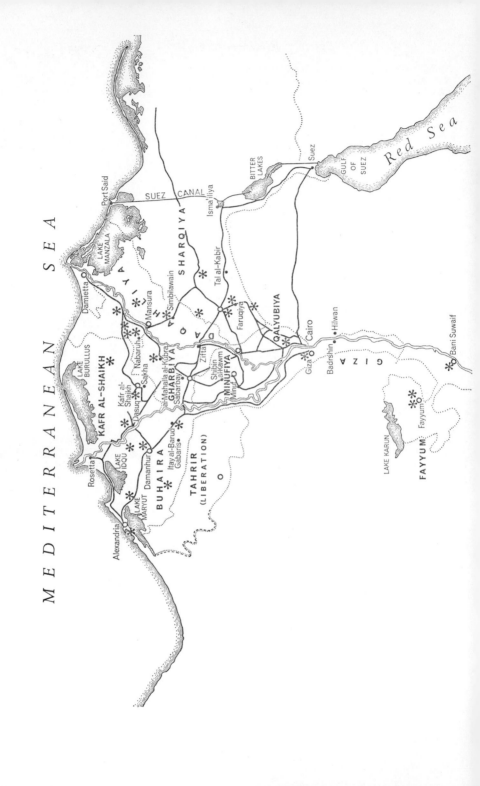

Red Sea

M E D I T E R R A N E A N   S E A

SUEZ   CANAL

Port Said

GULF OF SUEZ

BITTER LAKES

Suez

Isma'iliya

LAKE MANZALA

Damietta

SHARQIYA

Tal-al-Kabir

Simbilawain

Mansura

Faruqiya

Cairo

QALYUBIYA

Hilwan

Bani Suwaif

Nabaruh

Sakha

Ziffa

Giza

Badrshin

GIZA

LAKE BURULLUS

KAFR AL-SHAIKH

Kafr al-Shaikh

Dasuq

al-Mahalla al-Kubra

Sabarbay

GHARBIYA

Shibin al-Kawm

Minuf

MINUFIYA

Rosetta

LAKE IDQU

Damanhur

Itayal-Barud

Gabaris

BUHAIRA

TAHRIR
(LIBERATION)

LAKE MARYUT

Alexandria

LAKE KARUN

Fayyum

FAYYUM

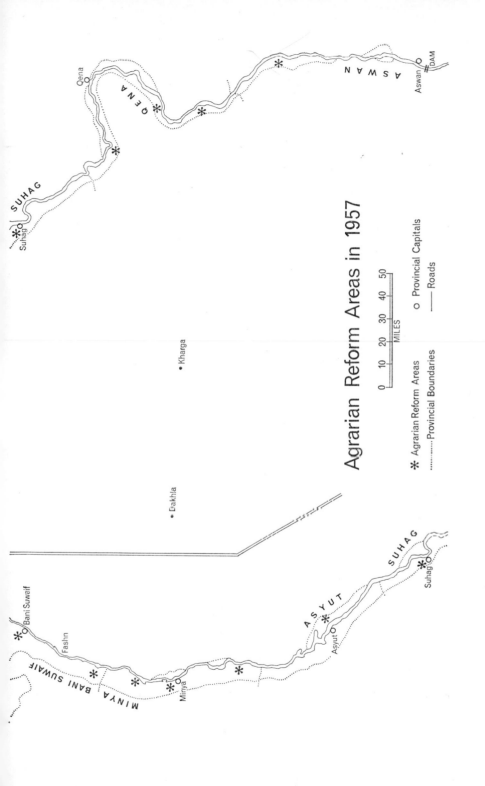

Agrarian Reform Areas in 1957

* Agrarian Reform Areas   o Provincial Capitals
.... Provincial Boundaries   —— Roads

0 10 20 30 40 50
MILES

Aswan
DAM
ASWAN
Qena
QENA
SUHAG
Suhag

Kharga

Dakhla

Bani Suwaif
Fashn
BANI SUWAIF
MINYA
Minya
ASYUT
Asyut
SUHAG
Suhag

INDEX

(AR = Agrarian Reform)

Index

134, 139 n.; in reclamation areas, 161, 179, 215.
Hugmin, 93.
Human factor, 138–40.
Hungarian cattle, 209–10.

Idarat al-Bur, see Waste Land Dept.
Idarat al-Ta'awun, 53 ff., 64 f., 68.
Idfina, 40, 114 n., 122, 210–12.
Idqu, 116, 210.
Illiteracy, 6, 125 n.
Income, ceiling for personal, 181; see also under Beneficiaries.
India, 113, 126 n.
Industrial companies, exemptions from (1952) law, 18.
Industrial infrastructure, 159.
Industry, 169 n.; role of in 1952, 1; national income from, 173.
Infant mortality, 125.
Inheritance laws, 9, 148.
Insecticides, 58, 77, 83; supply and use of, 85; effect of, 110 ff., 170; spraying of cattle and poultry, 114; at Nawag, 190 f.; new types, 218.
Inshas, 32, 71, 114 n.
Insurance, 61, 205; see also under Cattle.
Investment: in land, 12, 125; not being accelerated, 126, 172; in orchards, 128–9; of co-op. profits, 134; desirable and undesirable forms of, 134, 137–9, 172, 177; in Liberation province, 138; AR plans for, 139; see also Savings.
Iradat al-gam'iya, 43–44, 130.
Irrigation, 68, 79, 211, 213 f., 218 f.; wasteful use of, 3 f.; networks, 56, 73–76; ACS and, 58; distribution of water, 73–75; engineers, 73–75; upkeep of, 74–77; credit service, 86; use of draught animals for pumps, 104 ff.; co-operative profits, 132, 197 f.; at Nawag, 149, 193; Nasir programme, 160; on reclaimed land, 160 ff.; mechanization hindered, 162; 'irrigation opening', 164; see also Drainage; Water.
Irrigation pumps and equipment, 5–6, 57, 59, 139 n.
Irrigation wardens, 74.
Issawi, Prof. C., 180 n.
Istislah and *istizra'*, 158 n.
Italconsult, 161–2.
Italy, 19, 52 n., 109, 113, 138; see also Borgo à Mozzano; Maremma region.
Itay al-Barud, 40, 85 n.; indebtedness in, 50, 93, 97, 99; water shortage in, 74; loans diverted, 83 n.; cotton-seed cake, 85 n.; pest control, 103 n.; mechanization, 107–8; veterinary unit, 114 n.; calf-fattening, 116;

milk-processing, 118; smallholders income, 120; dissatisfied smallholders, 122; livestock project, 206–9; see also Qism Awwal Rub' Shandid.

Kafr Bahut, 99.
Kafr al-Dawar, 114 n.
Kafr Damira Jadid, 74 n., 202 ff.
Kafr Katta, 99.
Kafr al-Shaikh province, 29, 40, 124, 171.
katib, 55 n., 151 n.
khadamat, see Services.
Kharga, 64, 161.
al-Khazan, 11 n., 93, 111, 114 n., 124.
Kuta project, 212 f.

Labour, 157, 181; co-operative and hired gangs, 74–76, 102–3, 196; see also Agricultural labourers; Employment; Manpower; Wages.
Labour unions, 164 f.
al-Lagna al-Ulya l'il-Islah al-Zira'i, see AR: High Committee for.
Lagnat al-Musalahat, 48 f., 204.
Lagnat al-Nazafa, see Street and House Cleanliness, Committees for.
Land: shortage of arable, 3; values, 12–13, 20, 24, 193; requisitioning of, 19–20, 21–24, 27 f.; low-productivity, 109 n., 184, 210 f., 213; state-owned, see State Domains. Reclamation and improvement, 3 f., 10, 157–65; development companies, 3, 29, 158 f., 165 ff., 178–9; area benefited, 9, 109 n., 129 n., 158 f.; area expropriated or redistributed, 28 f., 109 n., 188; Permanent Organization for, 29, 159, 164; control of AR authorities, 60, 63 f., 161 f., 164, 213 f., 216; General Organization for, 63 f., 164; projects, 159–62, 188; private enterprise and, 163–5, 178–9; see also Abis; EARIS; Idfina; Liberation province; New Valley project.
See also AR; Expropriated estates.
Land tax, 42–43, 178, 193, 211; as basis of assessing compensation; 24; — beneficiaries' payments, 41 ff.; collection and payment, 54, 83, 130.
Landless peasants: income of (1952), 13; transfer of land to, 28, 34; and Nasir buffalo project, 116–17; still numerous, 172; Second Reform and, 185; probable no. after further redistribution, 188; see also Agricultural labourers.